Learning
and
Teaching Style

In Theory
and Practice

KATHLEEN A. BUTLER Ph.D.

CORBAN COLLEGE

5000 DEER PARK DRIVE S.E.
SALEM, OREGON 97301

The Learner's Dimension
P.O. Box 6
Columbia, CT 06237

TABLE OF CONTENTS

FROM THE AUTHOR

Dear Reader,

From 1976 to 1981, I had the priviledge of studying with Dr. Anthony F. Gregorc at the University of Connecticut as he began ground-breaking research into the field of learning style. As a result, I realized that my life's work as an educator would take shape as an interpreter of this model.

My interest in this model is multidimensional—at once personal and professional. Personally, I have seen its value and felt its impact as I learn to understand myself as a child of my own parents, an individual, a wife, a parent to my children, and now as the grown child of my parents. If it had no further impact, this understanding has brought me great insight.

Combining the personal and professional, I see my own work as a teacher magnified before my eyes when I consider style. I am compelled to examine the implications for teachers and administrators. Perhaps, as the mother of two children with very different styles, my writing reflects a wish to tell their teachers more about them! I know all children would face fewer needless obstacles if their schooling included a true understanding of style. I know that the worthy obstacles learners face could be overcome with important learning impact if teachers could work appropriately with style, rather than experience the frustration of its invisible forces. I know I am a better teacher because of style.

As a staff development specialist in style, I hear the request a thousand-fold, "What are the practical applications of style?" My reply usually is, "What do you mean by 'practical'?" If you mean a sure-fire formula for immediate, concrete use in the classroom without need for thought, I have nothing to offer to you. If you mean, how can I take my understanding of theory to improve the quality of life in my classroom? how can I increase my ability to know more about children's minds? how can I offer children an avenue for self-understanding? and how can I use instructional strategies to convey my curricular goals and objectives with integrity?—then I have much to share with you.

This second edition reflects my own refinement and understanding of style as I have worked with it and researched its applicabilities to real classroom life since the first edition in 1984. Teachers throughout the country have worked hard with me to find appropriate ways to implement style. We know clearly, there is no single approach or method to implement this complex concept but many.

One feature of style research continues to stand the test of time—the teacher alone makes the significant difference for application of style in the classroom. Every aspect of instruction, all planning steps, and each application strategy filters through the mindscreen of the teacher. Training for style application in and of itself is an exercise in wishful thinking. Rather, we educators must all work together to develop a refined understanding of style. But I must forewarn you that every teacher enters a study of style at an individual stage of readiness and receptivity for style. Some teachers become style-technicians in the classroom, forever applying one step after another without true understanding of what they do. Others intentionally integrate style principles into teaching and instructional practice, making a true difference for their learners. And some very special teachers *live* a style philosophy in the classroom, revealing a genuine receptivity to the natural dimensions of style created from their own understanding of style differences.

These teachers, the master teachers of style, offer us individual role models for the authentic, personalized, and respectful application of style with learners. They bring style from idealized theories and models to the reality of a child's learning world. They have taught me well that to make a difference for children, we must invest in our teachers' minds and hearts, not just in their curricular packages.

To all who teach in the spirit of style, thank you for your courage in defying the norm and for working to retain the integrity of learning as an individual joy. To all who have helped me with the details of this book, thank you for your belief in the worth of these ideas. And, to my husband, Kerry, thank you for your love and confidence in me. I value beyond measure your support and help during this revision.

Kathleen A. Butler
September 1987

FOREWORD

The teacher **is** the primary decision-maker in the classroom. This is a phenomenological fact! The tool for making decisions is the teacher's mind. He/she uses the mind to select, accept, reject, enhance, ignore, highlight, obscure, activate, and avoid ideas, philosophies, psychological truths, subject matter content, technical skills, system expectations, and ethical demands. The various aspects of the teacher's mind become manifest for all to see through the teacher's style (behaviors, characteristics, and mannerisms). By personally studying style, the individual teacher can come to know many of the conscious and unconscious biases and prejudices that guide his/her thinking and decision-making. He/she can also examine the sources of his/her style. Are they reflective of his/her natural ways of dealing with existential realities? Do they represent currently accepted opinions, i.e., orthodox approaches to teaching that have been acquired. Do they consist of a potpourri of rules-of-thumb, fragments of research, biases of a favorite professor, or things other teachers do? Are they reflective of all of these?

The in-depth study of style can also open the teacher's eyes to the mind qualities used by learners. No longer will teachers be able to support the Average Child Concept that states, in part, "that all children, except for a rare few born with severe neurological defects, are basically very much alike in their mental development and capabilities...." The teacher will come to recognize and deal with the fact that children (little ones and big ones) naturally learn and present their ideas in various ways. With this realization comes a professional obligation to relate to the learners' minds. This is supported by *The Aquarian Gospel* by Levi:

> And hear me once again, he who shall cause
> a little one to stumble and fall is marked,
> accursed; and it were better far if he had
> drowned himself.
> (Chapter 131, Verse 115)

Because the study and subsequent application of style and mind-quality principles are no small tasks, bridges are needed to aid individuals. This book by Kathleen Butler offers a valuable bridge for teachers. It reflects the view that there are no definitive answers to psychic realities. There are, however, guidelines to a study of style. Kathy has provided these for teachers.

Anthony F. Gregorc
September, 1983

To
My daughters, Erin and Johanna

I can sense the dreams within you...
Listen to their calling

INTRODUCTION

Just as a building reflects the vision of its architect, my interpretation of learning style reflects my vision of the learning and teaching process. You, too, have a vision of this process. Through this book, I share my ideas with you as a point of departure on a study-journey into style. We will consider theory and its personal and professional application to learning and teaching, and assess how ideas about style apply to you in your classroom. This approach allows you to address the influence of your own style, it encourages you to listen to your students and observe them in relation to your style, and it gives you the opportunity to create a style approach that enhances and actualizes your own teaching style.

We have a journey to start. Along the way, you will have the opportunity

- *to look closely at your personal style—its source, its use, and its effect on you and on others.*

- *to assess your role as an instrument of thought in classroom.*

- *to look at each student as a unique human being with unique goals and needs, whose differences in style reflect individual mind patterns.*

- *to use a style-differentiated approach to instruction by considering interpersonal, curricular, and instructional options that address and broaden individual student styles.*

Clearly, consideration of style in the classroom takes both teacher and student into account. We cannot isolate teaching or learning into neatly examined and categorized components . Rather, we study them together in a holistic process. Learning flows between the inner forces of the teacher and of the students. All the learning-links that occur in the classroom have the influence of the lives brought together there.

ASSUMPTIONS

Five assumptions underlie my position on learning and teaching style.

The first assumption: **As a teacher, I must understand myself and my own goals before I can understand or accept others and their goals.** I cannot walk in others' shoes before I am comfortable in my own. Let us put our goals as persons and as teachers into perspective.

The second assumption: **As a teacher, I bring to the classroom a unique and natural set of qualities that have positive and negative sides—in intent as well as action.** In my role as a teacher, I am charged to enhance my positive qualities—those that help me, others, and the environment to maintain, grow, and develop. I need to diminish my negative qualities—those that block, harm, or destroy me, others, or the environment. In studying the concept of style, and in trying to meet the specific styles of all students, I will not give up my own personal style. I expect to understand the forces of my style and to work with my style rather than in defense of it.

The third assumption: **As a teacher, I should not try to "fit" someone's model of the competent teacher.** I need to self-assess, and to find and accept constructive assistance. I believe I can meet the needs of others by understanding their needs and by providing them with options. However, I know I must be free to operate from the strength of my teaching style. As Emerson wrote, "The only gift is a portion of thyself." Teachers must be allowed to give of themselves. We must teach from the strength of our own positive style. This does not excuse incompetent behavior, but it does require a more sophisticated approach to supervising teachers.

The fourth assumption: **As a teacher, I have the power and capacity to do more than teach the content. I have the potential to aid students on their lifelong path toward self-actualization.** I can provide conditions that permit students to learn and work with a positive view of themselves. I can help them learn techniques for style flexing, coping, or adapting to the legitimate demands of the world. I have this potential.

The fifth assumption: **As a teacher, once I accept that people use their minds to think and to learn differently, then I am duty bound to develop teaching techniques and approaches based on my knowledge of the different ways in which my mind and my students' minds work.** As teachers interested in applying style to the classroom, we look for personalization of learning and reasons for success, not diagnostic and prescriptive learning. We must know why we teach as we do and be intentional about our teaching!

THE PRESENT

Demands for high school competency tests, teacher competency tests, the stress on "basics," and the drive to teach "thinking" skills proclaim the public's belief that teachers do not know how to bring about learning. If we cannot back up what we do in the classroom with reasoned explanations of the how and why of learning, the public may be right—we don't know why we direct and diagnose as we do. We can confront this problem head on if we understand how style affects learning.

Although researchers, policymakers, curriculum writers, and textbook publishers have become aware of style, few are asking serious questions about how the mind works. Most publishers have not incorporated a style-based theory into their curriculum development. Because they are geared to make a profit with the fewest changes, publishers are not likely to do so in the near future. With many, many schools wedded to textbooks, teachers do not have easy access to content-based, style-differentiated ways to provide for student needs, unless they write it for themselves.

Some teachers force students to adapt to only one method because they understand few differentiated ways of teaching. Preservice teacher education programs have just begun to include learning style. Most inservice training on style has little depth. And, teachers have little time or administrative support to implement change on their own.

Most teachers who can offer alternatives to students do so because (1) they were trained to recognize how minds work in various ways; (2) they personally experience multiple ways of learning; (3) they have taken specialized training and have sought content methods to address these differences; (4) they have devised differentiated options through their experiences with students.

Every content area needs content specialists from all styles of learning to help teachers to develop stylistically differentiated approaches to subjects. Peer coaching holds great promise for teachers of different styles to help one another in these ways. Some teachers can differentiate learning activities simply by knowing the principles of teaching and learning styles; others cannot. Teachers who experience, learn, and understand content through only one or two styles find it extremely difficult to teach content from a style that is not their preferred style. Those who cannot differentiate witness the strength of their own style preferences! They truly understand the meaning of style dominance because they experience the difficulty of style mismatch.

Will we ever have precise, diagnostic tools to predict how a student's mind works? At present, we know too little about the mind to create these tools. We delude ourselves if we think that we can achieve predictability. Like weather forecasters, we can apply all our knowledge against conditions, but then must use our powers of observations, judgment, feeling, and intuition to monitor and revise our approach.

WHO SHOULD READ THIS BOOK

This book is designed for you if you are interested in the process of learning and teaching, if you seek guidance backed by theory and field research, and if you are attuned to self-discovery. For those of you familiar with Gregorc's work, this book will help you consider elements and implications of the Energic Model of Style from a classroom point of view. It may also serve to validate the way you have applied style in your own classroom. For those who have limited experience with learning style, this book will introduce a qualitative approach to teaching and classroom dynamics.

In spirit, the writing of Carl Sagan helps us parallel this qualitative approach to style with "doing science":

> *Science is a way of thinking much more than it is a body of knowledge. Its goal is to find out how the world works, to seek what regularities there may be, to penetrate to the connections of things....[It is] based on experiment, on a willingness to challenge dogma, and on an openness to see the universe as it really is. Accordingly, science sometimes requires courage—at the very least, the courage to question the conventional wisdom....The scientific cast of mind examines the world critically, as if many alternative worlds might exist, as if other things might be here which are not....If you spend any time spinning hypotheses, checking to see whether they make sense, why they conform to what else we know, thinking of tests you can pose to substantiate or deflate your hypotheses, you will find yourself doing science. And as you come to practice this habit of thought more and more, you will be better and better at it. To penetrate into the heart of the thing, even a little thing, a blade of grass as Walt Whitman said—is to experience a kind of exhilaration that, it may be, only human beings of all the beings on this planet can feel. We are an intelligent species and the use of our intelligence quite properly gives us pleasure....Understanding is a kind of ecstasy. (1)*

You will find yourself "doing style" when you question why you think as you do, when you challenge traditional assumptions about how students learn, when you spin your own hypotheses about how to help students learn, and when you finally gain a glimpse into the mind of a child. Indeed, understanding **is** ecstasy.

Certain attitudes and conditions make your work with style smoother. Three conditions seem to make application of learning style concepts in the classroom an easier process. First, you must like children and young people. This may seem to belabor the obvious, but...teaching is not just a job! As Martin Buber suggested, "Teaching is a situation that has never been before and never will come again. It demands of you a reaction that cannot be prepared beforehand. It demands nothing of what is past. It demands presence, responsibility, it demands you." How can we give of ourselves in service to others if we don't like the persons to whom we minister?

Second, you must believe in tapping the potential inherent in human nature. In spite of the anxieties of living in the nuclear age, we must either believe in the power of education to shape and direct humankind to purposeful means and ends or ask ourselves why we are educators. To my way of thinking, unless we can help our students to recognize and develop their own capabilities, talents, and aspirations—in part, by addressing their natural style—we can give them only existing knowledge. We must also aid them to understand their potential. People are both citizens of the world and agents of their individual selves. They can interact with one another in an infinite number of combinations. Education can be one vehicle by which individuals gain access to their own potential as well as find a citizen role.

Third, teachers must have content knowledge of their subject area. Teachers need depth of content as well as breadth of methodological approaches. We cannot generate optional ways to teach a subject without content expertise. For example, a teacher who knows the field of history only through the content of the textbook has little ability to design, or even recognize, other ways to approach the study of history. However, we can acquire content knowledge and use multiple resources. In this book, you will blend an assessment of self and a willingness to consider multiple ways of viewing students with diversified instructional practices within your content area.

OUTCOMES

If these goals and assumptions are, or can be part of your own thinking, then this book can assist you to address the following kinds of objectives.

Assessment Objectives

• *To understand the meaning of individual differences from the perspective of the Gregorc Model.*

• *To consider the stylistic reasons for differences in teaching styles.*

• *To appraise the communication process with students through an understanding of stylistic differences.*

Knowledge Objectives

• *To differentiate among the four learning styles of the Gregorc Model.*

• *To apply learning style as a concept to teaching style as a process.*

• *To explain the learning style demands of various instructional techniques, curricular programming, and classroom approaches.*

Implementation Objectives

• *To develop a plan for broadening personal teaching style through use of interpersonal strategies and classroom options.*

• *To develop a plan for expanding effective teaching approaches by diversifying curricular options, and instructional strategies.*

These objectives intend to aid you to understand yourself better and to enable you to put yourself in perspective with your students and their learning needs. With understanding and information about learning style, you can help students to know themselves, to understand others, and to see the relationship of learning to their own style and achievement.

A study of style can help you to manage your behavior, and to predict and respond to the behavior of others in more clinical and efficient ways than you do now. It can help you to fulfill your obligations by showing you how to work in other styles. **Or, it can open you to an examination of your belief system and the educational practices built on principles that defy current knowledge about human learning.**

Part I

Learning Style
In Focus

Life should be a stately march to an inner tune.

—Henry David Thoreau

PART I

LEARNING STYLE—IN FOCUS

*As we come to understand more about learning
and teaching styles and how the mind operates,
I believe we will improve mental health and
self understanding as well as increase learning.
Learning styles and teaching styles have
already revealed much to us and continued
research will undoubtedly reveal more. This
trust can lead to the revitalization of "the
noblest of professions."*

—Anthony F. Gregorc

Learning Style is a generic term, an umbrella concept, and a name for recognizing individual learning differences. Learning style has also become a complex field of study. Just as we can identify schools of psychology by examining their philosophical beliefs and subsequent operation and implementation strategies, so, too, can we identify several approaches to learning style. No one has a monopoly on the terms *psychology* or *curriculum*. And no one can claim to represent learning style in its entirety.

Learning style research supports several branches of theoretical interest and operational models, each stemming from a different perspective on how the human mind operates. Each makes a notable contribution. Further, just as the various branches of psychology meet the needs of certain people, so do the various models of learning style. Some models serve specialized populations or specific points of view, and some are more broadly based.

Through this book, I will attempt to meet the needs of those interested in an interpretation of the model of learning style developed by Anthony F. Gregorc, Ph.D. and offer application of this model for classroom teaching. I will interpret the model's major theoretical principles, provide a descriptive analysis of learning and teaching style for teachers and students, as well as introduce my approach to implementing style, Style Differentiated Instruction (SDI). SDI proposes application guidelines, approaches, and strategies for using the Gregorc learning style model in the classroom.

In Part I we begin with a review of Gregorc's Mediation Ability Theory and Energic Model of Mindstyles,* discuss the implications of working with a psychological model of style, and offer you a way to examine your own style.

*Mindstyle is a trademark registered by Anthony F. Gregorc, Ph.D.

CHAPTER 1

A THEORETICAL FRAMEWORK FOR UNDERSTANDING STYLE

The asking of a question with passionate concern for its answer, a concern which demands life investment, suggests a door which will sooner or later be found....A new idea fails if it involves too great a sacrifice of invested belief. If the new idea triggers a passionate enough pursuit to make suspension or abandonment of previous beliefs, or current criteria worth the risk, however, the new idea can change reality structure.

—J. C. Pearce

Significant ideas often begin with significant questions and from time to time do change the shape of reality. Anthony F. Gregorc began with the question, How and why does the human mind work? His pursuit of answers has changed the shape of reality for us in education by redefining the nature of human learning.

A PHILOSOPHICAL BASE

Our own views about the nature of human learning begin with our views of our philosophy of life. Gregorc states, **"The primary purpose of life is to realize and actualize one's individuality, spirituality, and collective humanness."** (2) Our beliefs about what, how, and why we learn as individuals, as members of our society, and as world citizens develop from our philosophy. Given his philosophy, Gregorc investigates learning as it is experienced by the individual human mind.

THE RESEARCH APPROACH

The research approach that lent itself best to considering the nature of human learning, and how people experience learning, was phenomenology. Phenomenology aims to uncover the nature and role of individual perceptions. It allows the researcher to gain an understanding of fundamental consciousness—a person's essence and driving forces—the essential self

With a phenomenological approach to study a person's mind, we ask, What forces drive the individual? How does the individual reveal these forces? What is the relationship of the individual's internal driving forces to the way the individual experiences learning? How can we encourage people to consider these questions about themselves?

Phenomenological research reveals that invisible, driving forces lie at the core of being, the individual essence, and that the mind is the vehicle that expresses one's individual essence. Individuals must seek the nature of these driving forces for themselves, for that is part of the purpose of being human. This quest can be made easier if people have ways to recognize and consider how the primary conveyor of the individual essence, the mind, operates.

MEDIATION ABILITY THEORY

Gregorc's Mediation Ability Theory and the Energic Model of Mindstyles provide an organized way to consider how the mind works. Gregorc theorizes that the mind of each of us possesses an overarching set of natural qualities that help us to realize and to actualize our personal essence. These qualities are expressed through mind channels. He states, "The power, capacity and dexterity to utilize these channels are collectively termed mediation abilities."(3) Gregorc identified "four qualities found within four basic mediation channels."(4)

Gregorc's understanding of natural qualities, mediation abilities, and mind channels led to his interpretation of style. His early definition of style stated, "Styles are symptoms of underlying psychological frames of reference and of driving mental qualities of the mind." (5) His recent refinement of that definition reads, "Generically, style consists of outer behavior, characteristics, and mannerisms which are symptomatic of the psyche and of particular mental qualities. Specifically, an individual's outer, visible style characteristics provide clues as to the inner invisible nature and capacity of his psychological and mental makeup."(6) People tell us about themselves, their driving forces, and the way they learn through their style, their outer behavior.

Understanding individual styles, however, requires careful analysis. People must feel free to use their own style and act at their natural best before their style can act as an effective interpreter of true capacities and abilities. Whereas some people feel free to be themselves under all circumstances, for various reasons, others assume behaviors that do not represent their natural style. People need unguarded moments—times when they do not role play— to reveal style. We cannot interpret a person's natural abilities and capacities if that person consistently plays a role.

Through a phenomenological approach and by using style as a tool for personal interpretation, we come closer to understanding our own core and essence, and to permitting others to reach their own as well. But even when we understand ourselves, we may not find it possible to express that under-standing fully, and we can never understand others completely.

Style gives us a common language that makes it possible for one mind to translate itself to another. But as French philosopher Ignace Lepp warns, *"Experience proves that every human being possesses a central core that is so intimate that it is practically incommunicable."* Even when we achieve a sense of our own forces, abilities, and style, the nuances of our own makeup may appear too subtle to allow full expression of them to others. Michael Polyani asserts, *"We know more [about ourselves] than we can convey."*

Mediation Ability Theory defines four types of mediation abilities: perception, ordering, processing, and relating. This guide concerns two of these four mediation abilities—perception and ordering—and how they influence learning. Remember that because we will consider only two aspects of the mind, we will not examine the whole picture of learning. At best, we glimpse the whole when we consider some of the parts.

Gregorc writes that *"perceptual abilities are the means through which you grasp information....Ordering abilities are the ways in which you authoritatively arrange, systematize, reference and dispose of information."* (7) He explains that every mind has the perceptual ability to perceive the world in concrete and abstract form, and the ordering ability to order the world in sequential (linear) and random (nonlinear) ways. Even though everyone uses all four qualities—concreteness and abstraction, and sequentialness and randomness—some people perceive the world more abstractly than concretely, and others do the reverse. Similarly, some people are more random than sequential in their ordering of information and vice versa. Others exhibit a balance among the four qualities.

Each person is qualitatively different from every other human being. We each have our own personal essence and express it through mind qualities. The way in which the individual displays the four qualities to others is his/her mind's style—Gregorc's mindstyles.

> **EACH PERSON IS QUALITATIVELY DIFFERENT FROM EVERY OTHER HUMAN BEING.**
>
> **WE EACH HAVE OUR OWN PERSONAL ESSENCE AND EXPRESS IT THROUGH MIND QUALITIES.**

Perception:
Abstract/Concrete

The perception quality of abstraction allows each of us to experience the abstract world of emotion, feeling, spirituality, and intellect—all invisible and nonphysical. Through our abstraction abilities, we appreciate aesthetics, experience emotions, understand relationships, conceive ideas, analyze concepts, live vicariously, and know God. Gregorc defines the quality of abstraction in this way: **Abstraction**

> *...enables you to grasp, conceive and mentally visualize through the faculty of reason, and to emotionally and intuitively register and deal with inner and subjective thoughts, ideas, concepts, feelings, drives, desires and spiritual experiences. This quality permits you to apprehend and perceive that which is invisible and formless to your physical senses of sight, smell, touch, taste and hearing. (8)*

On the other hand, the perception quality of concreteness permits us to experience and to understand the physical world, as well as to express ourselves in physical media. Using concrete ability, we construct everything from bridges to bulletin boards, and create in a technological sense. Gregorc states: **Concreteness**

> *...enables you to grasp and mentally register data through the direct use and application of the physical senses. This quality permits you to apprehend that which is visible in the concrete, physical world through your physical senses of sight, smell, touch, taste and hearing. (9)*

CONCRETE   ABSTRACT

Perception
Abilities

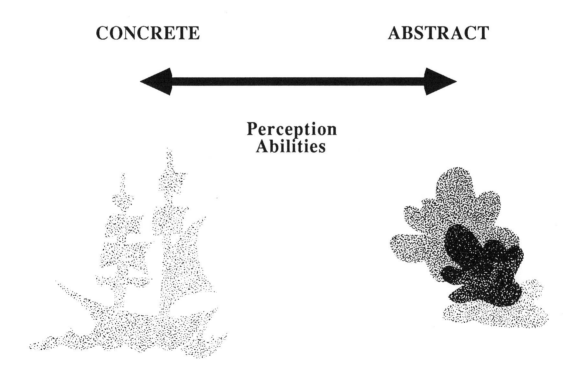

Ordering:
Sequential/Random

The ordering quality of sequence permits us to order the world in crisp, clear, linear, organized fashion. Some people have strong dominance in their lives for sequential ability —"there is a place for everything, and everything is in its place." Gregorc defines **sequence** as

> ...the quality which disposes your mind to grasp and organize information in a linear, step-by-step, methodical, predetermined order. Information is assembled by gathering and linking elements of data and piecing them together in chain like fashion. This quality enables you to naturally sequence information. It further encourages you to express yourself in a precise, progressive and logically systematic manner. (10)

Finally, the ordering quality of randomness allows us to operate in nonlinear fashion, choosing intermittently, and selectively, from among things that are of equal value. **Random** ability permits flexibility, split-second decisions, changes, and tolerance for ambiguity. In Gregorc's words:

> This quality disposes your mind to grasp and organize information in a nonlinear, galloping, leaping, and multifarious manner. Large chunks of data can be imprinted on your mind in a fraction of a second. Information is also held in abeyance and, at any given time, each piece or chunk, has equal opportunity of receiving your attention. Such information, when brought to order, may not adhere to any prior or previously agreed upon arrangement. This quality enables you to deal with numerous, diverse, and independent elements of information and activities. Multiplex patterns of data can be processed simultaneously and holistically. This quality encourages you to express yourself in an active, multifaceted and unconventional manner. (11)

SEQUENTIAL   RANDOM

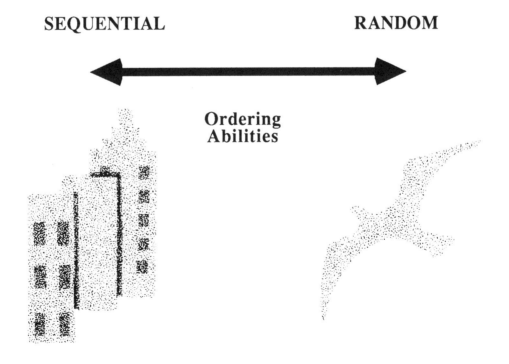

Ordering
Abilities

Qualitative Differences

According to Mediation Ability Theory, every mind has all four qualities—concreteness, abstraction, sequence, and randomness—but we use these qualities with different intensity. However, we can miss these qualitative differences in several ways. We may believe that people are all the same because most of us appear to relate to ideas, emotions, facts, and possibilities. We do share this likeness, but we are also much more complex. We can also miss qualitative differences if we believe people differ on the surface but are basically the same underneath. For example, if we believe that no two persons have the same looks, preferences, and talents but that such outward appearances cover millions of hearts beating as one, then we cannot see qualitative differences.

Through style, we search to find the point at which the individual can recognize and express personal forces—the essential self. Gregorc explains qualitative differences through the imagery of the rainbow. Unlike a continuum running from black through shades of gray to white, the rainbow begins with a common source, but then separates into qualitatively different colors, each different, yet equal. So, too, minds are qualitatively different yet equal.

Four Mind Channels

When Gregorc combined the two sets of mediation abilities— abstract and concrete, and sequential and random—he characterized four types of "transaction ability channels": concrete sequential, abstract sequential, abstract random, and concrete random. Each of these channels has particular behaviors and characteristics. That is, each shows its own style.

FOUR MIND CHANNELS

CONCRETE SEQUENTIAL

CONCRETE RANDOM

ABSTRACT SEQUENTIAL

ABSTRACT RANDOM

Learning and Teaching Style: In Theory and Practice

primary reference, *An Adult's Guide to Style,* Gregorc explained how each of the four styles reveals itself from its own vantage point according to

World of Reality	Ordering Ability
View of Time	Thinking Processes
Creativity	Approach to Change
Approach to Life	Environmental Preferences
Validation Processes	Use of Language
Focus of Attention	Primary Evaluative Words

Although each style has its own complete view of the world, none of us operates solely with one style. First, all four styles exist in every individual mind; second, we deny expression to part of ourselves if we insist on using only one style. Likewise, if we try to operate equally in all four styles when we actually have a dominant style, we may deny ourselves access to our essential selves. We refuse to recognize and develop—to realize and to actualize—our most natural gifts.

In the coming pages, we will see that each person has a natural style, emerging from one's personal essence; each person must develop style flex-abilities or versatility to meet the legitimate demands of others; and each person must find ways to cope with style mismatch or experience considerable stress.

Natural Abilities

Each style has its own distinguishing characteristics, natural abilities, and creative energies. Some highlights...

Concrete Sequential

People with a strong concrete sequential (CS) channel have a style that distinguishes them as **practical, predictable, to-the-point, organized, and structured.**

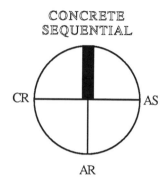

CONCRETE SEQUENTIAL

Dominant concrete sequentials are "naturals" in the physical, hands-on world and relate to it in a structured way. For example, a CS technician is a "natural" at servicing predictable but extremely sensitive machinery. Or, a dominant CS accountant is a "natural" auditor of the most complex set of business books, with or without a computer! The dominant CS teacher is a natural at devising schedules, records, projects, and learning centers, as well as other areas that are important to his/her productivity.

CS people express their creative energies in the context of the concrete world of physically identifiable projects and products through a sequential or linear approach. Thus, a dominant CS artist may produce the highest-quality still life, or a dominant CS chef may refine a complex recipe to perfection.

Abstract Sequential

Individuals with a dominant abstract sequential (AS) channel have a style that individualizes them as **intellectual, logical, conceptual, rational, and studious.**

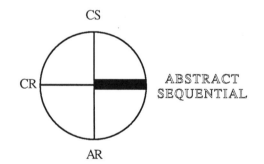

Dominant abstract sequential types are "naturals" as reflective thinkers, researchers, and idea specialists. Their natural abilities drive them to use their intellectual powers in search of knowledge and truth, and to refine our understanding of the rational, logical world. The intellectual drive is at the core of their being. Some AS individuals may prefer the "ivory tower" of academe; others may join "think tanks." Some seek the professorial role to do research, and to convey significant ideas to new generations of thinkers; others take on the role of teacher, critical thinker, or content specialist to hone the content and the thinking skills of students and themselves. Still other AS persons want to be in the thick of things and may be active in organizations that provide them with a forum for ideas, or they may espouse a cause through political activism so as to represent "reason's viewpoint."

AS people express their creative energies through the area of ideas, using a sequential and structured approach. For example, the AS researcher may revel in thoughts and concepts that can be analyzed and synthesized into theories, research reports, and state-of-the-art publications.

Abstract Random

Individuals with a strong abstract random (AR) channel have a style that individualizes them as **emotional, interpretative, sensitive, holistic, and thematic.**

Dominant abstract random types are "naturals" in areas that involve relationships, emotions, and personalized interpretation. They may appear as tour guides who love sharing their experiences, as singers who capture your heart (or at least as shower soloists), as writers who move you to tears, as teachers who thrive among children, as sensitive and interpretative counselors, doctors, and caring next-door neighbors. The AR is a "natural" in the world of relationships, whether with people, poetry, music, canvas, or aesthetic environments.

AR people express their creative energies in the abstract, nonphysical realm of emotions and spirituality through nonlinear form, for example, as creative writers, artists, actors. These types of ARs absorb the world around them, then interpret it so that we can understand it better. To illustrate, an AR musician's song may lift our spirits by helping us to appreciate what we have, or have forgotten. Or an AR writer may depress our mood with memories of a loss.

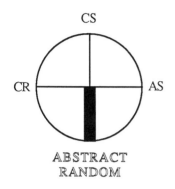

ABSTRACT RANDOM

Concrete Random

Individuals with a strong concrete random (CR) channel have a style that individualizes them as **original, experimental, investigative, option oriented, and risk taking.**

Dominant concrete random types are "naturals" at exploring people, places, things, and ideas. They may be the creative cinematographers, the organizational change agents, the troubleshooter engineers, or the revolutionists, but their driving force is to experience what has not been, to do what has not been done.

CR people express their creative energies in the concrete world of the here-and-now problems that can be solved by random (nonlinear) means. They may be the admired inventors and investigators, the dreamer and doer personalities, or the ones who can never settle down.

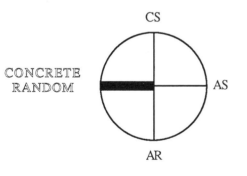

CONCRETE RANDOM

The point to remember is this: the mind's abilities drive natural behavior. "Naturals" do not simply learn behaviors, nor do they solely adapt to the environment; naturals draw their behavior from qualities integral to the core of their being.

We value variety among people, and we praise certain types for their performance in particular ways. We rely on CS individuals. For example, we expect builders, bankers, nurses, shoemakers, repairers, mail carriers, toolmakers, secretaries, fire fighters, lawyers, editors, engineers, plumbers, truck drivers, computer specialists, and technicians—people responsible for the well-being and functional aspects, of our physical world—to have dominant concrete sequential qualities and abilities. Regardless of our own degree of flexibility, we find it inconvenient, uncomfortable, and inefficient when individuals who do not have natural concrete sequential strengths take on these roles.

We assume that the research and instructional components of most professions attract people with abstract sequential qualities. Thus, naturally abstract sequential people in the medical profession gravitate to teaching hospitals and programs. An AS law enforcement person might teach a college course in such areas as criminal justice. AS individuals often create the theories that others test in the real world. However, when such theorists or teachers lose sight of the fact that they are working with theory and not actuality, they may also "lose" those who work in the day-to-day world of physical reality. For example, a sociology professor who expounds notions about community relations but who has never been a part of a varied community risks the scorn of students from that background.

We assume that people in the visual and performing arts have abstract random qualities and abilities. We also expect ARs to work in the helping professions, such as counseling, in roles that demand individuals with natural interpersonal skills, and in positions that require a high degree of flexibility, imagination, and interpretation. Their abilities to empathize and relate lead to their being relied upon by others as sounding boards and support persons. With their ability to interpret, they may also serve as buffers or mediators between different types of people.

And, we expect CRs who take the roles of troubleshooters, inventors, investigators, change-agents, and entrepreneurs to have dominant concrete random qualities and abilities. The concrete randoms' extraordinary ability to think divergently, to see many sides of a problem, and to risk experiencing different solutions allows them to do such things as become criminal investigators, start new businesses without sure guarantees of success, or try techniques never before used in a profession, a la Christiaan Barnard's open-heart experiments or Barney Clark's artificial heart.

Nondominant Channels   Most of us do not have well-developed channels in all four styles, yet most of us use all four of them **to some degree**. Theoretically, people use their nondominant channel in several ways.

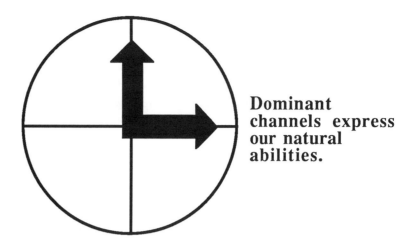

Dominant channels express our natural abilities.

Learned versus Natural Behavior

We ourselves can nurture and develop a nondominant channel, others can assist us, or our environment can facilitate this channel. For example, we can learn AR behaviors. We can take sensitivity training and group-process courses, read about effective ways to communicate, use style as a vehicle to relate better to ourselves and others, make a conscious decision to pay attention to our emotional signals, or broaden our AR experiences through theater and conversation, or just by listening to others. But, dominant ARs have a sense about or attraction to the world of emotions, relationships, and interpretation that is not learned; it is simply integral to their core.

Style Skill Building for Versatility

We can broaden a nondominant channel, allowing us to use it spontaneously when necessary for short periods. For example, we can take courses in time management to help us broaden our skills in this area. When we learn to use a variety of styles with reasonable comfort, we can become more versatile and more able to use the styles we generally do not access. Style skills for versatility help us develop healthy responses to the legitimate demands of others.

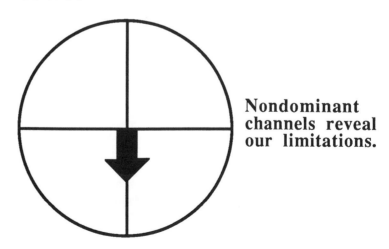

Nondominant channels reveal our limitations.

Coping with
Style Demands

We can recognize and respect a nondominant channel as a limitation that requires careful attention and directed energy. To illustrate, if you ever had difficulty in producing a researched and documented paper, you appreciate the natural abilities of the abstract sequential as well as recognize your own limitations in this area. Some students will not enroll under certain teachers because the demands of their required research papers call for more abstract sequential ability than the students can or will use. In effect, such behavior confesses to the students' difficulty with abstract sequential work. As we went through school, why did some of us have to relearn how to write a research paper each time we received a research assignment? We did not internalize the process the first time because it was not natural to the way we think.

If we do not develop coping strategies to deal with style demands, we can expect to develop stress. Stress results when the coping strategies change from useful techniques to help us manage demands into survival skills to meet demands beyond our capacity.

Ignoring a
Nondominant Channel

We can ignore a nondominant style channel. For instance, all of us must use abstract sequential channels in the course of schooling when we learn to read. From reading to test taking, we face the abstract world of ideas presented in logical, written fashion. However, once we can satisfactorily demonstrate reading skills to the teacher, we can ignore reading as the way to gather information for ourselves. Thus, in effect, many students can read but choose not to do so. Others read only what is necessary to meet school or work demands. Still others "slip through the cracks" of the school system, never learning to read because their lack of abstract sequential ability was ignored. Students who have little abstract sequential ability often cannot learn to read at all without a personalized program to help them approach reading from their own stylistic point of view.

Repressing
a Dominant Style
Channel

We experience fatigue, self-doubt, and self-consciousness, or even put on masked behavior when forced to use a nondominant style. As a result, we inevitably repress a dominant style. For example, most of us can "flip" into our abstract sequential channel when necessary, but not all of us find joy and reward through it. Yet, some people developed the abstract sequential style so well during school years they carried it through their adult life without questioning its relationship to their own natural drives.

What happens if people mask style, pretend to be a particular style? Three case studies show some effects on people who pretended to be abstract sequential.

> *Sam listened to a colleague's general ideas, then treated them as if they were absolute facts. Sam's job required him to think like an abstract sequential, but his strengths were concrete sequential. Thus, he prematurely turned abstract considerations into CS hard data.*

> *Joe pretended to be an abstract sequential, but his true style strengths and needs were abstract random. He repressed his strong emotional side on the surface. He released it, however, every time he engaged in an intellectual debate by creating an emotional scene.*

Sara, a person with strong concrete random gifts and abilities, has a need to question every idea for the sake of thinking differently than everyone else. She could find no "truths" anywhere.

Examples abound of people who developed an abstract sequential channel for school's sake. Along the way they came to believe that intelligent people had to have the AS approach. Even though most of our present schooling experiences afford us the opportunity to develop the abstract sequential channel, it is imperative that it not be accepted as our only channel. If we persist in using a false style point of view as our own, we deny our own forms of intelligence and open the door to resentment, anger, hurt, and harm to ourselves or others.

Some people have become negative people because they repressed a natural quality, ability, or capacity. Those natural energies must come out in some way. If not expressed in a positive manner, they will emerge in a negative way.

What about Nondominant Channels?

To conclude, we learn nondominant style behaviors and adapt to our environments to varying degrees. Some people cannot or will not learn these behaviors; they would rather fight the system than switch. Well-adjusted individuals function very well as long as they have room in their lives for their natural style to emerge and opportunity to develop versatile skills. On the other hand, some people have lost jobs or failed in situations because they could not or would not learn certain style behaviors and skills. Jonathan, a teacher with a dominant CR style provides a good illustration. He works within the system. He knows the "rules of the game" and adapts to them. He conforms to the dominant expectations and reserves his CR abilities for the appropriate phases of his teaching and for private times. But Terry is a CR maverick. She does not conform. She challenges others to change, and uses her persuasive powers to achieve her ends. Other types of CR's cannot or will not work within organizational roles, be it in a marriage, an institution, or a particular field of work; they consistently fight the system and go against established norms.

Questions

When assessing the relative uses of each of the style channels for self-realization and self-actualization, how does each serve you? Which channels reveal and realize your driving forces? Which are used as a means to an end? Which channels direct your creative energies? Which channels represent learned behaviors that allow you to style flex, adapt, cope, or survive in certain situations? We all appear to operate in one of the four styles from time to time. But, I ask you to answer these types of questions. In which channel do you find hard work fulfilling? As you look back on your life, through which channels do you find your greatest joy, satisfaction, and accomplishment? Would you be freer to be yourself if you could give away one of your style channels for a while?

For each of the style channels, probe for your natural style dominance. Which styles reveal your natural abilities rather than learned behavior? Which style do you value in and of itself, regardless of its functional role?

Chapter 1: A Theoretical Framework for Understanding Style   23

Concrete Sequential

____ Do you naturally prefer to order and organize in a conventionally recognized way?

____ Do you judge value according to practicality?

____ Are you more concerned with finishing a job than with how you or others feel about the job?

____ Is time and efficiency of primary importance to you?

____ Do you feel you have met the challenge of the day when you have accomplished something?

____ Are you task oriented?

____ Do you seek directions because you assume there is a correct way to do the work?

____ Do you relax by puttering, straightening out, fixing this and that?

____ Would you choose physical activity or hands-on assignments if given a choice?

____ Do you take things as they are rather than considering alternative ways of evaluating?

____ Do people praise your reliability, steadiness, dependability?

____ Are you recognized for your efficiency, exactness, accuracy?

Abstract Sequential

____ Do you love argumentative debates?

____ Do you prefer to do a library report rather than invent a product?

____ Do you scan the best-seller list with anticipation?

____ Do you regret having too little time to read?

____ Do you treat yourself to a book whenever you can justify the time—bedtime, traveling, sicktime?

____ Do you find that you never pass a bookstore without stopping and purchasing?

____ Do you head to your papers, desk, library, or the latest journal as a matter of course?

____ Do you love the world of ideas, research, analysis, and evaluation?

____ Do you gravitate toward documentaries?

____ Do you consider yourself a thinker? researcher? idea specialist?

____ Are you driven by the need to use your intellectual powers in search for knowledge and truth, and to refine our understanding of the rational, logical world?

____ Do others see you as intellectual, analytical, evaluative, critical?

Abstract Random

_____ Are you driven by your emotions, or do emotions easily control you?

_____ Is a comfortable, aesthetic, or personal environment important to you?

_____ Are relationships more important to you than accomplishments?

_____ Do your moments of greatest fulfillment occur through relationships? self-understanding? self-healing? emotional release?

_____ Are you a flexible person, more able to "go with the flow" than stick to a schedule?

_____ Do you avoid competition?

_____ Do you have difficulty with detail and directions?

_____ Do you tend to see the whole rather than the parts?

_____ Are you a good judge of character?

_____ Do you read the tone of an environment quickly?

_____ Do the visual or performing arts, or music and poetry hold special meaning for you?

_____ Do your environment and surroundings play an especially important part in your comfort level?

Concrete Random

____ Are you driven by the need to envision and do what has not been done before?

____ Are your natural responses unusual in light of others' responses?

____ Do others find your points of view unusual?

____ Do you gravitate to the unknown, the new experience, the unusual approach, the possibilities?

____ Is frequent change appealing to you?

____ Do you consider yourself a risk-taker?

____ Given circumstances that are important to you, do you usually need to find several equally acceptable ways of seeing that situation?

____ Do you find yourself "seeing the picture" differently than most of your colleagues?

____ Are you a problem-solver?

____ Do you create your own life-problems just to have a problem to solve?

____ Would you describe yourself as one who thrives on diversity and change (or, perhaps, organized chaos)?

____ Do others look to you to solve problems that they find too complex to address or too annoying to do?

You have considered style theory and some aspects of style in yourself. If you wish to probe your own style further, read Dr. Anthony Gregorc's work, **An Adult's Guide to Style**, another phenomenological approach.

Unlike traditional educational studies, primarily quantitative in nature, qualitative approaches to learning , such as phenomenology, consider how and why the individual actually relates to the world and can aid us to understand the role of the mind in the experience of the individual.

One of the values of phenomenologic methodology as a research tool lies in its ability to uncover previously unrecognized variables. One such variable—a psychological base for learning style—is the result of phenomenological work. Phenomenology can also serve as a check against the assumptions, findings, and implications of standardized studies by going to the individual source to search for personal interpretation—in this case, how we learn.

Phenomenologists interested in learning style seek always to understand the individual's perspective and to comprehend the forces that drive the person—the reasons the individual perceives the world in certain ways. As we shall see, knowledge about learning style can help us to recognize various worldviews. Style becomes a sorting mechanism, a differentiating tool and a mind translator. A style-based approach to working with others offers a beginning means to understand the driving forces of the essential self.

In trying to come to grips with learning, phenomenologists assume that we must reflect individually upon our experiences before we can begin to grasp the meaning of our actions. In effect,

> ...like glasses for our eyes, our experience remains silently and unseeingly presupposed, unthematized. It contains within itself the uninterrogated and overlooked beliefs and actions which we daily live through but do not critically examine. (12)

As you read this book, assume a phenomenological attitude. By this approach seek to recognize not only your own behavior and your experiences but also the meaning of your behavior and experiences. Then, try to see the behavior of others as they experience life, not as you would. So, when we describe one learner as detail oriented and another as thematic, try to think as they do, and provide the rationale.

Uncovering the basis for our individual learning styles, through phenomenology, frees us to be ourselves. The process seeks out essential self. For this, we must seek the why in I.

CHAPTER 2

THE NATURE OF A PSYCHOLOGICAL MODEL OF STYLE

The success or failure of any idea is subject to an enormous web of contingencies. Any idea seriously entertained, however, tends to bring about the realization of itself, and will, regardless of the nature of the idea, to the extent it can be free of ambiguities.

—J.C. Pearce

A psychological model of style considers the behaviors of individuals and the reasons for those behaviors. Gregorc's Energic Model of Style, therefore, identifies behaviors (style) but also attempts to understand why individuals behave as they do. The four categories of learning styles

Concrete Sequential (CS)	Abstract Sequential (AS)
Abstract Random (AR)	Concrete Random (CR)

serve to identify types of behaviors and to suggest how and why persons who exemplify them behave in certain ways. When people identify themselves as CS, AS, AR, or CR, they intend to mean that they have a majority of characteristics common to a particular style, that others will recognize or predict their behaviors according to the pattern of that style, and that they have certain preestablished preferences.

STYLE AND BEHAVIORS

If we look just at behaviors, then we quickly recognize some people as natural CS, AS, AR, or CR styles because their behaviors broadcast their style. They "fit" a style pattern—the signal system for standard identification—and they are comfortable with the behaviors of that style. They work easily, efficiently, and effectively within their style and appear to have a sense of self, inner peace, and spontaneous energy flow when they use their own style.

People who have a natural ability in more than one style show behaviors in each style. However, when people have strong abilities in more than one style, their behaviors are more difficult to predict, unless they consistently use the same pattern for particular situations. For example, John, a sales manager, has three natural styles: concrete sequential, abstract random, and concrete random. When he faces a problem, his co-workers do not know whether he will assume a supervisory role and inform them how to solve it (CS), call an impromptu meeting to share his feelings and get reactions (AR), or turn a staff meeting into a brainstorming session to gather alternative solutions (CR). John weaves in and out of his three styles with ease, and matches them to problems as he sees them.

On the other hand, Susan, also a sales manager, has the same three styles but consistently behaves as a CR at work. She delegates decisions that do not require problem-solving, and assumes a leadership role for all problems without evident solutions (CR). She reserves her AR style for socializing outside the office, and assumes a CS task-oriented approach in organizing her home, family appointments, and money matters.

Beyond Natural Style

If one defines *natural style* as behaviors that reveal the mind's natural abilities, then how do we relate to environments that do not cultivate, accept, refine, or permit use of a natural style? It appears that we must develop nondominant channels or, in other words, "stretch" our style.

Ideally, by using both dominant and nondominant channels, individuals can develop the "total style response"—if there were such a thing! More realistically, with awareness of style abilities and style expectations, we can understand better our own style responses, our reactions, and resultant efforts. There appear to be at least six ways we can describe our style in different circumstances.

OUR STYLES APPEAR IN MANY WAYS:

NATURAL
FLEXED
ADAPTED
COPING
RESISTANT
MASKED

Natural

When we use our **natural** style, we work through the mind's strengths.

Flexed

When we use a **flexed** style, we purposely and successfully work in another style. One's style flex-abilities can appear to others as a natural style. Flexed style stems from an integral part of one's own style repertoire, requires little extra energy, and does not diminish one's natural style. Steve, a dominant concrete sequential, illustrates my point. Steve's principal allocates twenty minutes of each faculty meeting to small-group discussions on an announced topic. Four teachers from as many departments, who do not share prep-periods, use the time to raise questions about the principal's topic. The principal expects them to suggest ideas on the topic, and to get to know one other as professionals. Steve says he would normally view such an activity as a waste of time, but has purposely given his principal a fair chance. He attempts to respect the group process of open contribution by raising questions and issues in a nonthreatening manner, by helping other teachers become comfortable with group discussion, and by according value to the approach.

Adaptive

Adaptive style appears when the individual must call upon a limited style within himself or herself. One's adaptive style does not appear to be natural. To use the adaptive style requires extra concentration and energy, and if successfully used over time, may cause the individual to question the legitimacy of his/her own natural style. For example, Sue has a strong abstract random style, but in curriculum committee meetings she consistently assumes responsibility for the research on study units for the newest materials—a task that requires abstract sequential ability. This process requires extraordinary time and is a chore for her. Yet, Sue believes that others expect her to do it, teachers praise her for it, and so she persists. Superficially, she appears to have a natural ability for this work. In reality, she adapted her style to the demands, with resentment.

Coping

Coping style occurs when the individual overlooks his/her driving forces and natural mind channels in order to survive the needs and demands of others. Coping style never appears natural, and calls for maximum concentration and energy. Steady use of coping style may cause the individual to forget the importance of his/her natural style and forces. For an example, Roger has a strong concrete sequential style. He enrolled in a graduate course in administration. His professor, a dominant concrete random style, uses simulations to convey the material in the course. Roger devotes much energy to "playing the game," and considerable time trying to figure out the point of the course. His discomfort in simulations in which he has to create a character's responses breeds disdain for the course. He sees little value in pretending to be someone he is not. He complains about his "stupid" course but has arranged to meet with other class members to sort out the main points for papers and exams.

Resistant

Resistant style indicates a person puts maximum energy, effort, and concentration into resisting the style demands and goals of others, but may or may not recognize or realize his/her own. For example, Jon presents a strong concrete random style as a person and as a teacher. His new principal is a concrete sequential who would like to reorganize the school schedule and develop a standard curriculum. Jon ignores her plans, and takes every opportunity to subvert faculty meetings and to question the value of her ideas. Jon has assumed he cannot and will not work with her. He refuses to consider her alternatives and resists all attempts to implement the new plan.

Masked

Masked style results when the individual does not recognize style strengths or needs. In effect, a person with a masked style comes to believe the mask is real. Masking requires a large investment of time and energy. Consider Nancy, who learns and teaches in a dominant abstract sequential style. She views herself as an imaginative and media-oriented abstract random teacher. Actually, she uses media once a month and predominantly lectures to the class on material from the text the rest of the time. Her students complain that she runs an extremely structured class, and gives heavy reading assignments and long essay tests. Nancy's self-evaluation indicates she has lost her ability to see herself as she is in favor of pretending to be someone else.

We cannot underestimate the strength of our own styles, but we also must recognize the ways in which we actualize, support, adjust, or defend our styles when others place demands on us. No one ever said that understanding style would be a simple task!

STYLE AND ENVIRONMENTS

We pursue professional and personal goals, assume responsibilities, and perform tasks in many environments—home, workplace, school, marriage, family, and organizations. We naturally feel satisfied when we can use our own dominant style.

Individual Accommodation to Environmental Demand

Environments may not always accommodate our needs or our desire to use our preferred, natural styles. Environments may call for one style of behavior. For example, a police department may mandate a standard uniform and certain decorum for its troops. A principal may require that students march out single file through a designated door in a fire drill. A restaurant may insist on jacket and tie for its adult male patrons. Or, a family argument may require parents and children to listen to one another rather than walk out during conflict. In each situation the environment's demands appear to take precedence over the individual's predilection.

Some people can easily style flex or adapt to situations like these. They may even appear to function naturally in it. But others do not.

Individuals in Conflict with the Environment

What if the individual and the environment conflict? Either party can take one of several courses of action available. First, the individual may choose to work for a change or to opt out without a defensive approach. For example, in the former situation, if a teacher thinks a certain type of test does not reflect student ability and leads to placement, then he or she may attempt to change the criteria for using test scores and provide counterevidence to the administration and work to change policy. In the latter situation, a teacher who knows he or she cannot work with special education children may aid both himself or herself and the students by refusing such a position.

Second, if individuals believe that the environment deserves attention, then they may learn how to meet the environment's expectations. Perhaps they look for training, try to gain experience, get a clearer explanation of expectations, or change attitude. They might even choose another solution: learn how to become neutral in the environment by controlling certain of their own behaviors. For example, if a teacher agrees with the need to attend to student learning style, he or she can learn about style in several ways. Choices include inservice training, hands-on classroom experiences with peer coaching, independent study, administrative coaching, experimenting with programs....

Many inservice training fiascos occur because teachers do not accept the need for training. When administrators require teachers with this mind to take inservice training in the area of style, the instructor must break the attitude barrier before he or she can realistically convey training materials, resources, and programs.

Third, if parties in conflict can find a variety of ways to address a problem, then they come closer to resolving conflict. For instance, a restaurant can mark off smoking and nonsmoking sections to accommodate the legitimate desires of its customers. Schools can accommodate the different environmental needs of children by providing multiple types of environments ranging from quiet, structured areas to informal settings.

Fourth, concern that an individual will do harm to himself or herself or to others demands action, but such action should preserve the dignity of the individual. For example, a school system may offer early retirement incentives for teachers whose lack of ability leaves no question as to their unsuitability.

OUR ENVIRONMENTS REQUIRE RESPECT

BUT MUST ALSO RESPECT US.

Environmental Impact and Style

To this point, we have talked only about individual behaviors as they relate to the environment. What happens if the environment can demand, accept, or reject style behaviors—positive or negative ones?

For example, the school can demand CS behaviors from teachers by requiring them to turn in report cards by Friday at three o'clock. It can demand AR behaviors by calling upon teachers to keep a steady line of positive communication among parent, teacher, and student. It can demand AS behaviors from students by preparing them to achieve certain scores on tests. And it can demand CR behaviors from teachers by asking them to find multiple ways of teaching different types of children in the classroom. As we discussed in the previous chapter, individuals are most likely to meet the environment's style expectations if they consider them worthy, necessary, or legitimate.

Some people assert that they can flex into any style on demand. In most cases, they mean that they can assume the behaviors of the style. They can balance a checkbook in concrete sequential fashion, they can enjoy an abstract random party, they can write an abstract sequential term paper, or they can throw caution to the wind and flow with the potential results of a concrete random decision.

Theoretically, we access our natural qualities of concreteness, abstraction, sequencing, and randomness through the four learning channels: CS, AR, AS, and CR. We therefore should be able to work in all four styles. This is much more easily written than accomplished! And we should understand why we act in the style we choose, one of life's great challenges.

The more strongly developed each of the learning channels is, the more easily we show representative style behaviors and the more quickly we can recognize those style behaviors in ourselves and others. For example, Sandra is dominant in the abstract random and abstract sequential channels, with fewer abilities in concrete sequential and still fewer in concrete random. If she listed her behaviors according to a style profile, she would find more in her dominant channels than in the others.

Environmental Power and Style

The environment—people and organizations—brings about our style responses in several ways: by its ability to nurture our natural style; by its delusion that all people can become well rounded if they truly want to; by its willingness to allow only one type of style; or by its influence to blind us to all but one type of style. For example, teachers may nurture students' natural styles by helping them to understand, express, and refine their natural abilities through activities, experiences, and personal conversation. Students may nurture a teacher's natural abilities with positive responses to the unique experiences and opportunities provided.

Teachers can also cultivate nonnatural styles when they require students to use many different types of skills and abilities. Likewise, students force a teacher to develop many style skills and abilities.

Environments can also force people to use only one style. An elementary school that requires teachers to adhere to a tight schedule of lesson plans complete with behavioral objectives compels a CS style. A language arts curriculum oriented toward creative writing obliges teachers to develop their random side. Or, a teacher who uses only one or two styles of teaching makes students work within the concomitant demands or be unsuccessful.

And, environments can convince us of the value of one style over others. A strong parent can influence, cajole, or intimidate a child into a desired pattern of behavior. A parent may model a style of behavior and thereby teach a child to behave in that style. For example, a CR mother may teach her children to enjoy exploring and investigating the unknown by doing such things with them. Or, a parent may ridicule, insult, or shame a child into giving up his or her natural style for "the right way." Comments like "What's wrong with you that you can't keep your room neat?" eventually lead a child to the demands for linear structure. Or a parent can shape a child into one style by praising and rewarding only certain types of behaviors. Thus, a sensitive and emotional child may hide AR proclivities if parents recognize only AS behavior—"model student behavior."

The people and the world around us continuously signal approval and disapproval of our behaviors, thereby guiding and shaping our view of ourselves and our ability to accept our natural style.

Developed Style

It seems that some of us always operate with our natural style regardless of environmental demands. Mrs. Lucas, mother of seven-year-old Rob, related that she could see abstract random dominance in her son before preschool. She realized that he had a natural capacity to make friends. She said, "He could make friends with a polar bear!" As a youngster he loved the arts, plays, and opportunities to create imaginative stories.

People with a well-**developed** style let their style shine through for the world to see. Some use their style with elegance, in an unobtrusive manner, and without alienating others. They manage to seem amenable even though they use their own style. However, others with similarly well-developed styles manage to have their own way regardless of others. This leads to resentment in others.

The Emerging Style

Some people have a dominant, natural style but need time for it to emerge as developmental stages and maturing experiences allow. With patience and opportunities to refine the abilities of their natural mind channels, these people blossom from an **emerging style** into a natural style. For some, the opportunities occur during school years; for others, not until adulthood. One thinks of children who have school experiences strictly channeled in one style; they may never gain the psychological freedom to have positive experiences with their own style. Many such children often become behavior problems in school, or are diagnosed as underachievers. A few develop into gifted adults once they regain their freedom and sense of self.

STAGES OF STYLE DEVELOPMENT
DEVELOPED
EMERGING
EXPERIMENTAL
ADJUSTED
HIDDEN

The Experimental Style

Some people need many experiences with using different mind channels before they recognize their own natural channel. They must have these multiple exposures before they claim a dominant style or they may miss their best channel. Their style is **experimental**. For example, some students achieve high grades and school success throughout their educational career. But because they have had few qualitatively different experiences, they do not know which career path to choose or how to thrive in other than an educational environment. For such people, experience really is the best teacher.

The Adjusted Style   Some people have an **adjusted** style. They style flex or adapt so well they continually defer use of their best channels in favor of pleasing others. And some may mask so well that natural mind channels atrophy.

The Hidden Style   Finally, some people have a **hidden** style. They have many environmental pressures or innate problems not related to style. They will not recognize natural mind channels until they can solve these problems.

Implications   By definition, learning style is a set of outer behaviors that signal our mind's style to others. It is up to us to decide how our style serves our self-realization and actualization, whether we activate our naturally dominant mind channel, and how our interpretation of style influences our future assessment and direction of self.

STYLE AND REASONS FOR BEHAVIORS   The phenomenological approach to style moves beyond the behavioral characteristics of different styles in order to probe why styles evidence different behaviors. Once we move to a phenomenological level, we begin to investigate how the behaviors relate to the individual's driving forces, and, ultimately, personal essence. We ask how style relates to the individual's internal goals, and how style helps or hinders achievement of the goals.

Because we can never truly become another person, we will never know another's personal essence, but we can seek it in ourselves. And, we can go as far as possible to understand it in others. One of the rules of thumb for understanding others: check their perceptions; don't project your own onto them.

We have seen that environments—people, organizations, and situations—can help individuals self-realize and self-actualize, or they can deter individuals from their goals. In summary, environments produce a range of possibilities. They can

- let us be ourselves and use our own style;

- encourage us to use our own style, and to develop additional style responses;

- guide us to recognize personal forces and use of natural style;

- ask us to subordinate our dominant style channel in favor of another for its convenience or use;

- require us to submerge our dominant style channel and work consistently through a nondominant channel.

We can respond to these environmental demands in different ways. We can

- be ourselves and use our own style;

- develop style flex-ability—the ability to know and retain our own style but at the same time to read different types of style demands and flex with ease to meet legitimate ones;

- develop our own understanding of personal forces and style;

- learn adaptation skills—skills that permit us to work in nondominant channels at a satisfactory level within the environment;

- learn coping skills to help us survive in the environment;

- develop the ability to resist—to fight the environment overtly or covertly, through confrontation or by sabotage.

We run into difficulty if we rely solely on behaviors as a measure of individuals' dominant learning channel. In fact, they may have adjusted their behaviors to meet environmental forces and expectations. It is paramount that people have the opportunity to be understood beyond their behaviors, for the reasons under the surface.

CHAPTER 3

USING A PSYCHOLOGICAL MODEL OF STYLE

The nature "discovered" is determined to an
indeterminable degree by the mind that sets
out to discover.

—J. C. Pearce

THE VALUE
OF STYLE

A psychological model of style is valuable as an individual and organizational tool, and serves several functions. As a vehicle for personal analysis, interpersonal understanding, and organizational change, it plays many and varied roles. The results of using a psychological model of style depend upon the individual's or organization's willingness to recognize the possibilities of style, and implement them after proper training.

The determination of style for an individual is not an end in and of itself but primarily a tool to achieve ends. Thus, I gain little of value by knowing I have an abstract random style unless I develop the ability to register this information, to cause a change in my attitude, a change in the reasons for my behavior and ultimately a change in my behavior.

For individuals to find value in a psychological model of style, they must be open to its possible uses, which range from an attitude shift to physical action. Although most educators want the practical applications of a theory without the background, for this model the most practical application begins with the theory, then moves to the concrete applications of activity in the classroom.

According to Gregorc, most people move through five stages of style understanding before they achieve a full grasp of the possibilities.

Alert

During the first stage, the **alert stage**, people need to gain knowledge about learning style theory, hear that researchers test it and that practitioners are at work with it in the field. During this phase, educators see that style is a serious issue that affects their personal and organizational lives.

In effect, the alert stage serves as the alarm clock: a signal that we need to move from one state of existence—inattention to style—to another.

Awareness

During the second stage, the **awareness stage**, individuals examine the concept of style and apply it to their own lives. They identify their behaviors and observe their lives. At this point if they can recognize that their style patterns exist, and concur that these patterns affect the quality of their lives, then they are ready to move to the next stage.

Attitudinal

In stage three, the **attitudinal stage,** individuals examine and assess their perceptions of themselves, the way their perceptions form their worldviews, and the way the worldviews serve their ability to self-realize and self-actualize. Individuals feel the challenge of style in this phase. This phase causes the most introspection and lingers throughout a lifetime if it is seriously addressed.

Appreciative

In stage four, the **appreciative stage**, individuals incorporate their knowledge of self with a re-view of others. During this stage they perceive others in a new light, move from tolerance for differences to an appreciation of the unique worth of others. In this stage people no longer equate qualitative differences with deviance, a technique used to verify their own style. Rather, they examine similarities more closely to determine the difference between superficial and meaningful similarities, and they begin to interpret common experiences with others with new understanding. Further, with attitudinal shifts, individuals open themselves to receive the gifts of self that others offer.

Activation

Finally, in stage five, the **activation stage**, individuals address their own stylistic needs as well as those of others. They understand their own "truths" and how they differ from the "truths" of others. They become more conscious of how to read the signals they send to others and the signals that others send them. They decipher when to use their natural style and when to style flex. They become more aware of the stress incurred during adaptation and coping periods, and understand the difference between their style-flexing abilities and their adjustment skills. And they more fully tune in to their own self-signals that invite personal growth.

During the active stage, individuals make conscious choices and decisions based on their knowledge of qualitative differences rather than reacting to their experiences. They determine the course of their actions rather than begrudgingly adjust to others or mourning for nonexistent skills. In working with or teaching others, individuals who have reached this stage differentiate their activities and actions with others in a qualitative way.

UNDERSTANDING STYLE IS A GRADUAL PROCESS.

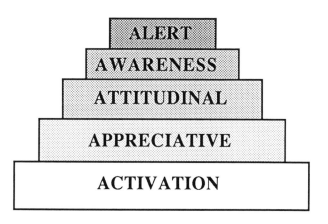

```
        ALERT
      AWARENESS
     ATTITUDINAL
    APPRECIATIVE
     ACTIVATION
```

The Possibilities of Style

A psychological model of style recognizes and values the multiple ways by which we define, pursue, and achieve our goals. If we apply style to the way different types of people experience the world, we validate the way an individual learns, works, and thinks. If teachers accept and recognize that all styles of learning are valid and valued, teachers develop or increase positive self-concepts in their students. If teachers approve of many different ways to learn, children gain the opportunity to see themselves as good learners. With a positive sense of self-worth and belief in their abilities, they have greater chances of school success.

Knowledge about our own style helps us to recognize and develop all our style channels rather than allowing us to rely on one channel regardless of the circumstances. It encourages us not to cling to our own style and to defend it less. Understanding our style promotes self-confidence.

If we address style differences and attempt to develop all our style channels, then we increase the number and qualitative range of our responses in different situations. As we do this, perhaps we will meet our own as well as others' legitimate needs. And with improved understanding of style preferences and style demands, we will make better choices when faced with decisions.

A study of style opens the door to in-depth self-assessment. By our appraisal of how and why we respond to our world, we have a greater chance of understanding our "essential self" versus our role-playing self. We equip ourselves better to distinguish between natural behaviors, those we adopt temporarily to accommodate a nondominant style.

Finally, a study of style can bring about systemic change in an organization by providing the tools to incorporate policies and standards that acknowledge, value, and act upon the contributions of individuals' differences.

POTENTIAL OUTCOMES

In the study of the Gregorc model of learning style, an individual usually moves through levels of sophistication. An individual may find that he or she may

- *move from one of the five stages—alert, awareness, attitudinal, appreciative, activation—in a linear manner, to complete and internalize each stage before moving on, or may internalize two or more stages simultaneously;*

- *stop at any one stage and not be able to move on to another stage; and*

- *address parts of each stage but not fully complete any stage.*

In a holistic study of style, individuals consider not only how style impacts upon them but how they impact upon others. As in the stages of development about style, there are levels of sophistication in applying style to self and to others. And as in the stages of development, there is no guarantee that the individual will complete all the levels in each category, or even address each category.

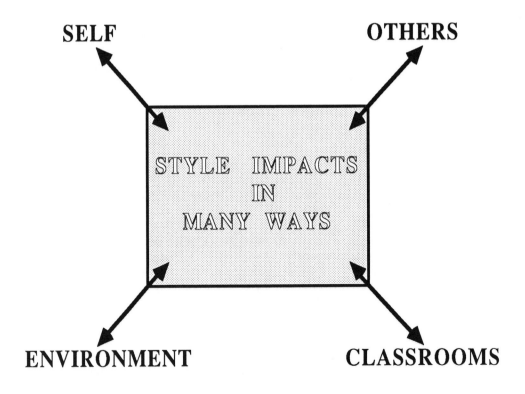

SELF   OTHERS

STYLE IMPACTS
IN
MANY WAYS

ENVIRONMENT   CLASSROOMS

POSITIVE USES

My own interpretation of the Gregorc model suggests to me these positive ways to consider its applications. It may be viewed as

- a system designed to consider personal driving forces—personal essence;

- a model for self-assessment, self-realization, and self-actualization;

- a means to define personal and environmental integrity;

- a guide to increase our ability to recognize the stylistic forces in an environment and to respond appropriately to many legitimate needs of people, places, and situations;

- a guide to observe, check, and correct our perceptions and behaviors; to balance personal stylistic forces with the environment's forces; to recognize when the environment compromises our own integrity;

- an opportunity to maximize our strengths and strengthen our weaknesses rather than maintain a defense of one style;

- a means to value style flex and adaptation;

- a signal system from others, so that we can "hear" what they are saying and "see" what they mean; a way to recognize that others' expectations stem from their minds' styles;

- a tool to predict the attitudes and actions of others and means to consider our own and others' perceptions so that we do not get caught "off guard" by others' perceptions and behaviors;

- a base of understanding from which to respond without infringement on others;

- a communication tool and means to value others;

- a method to create opportunities giving qualitatively different options to ourselves and others;

- a rationale: for not responding to certain situations that do not benefit from, require, or want our input; for recognizing when the environment will not or cannot compromise;

- an opportunity: to free ourselves or others from inappropriate or wrong expectations, demands, or situations; to know when the costs of the environment are too high in terms of health, psyche, spirit, emotions, intellect, or physical ability;

- a process that exposes negative behaviors and attitudes as harmful to self and others;

- an approach that provides "psychological safety" for us and others to experience different styles and develop unused, unrecognized, or overly controlled channels.

We can also misuse style if we disregard its intent to aid individuals' growth and development, and its goal to help them self-realize and self-actualize. We misuse this model when we diagnosis and prescribe for style. Webster defines diagnosis as "a careful investigation of the facts to determine the nature of a thing." We misapply concrete/abstract and sequential/random style when we use it

- *for its own sake—as a habit to identify and label people;*

- *to confine identity—if we simplify a person's being to a series of characteristics;*

- *to confine expression—if we determine, and permit, a limited number of acceptable responses;*

- *to limit options—if we recognize, provide, or allow only certain types of responses from certain types of styles;*

- *to avoid a phenomenological understanding of style— if we favor a mechanical approach to testing style;*

- *to create personality diffusion—if we identify only what we expect to see in others;*

- *to use difference to create deviants—if we identify one, two, or three styles as correct and appropriate" regardless of positive or negative behaviors, and make the other styles deviant; and*

- *to excuse inappropriate behavior—if we allow an "anything-goes" approach without an ethical and moral foundation.*

LABELING

The Gregorc model of learning style labels four types of learning style. Used appropriately, labels identify distinguishing characteristics. Labels should alert us and prompt us to examine our responses—in attitude and in action—to the differences.

According to Webster, the word *label* means "a rag, a shred." It means "a descriptive word or phrase applied to a person, group, theory, etc. as a convenient generalized classification." A label is a tag, a shred of evidence to identify someone or something. Many people, however, use a label as the person or thing itself. The label and person become synonymous. The attached part of identification itself becomes the whole. When a teacher says, "I am an abstract sequential," he/she may be giving up identity to the label.

In the hands of persons who do not understand their intended use, labels can cause serious harm. The danger in labeling students occurs if we do not attempt, or we stop trying, to understand the person and relate to the label instead. If the student does not behave and respond as the teacher expects a student of that style to respond, the student can be seen as wrong rather than as prey to the teacher's interpretation or as a case of mislabeling!

Before we go on to categorize people according to style, examine your reaction to being labeled according to style:
- *Does a label free you to be yourself without apology and with*

responsibility, or does it box you into a definition that may not be you at all?

• *What kinds of experiences have you had with being labeled? Were they positive or negative? Did they aid you to achieve a goal or make doing so more difficult?*

• *How would you feel if you were mislabeled and treated in accordance with the mislabeling?*

• *Are you attracted to the use of labels? Do you dislike the use of labels? How are these a function of your needs and qualities?*

• *Have you experienced labels used for convenience regardless of human cost? Have you attempted to counter such labeling in some way?*

• *What qualifications should a person have to be trusted with the use of labels central to a model of learning?*

Used positively, labels open the door to possibilities rather than hard and fast rules. Labels aid us to see further than we might without them. A label signals others about the way the person views the world. A label raises our perceptual antenna to receive the broadcasts others are trying to send. Labels help us "get on their wave length." Without labels we may continuously scan the information, and never tune in the channel. Labels, therefore, can serve as an early warning device: Another type of mind is here. Listen up!

LABELS AND INSTRUMENTS

When we work with style and its labels, we must transcend the simple use of labels and characteristics. We appropriately use labels as a departure point, not an ending point. Teachers who cannot recognize and work with different learning styles of adults or students without diagnostic scores may want to question whether they fully understand the meaning and implications of a psychologically based model of style.

Instruments are valuable tools to check style dominance and style limitations. With little time available to conduct in-depth interviews with students, teachers can find instruments efficient and effective. But before using style instruments, we advise teachers to "test" their real knowledge of, comfort with, and understanding of style. They accomplish this when they conduct in-depth interviews, make observations, and hold conversations with several students to verify their own perceptions of the students' styles. In this way teachers can assess whether or not their sense of style is consonant with identification instruments' findings.

In other words, teachers must understand and implement style phenomenologically before they attempt to use it diagnostically. By taking this phenomenological approach first, teachers see and understand that people live qualitatively different lives for qualitatively different reasons. With this perspective, we do not give up our power of evaluation to an instrument—which may be wrong at times.

The Gregorc model of learning style intends to aid individuals in their quest for self-realization and self-actualization. A component of Mediation Ability Theory, it provides guidelines and options through which people can consider themselves. It assumes that as people recognize and understand the fundamental forces in themselves, they will act upon such knowledge and bring about their own development.

Because the processes of self-realization and self-actualization never end, a model that intends to address these processes demands open-ended possibilities and serves as a catalyst for continued expansion of self. I consider the Gregorc model of style much more than an identification matrix of four styles. It provides the starting point for individual growth and development via phenomenological understanding of oneself and others.

This model serves individuals as persons and as members of organizations in their attempts to understand personal goals and driving forces and their resources. The power of personal goals cannot be underestimated. Thoreau noted their importance when he suggested that "life should be a stately march to an inner tune." The group Crosby, Stills, and Nash sang the same observation: "You, when you're on the road, must have a code, that you can live by."

The Gregorc model of learning style serves organizational goals because it promotes the development of members of an organization. As this model relates to schools, it aids educators and students to consider their own driving forces, possibilities as human beings, and expressions of themselves.

The model cautions educators to understand their own driving forces before they attempt to understand those of students. We cannot know others until we know ourselves. When teachers work with students, I expect teachers to apply the Gregorc model of style to help students understand their styles as they exist at each student's developmental stage.

There is no end to understanding one's style and its relation to self-realization and self-actualization. Therefore, identification of one's style profile must be complemented by lifelong self-awareness and self-assessment that leads to increasing ability to act in a self-fulfilling way.

We maintain the integrity of a psychological model of style when we employ the four categories of learning style—Concrete Sequential, Abstract Sequential, Abstract Random, and Concrete Random—to create general distinctions to understand differences in people. We maintain the integrity of the person when we recognize and act upon the principle that the individual has different patterns and assortments of style derived from internal qualities. We maintain the integrity of the environment when we recognize and act upon the belief that other people and places have legitimate goals that deserve respect.

*SEARCHING
WITHIN*

You have now spent time assessing your personal goals and their relation to your learning style. You may have thought about your own attempt to self-realize and self-actualize through achievement of your goals. And you may have considered whether how you interact with the world—your style—is conducive to the achievement of your goals. You may have found that you have never defined your driving forces, your goals as a human being. You may have discovered that your learning style is a natural expression of your essence, or that your learning style—your behavior—has changed with your perceptions of demands made on you.

The process of self-realization and self-actualization continues with hills and valleys along the way. Many have documented the difficulties. Others have provided base-line information about the process. Researchers in adult development have defined the role of developmental tasks and adult life stages that all of us face in our life cycles, and style theorists consider the role of style in adult development. Theorists, researchers, and practitioners in the field of learning style have identified some of the prevailing attitudes and behaviors that we use to define ourselves in relation to our world. The work by Abraham Maslow has afforded us the opportunity to understand the structure of our human-needs hierarchy. And, third-force psychologists have probed to uncover the nature of individual differences and mental health.

Professionals are rarely asked to assess the impact of their psychological history and their present mental well-being upon the way they perform in their jobs. Although the teaching profession is one field that necessitates that its practitioners understand the nature of the human mind, teachers seldom have or take the opportunity to be introspective. To become effective teachers, however, we must understand, accept, and attend to every type of mind entering the classroom. Yet, teachers have rarely been encouraged to do these very things for themselves.

Ultimately, we must accomplish the process of self-realization and self-actualization for ourselves. We can begin the process through introspection and self-examination. A personal search process causes you to reflect upon factors that influence your evolution as a teacher. In effect, our autobiographies enter into all our experiences. We cannot leave our histories or ourselves outside the classroom door.

We bring ourselves to our classrooms: our memories, our experiences, our needs for fulfillment, and our hopes for the future. In effect, we define and shape our reality as persons before we assume the role of the teacher. How we play that role is influenced by the person we bring to it.

Before you address the styles of your students, consider "the phenomenology of me"—the personal essence, driving forces, goals, and qualities that have interacted with experiences over the years to move you through life. Self-examination enables you to find what defines you, even before you walk into the classroom What is pre-set for you before you become the teacher in Room 105?

Through self-examination, you try to define your own psychological health and well-being. You attempt to understand your own psychological environment and definition of reality in order to recognize and nurture your natural energies. You ask, "How do my beliefs and attitudes about myself and teaching guide my decisions in the classroom?" You seek your own best self in relation to you, the teacher. And, you strive for an answer to the questions, Why am I a teacher? Why do I do what I do?

Four major questions help you to begin the self-examination process.

Who am I as a person?

___ the natural me?

___ the style-flexing me?

___ the adapted me?

___ the coping me?

What experiences have led me to see myself in these ways?

What conditions promote my mental health?

In what ways does my personal profile relate to my teaching self?

As you pursue these questions, consider your personal driving forces, individual mind channels, and personal style. Assume a phenomenological attitude: observe as well as reflect upon your experiences, probe the real you. Neil Diamond sings, "I am, I say!" Can you say the same?

Part II

Teaching Style In Focus

Teaching is a situation that has never been before and never will come again. It demands of you a reaction that cannot be prepared beforehand....It demands presence, responsibility, it demands you.

—Martin Buber

PART II

TEACHING STYLE—IN FOCUS

...An individual must come to recognize his
own qualities, characteristics, biases, and
world of reality before analyzing and applying
the tenets of mediation theory to others.
                                    —Anthony F. Gregorc

When we attempt to examine and interpret our learning style and the forces behind it, we probe our inner selves. We ask fundamental questions: What are my natural abilities? What is the range of my capacities? How do I use my self in my work? Why am I satisfied with myself, or dissatisfied? Energized, or enervated? Stressed, or relaxed? Investigation of inner self must come before investigation of role-related self. The inner self is the only meaningful starting point on the journey into the meaning of style.

Every teacher has a personal learning style. Every teacher brings a unique self to the classroom. Even though we value this unique self as beautiful and special, at the same time our qualitative differences also limit our vision of other possibilities in the classroom. The strength of our personal goals, expressed through natural style, pull in a fairly consistent direction and create our view of what teaching can and should be. But, our views tend to limit our understanding of different types of students. And our views restrict our choice and interpretation of teaching techniques, even when we have a variety from which to choose. Thus, as Alfred North Whitehead stated, "Value is limitation."

As with learning style, the concept of teaching style can help us to understand the person as a teacher. Teaching style can be considered from many points of view and for many purposes. Here we view it as a concept to gain perspective about the person in the process of teaching and as a way to see how the teacher, as an instrument of thought, shapes the reality of the classroom.

From a phenomenological point of view, teaching style is a set of "distinctive behaviors that place mediation demands upon the mind qualities of both the learner and the teacher." Although we can identify teaching style through the behaviors of the teacher in the classroom—many teaching-style questionnaires already address this task—identification is only the first step. Once we identify behaviors, we must ask the crucial questions: What mediation abilities must the teacher and the student use to meet the expectations of this class? Are these mediation abilities the teacher's natural abilities? How does the need to meet mediation demands affect the teacher and the learner? What changes in attitude and action need to take place in order for the teacher to use natural abilities and to extend the teacher's style-flex repertoire? If these questions can be addressed, then, the teacher will have the opportunity to examine why he or she uses a particular teaching style, and to consider options for change, growth, and development.

If we translate the above phenomenological teaching-style definition to the classroom, we create a more specific definition of teaching style:

Teaching style is a set of attitudes and actions that open a formal and informal world of learning to students. It is a subtle force that influences student access to learning and teaching by establishing perimeters around acceptable learning procedures, processes, and products. The powerful force of the teacher's attitude toward students as well as the instructional activities used by the teacher shape the learning/teaching experience and require of the teacher and student certain mediation abilities and capacities. Thus, the manner in which a teacher presents himself or herself as a human being and receives learners as human beings is as influential upon the students' lives and learning as the daily activities in the classroom.

Let's examine this definition. In part, the teacher's attitudes influence the classroom. In his working philosophical paper, THE ORGANON SYSTEM, Gregorc states that the mind is an instrument of thought. Therefore, **each human being acts as an instrument of thought in relation to every other human being. If we apply this principle to the classroom, then every teacher's being acts as an instrument regardless of content, subject, method, or grade level.** The guiding question in considering this principle is, How does the teacher act as an instrument of thought, shaping and guiding the course of classroom life?

The teacher's actions, furthermore, disclose how the teacher perceives (concretely or abstractly) and organizes (sequentially or randomly) the formal and informal content for teaching and learning. By using Mediation Ability Theory as the guiding structure, we can organize and identify styles of teaching representing the four types of style: concrete sequential, abstract sequential, abstract random, concrete random. Once we identify teaching style, we ask: How is the style used by the teacher compatible with his/her natural mediation abilities? How does the teacher's perception of his/her role influence the choice of teaching style? How does the teacher meet the learning-style needs of all learners? How does the person in the process of being a teacher self-realize and self-actualize?

In the next chapter we will consider some of the invisible ways teachers act as instruments of thought: by establishing the psychological environment; by orchestrating the class; by placing subjective, adaptation demands on students; and by creating classroom ambience. In the subsequent chapter we will discuss some of the visible ways the teacher operates in the classroom by discussing the teaching-style behaviors of each style.

CHAPTER 4

THE TEACHER AS AN INSTRUMENT OF THOUGHT

If one thinks back to his own school days, one will probably remember that the good teachers one has had in one's lifetime did not all behave alike or even with great similarity. Rather, each stands out as a person, an individual, some for one reason, some for another. Each had his own peculiar methods, values, and techniques. Good teaching is like that, an intensely personal thing.

—Arthur W. Combs

The teacher is like an orchestra conductor who brings unique presence and talents, a personal history, and an individual style to the persons with whom he/she works. These invisible and indivisible forces of the teacher shape the course of a class, determine its vitality, and influence the development of its members. Among the most difficult components of education to measure, yet one of the crucial factors for student success, the teacher as an instrument of thought influences the teaching/learning process in subtle, yet powerful, ways. Challenged to affect the lives of learners, teachers must balance their own needs and possibilities with those of their students.

PSYCHOLOGICAL ENVIRONMENTS

A few years ago I attended a concert performance by the cellist Rostropovich. As this elderly man walked across the stage and smiled at us, something changed in the tone of the audience. At the end of his performance, we rose in acclaim. He not only had impressed us with his performance but had also won our hearts. He had not spoken even one word, yet somehow he seemed a loving father to us all. He simply loved us through his music and we returned his love. This gentle person alone on the stage had wrought a personal relationship with each person who desired it. Out of the great space, he created an intimate environment.

I have watched a third-grade teacher in a basement of a worn brick school create the same atmosphere with her children. I have also seen a fourth-grade teacher in a modern, well-equipped school reduce her class to a group of tense, frustrated children.

In his writings, child psychologist Haim Ginott brings to our attention the psychological environment developed by the teacher. He sees the teacher as an instrument of thought and cautions us to appreciate our impact on children's lives. Of the many remarks that I have read about teaching, none has impacted me so strongly as the following quotation.

> *I've come to the frightening conclusion that I am the decisive element in the classroom. It's my personal approach that creates the climate. It's my daily mood that makes the weather. As a teacher, I possess a tremendous power to make a child's life miserable or joyous. I can be a tool of torture or an instrument of inspiration. I can humiliate or humor, hurt or heal. In all situations, it is my response that decides whether a crises will be escalated or de-escalated and a child humanized or de-humanized.*

—Haim Ginott

We create our psychological environment. Our unique presence can build rapport, cause fear, encourage divergent thinking, inspire academic excellence, or develop any number of healthy or unhealthy conditions for ourselves and for others. We might ask ourselves to what degree we create the good days and the bad days. How much do we ourselves determine our day's outcome? Is a good day one that supports our view of reality? Does our relationship with our students depend on their capacity to relate to us?

ORCHESTRATING YOUR CLASS

Earlier I mentioned that the teacher is like the conductor of an orchestra. Like the conductor, the teacher can bring about harmony or dissonance depending on his/her ability to bring together various gifts.

Using the analogy of the orchestra for the classroom and the conductor for the teacher, let us look at some of the possibilities for performance. The orchestra must practice as a whole. All musicians must identify the same notes, read music, and follow directions—basic skills if you will. But, each section of the orchestra plays in a qualitatively different way from other sections, just as each learning style works differently in the classroom. And each section of the orchestra offers a certain gift, variously tendered, as does each learning style.

When the sections of the orchestra play together, harmony occurs. In the classroom, if we have many ways for each style to perform, teachers can applaud all styles. If the arrangement favors the string section, the other sections of the orchestra can provide harmonic blend, or will they be silenced and go unrecognized. In the class, if the content favors use of one style, many other styles contribute their views or will we see them as having no function?

At some times an exceptional performer may give a solo performance because the person excels with his/her instrument. Talent, not choice of instrument, determines the soloist . In the classroom, "exceptional talent" cannot be determined by style. No one best style exists.

The conductor has the power to bring out the best in the musicians and to blend their forces in service to the score. So, too, the teacher must have the ability to bring out what students have to offer in order to meet the demands of the curriculum.

AMBIENCE

Each classroom has its own ambience: a mood, character, quality, tone, and atmosphere. Teachers create ambience, in part, by the ways they modulate their voices to affect others. How do you use your voice to shape your classes?

Teachers reveal themselves through movements and mannerisms. Your body language sends signals to others. One psychologist calls body language the "leakage channel" because our true feelings escape through it.

Teachers set a tone by the values they convey. For example, a teacher who values quiet, order, and authority creates an ambience very different from that created by a teacher who values an active, discussion-oriented class.

The teacher's style, too, creates ambience. Different styles of teaching foster different types of classroom atmosphere, each equally pleasing and productive in its own way. For example, the dominant concrete sequential teacher may run a more traditional classroom, and the dominant concrete random teacher may prefer an open classroom—different ambiences, but neither better in and of itself.

Teachers also set a tone that cultivates certain kinds of responses from students. The responses appear narrow or broad, to be of specific styles, or may reflect all shades of style.

Ambience makes its mark in several ways. For instance, by a first-grade child's refusal to get on the bus—her stomach suddenly aching after breakfast, or by a high school student's decision to skip class. Students from all over the school may stop in one teacher's room to meet others or talk when the atmosphere is accepting. Students frequently sign up for courses with certain teachers and not others because of the mood, tone, and quality of a teacher's classroom. And, some teachers cause their own discipline problems by establishing a mood or tone that begs for rebellion.

Different types of teachers and the classroom ambience create various types of responses in students. For example, an extremely structured teacher may bring out the negative qualities in a random student who cannot function in the class and therefore attempts to save face by disruptive behavior. Or an extremely random teacher may cause anxiety or disgust in a sequential student who cannot operate in a random teacher's flow of events.

Mood, quality, tone influence the impact of teacher upon student in invisible ways. All set an atmosphere that establishes many of the standards in the classroom.

Ambience appears in positive or negative ways. For example, let's look at teacher comments on report cards. One teacher consistently adds a note about deficiencies: "Sam must practice his math facts more," "Joyce needs to write more neatly," "Jon doesn't use any creative abilities." But another believes that report cards should measure success, and so attempts to write positive comments: "Sue is eager and innovative," "Lyle has improved his attitude." Remarks like these reflect the ambience teachers create every day.

You can witness the force of one's ambience with its positive and negative potential as you read the comments of a man discussing his school experiences.

> I was immediately transported back to my sixth grade
> class. I was sitting at my desk watching Mrs. Lynn writing
> on the board. This rotund woman with a twinkle in her eye,
> and a voice so soft it denied her massive presence, was
> indeed a fond memory for me. Mrs. Lynn took an interest
> in her students. She perceived the differences in needs

and attended to them. She encouraged me to write and in what I would now consider an expository manner. She understood the value of positive reinforcement, always encouraging me to do better, yet placing value on what I had already achieved. My parents noticed I did homework after school before I ran out to play ball. I began to enjoy certain subjects and look forward to school. I was experiencing success and personal growth. Best of all, some of these rewards were intrinsic. I didn't know this consciously at that time. But, in retrospect, I'm aware that I was beginning to do things of an educational (school related) nature that I drew personal satisfaction from.

In my school system, sixth grade was a transition year. A graduation ceremony was held that June, and all of the parents were invited to the graduating sixth-grade auditorium ceremony. This ceremony was complete with pomp and circumstance, and the appropriate awards for best students in all the subject areas. My surprise was to come at the very end of the ceremony when the principal made a short speech about the importance of growth in education and announced that Mrs. Lynn had a special award this year for the most improved student. Word had circulated prior to the ceremony who would be winning the academic awards, but this was a new and unexpected category. "Would Mitchell K. please come up and accept his award." It's funny because I remember Howard R. tapped me on the shoulder; it hadn't sunk in, or maybe I was daydreaming.

It's strange how this little piece of my past has ever greater meaning today. I had improved but not just academically. I was maturing, socially, physically, psychologically and academically. Mrs. Lynn came along at the right time, and she cared. Although I have not had any contact with this wonderful lady since that time, she remains a part of my life.

A fraction of a second later, Mrs. M. came to mind. The dichotomy is amazing. It was that very next year. I was sitting at my desk in English class awaiting the arrival of Mrs. M. She was out of a bygone era, she really wore a black dress, walked with a cane, wore her hair tightly cropped in a bun, and had a crackly tone in her voice that completed the picture. I wonder if she modeled herself after the stereotype schoolmarm of the 1800's —"spare the rod, spoil the child." But this was not a joke; if it were, it was rather a cruel one. The door swung open and we jumped to our feet. "Good morning, Mrs. M.," the class sang out. I kid you not. That was seventh grade in 1962 and we were at attention until we were given permission to sit down. I was not a trouble maker, and this woman scared me, both in reputation and presentation. I was determined to do well.

This teacher (and I use the term with hesitation)

terrorized her students. She concentrated her efforts on those who had the most difficulty with the subject. It was common for her to yell at a student, "Stop clicking your pen, you impudent little child." Several times her cane was used to what she called, getting the child's attention. She was into personality assassination. She was a master at ridiculing a child in front of the class and making jokes of sincere attempts of students who have difficulty. I had several run ins with Mrs. M., much to my dismay. The example I'll share was the culminating event. When she called the roll, she always called me Michelle, not Mitchell. I would correct her, but she would make some comment to get the class to laugh.

On one particular day, I was to make a class presentation. She called out, "Michelle, oh, I'm sorry, I mean, Mitchell." Humiliated, I went before the group. I had worked long and hard on my presentation for the past few weeks. I completed my presentation which was followed by class questions and evaluation. I was pleased with the class reaction. Then it happened. Mrs. M. swung her cane at me. She missed but I felt the pain. I ran out of the school crying and ran home. I was a mess, my mother was in shock. I had never had problems in school, and consequently my parents never had to go to school for a conference.

The meeting with the principal and Mrs. M. was unbelievable. She was atrociously sweet, and I couldn't even speak. The principal suggested I stay in the class and work things out. My mother insisted Mrs. M. apologize to me and stop calling me Michelle. She said she'd be happy to. Wouldn't you know it, the very next day, Mrs. M. while calling the roll, stopped at my name and said, "Mitchell's mother came into school and asked me to apologize for calling him Michelle because it was making him cry." Well, I survived that year, but the scars remain.

Yes! The teacher's being is powerful!

Abraham Maslow has long spoken to us about the force of ambience from a psychotherapeutic perspective. In his writings, he makes it clear that we impact on one another in strong and powerful ways. He warns us of the influence of our personal power, and raises us to new awareness of our individual capacities. As you read the following quotation, think about the teachers who have been a psychotherapeutic force for you, if even in a small way. In what ways do you act upon the potential of your own force?

Let people realize clearly that every time they threaten someone or humiliate or hurt unnecessarily or dominate or reject another human being, they become forces for the creation of psychopathology, even if these be small forces.

Let them recognize that every human who is kind, helpful, decent, psychologically democratic, affectionate, and warm is a psychotherapeutic force, even though a small one.

—Abraham Maslow

ADAPTATION DEMANDS

Our perceptions, values, biases, attitudes, and feelings influence how we define reality. Even though we attempt to teach objectively, impersonally and without bias, we cannot step out of our own definitions. Our view of the importance of the individual, our respect for differences in individuals, and our vision of the purpose of learning—in other words, our defined reality—influence the weight we ascribe to teaching and learning styles, and, in turn, influence our demands upon students.

As a classroom teacher, your objectives, your expectations of students, your values as a human being, and your attitude toward learning place subjective and adaptation demands on students.

Objectives

Webster defines *objective* as "something toward which effort is directed: an aim, or end of action." What is your aim in being a teacher? What is the end result of your teaching actions? What legacy do you wish to leave your students?

To assess our objectives, we have to look beyond the immediate, safe ones, such as "for all students to appreciate history" or "for all children to acquire basic skills." These rarely represent our real objectives. Appraisal of our real objectives requires us to step back from the day-to-day process of teaching—to look inward. How would you assess the following teachers?

Mr. King, a high school foreign language teacher, delights in students who excel in foreign languages. He thrives on students who have a natural talent for a language, who have a competitive sense, and who match wits with him. He wants to groom these students to excellence, to shape them into language naturals, and to use them as a validation of the worth of his superior language gift. However, he gives little attention to students who must work at learning a language, or to students who enjoy the textbook skills of a language.

For some students, Mr. King conveys information and tests progress. For the select few, he serves as a Rubik's cube—a constant challenge to outwit and master. He wants to convey his love of language as well as the power that mastery of any subject can provide. He prides himself not in his ability to teach all students but on his reputation as the most difficult foreign language teacher in the school system.

Teachers with objectives like these abound. Their colleagues admit that they serve certain students extremely well, but their techniques are ineffective and joyless for most. Administrators agree about the talents of people like Mr. King but object to their inability to address the needs of most of their students. One administrator solved the problem by offering his version of Mr. King a 2/5 teaching position. The administrator viewed him as a superior teacher for approximately 2/5 of his students, but someone else had to serve the other 3/5 because he could not. In effect, the administrator forced "Mr. King" out of teaching, causing him to leave behind a part of his life. This teacher also left one group of students who benefited from his teaching but a larger group who no longer had to adapt to his subjective demands.

Mr. Roberts, a professor of physics, taught introductory as well as advanced graduate-level courses. Unlike many of his colleagues, Mr. Roberts taught beginners with great enthusiasm. His test were simple measures of knowledge, not a means to weed out nonscientists. He believed that nonscientists deserve to experience the field in order to respect its potential and possibilities, even though they do not intend to enter it. He rarely lectured to his students, but most often provided guidelines, summaries, and experiments for students to try themselves.

His objectives as a teacher centered on making physics accessible, to meeting individuals at their ability levels, and to conveying his respect for the field of physics by helping others to appreciate it. He wanted to impart a sense of respect for individual abilities, his expertise, and the power of physics.

Do students who have teachers like both of these men feel the teacher's power as an instrument of thought, aside from the content of what is taught? Yes! Whether we work as preschool teachers or full professors, our objectives—the outer results of our inner resources—place adaptation and subjective demands on our students.

What do you expect as a teacher? Webster offers several meanings of the infinitive *to expect*:

- to anticipate, or look forward to the coming, or occurrence of,
- to consider reasonable, probable, or certain,
- to consider obligated or duty bound.

Take the first interpretation: to anticipate. The teacher looks forward to the results that will occur. Under this definition, a teacher may anticipate a number of outcomes: producing Merit Scholars, seeing that all students pass the math competency tests, enabling students to read, receiving respect from the students, or drawing out divergent thinking. This type of teacher holds no one responsible for exact outcomes.

If we use the second interpretation—to consider reasonable, probable, or certain—the teacher believes it highly probable that particular results will be achieved. If the teacher and the student share the desire to achieve a goal and work toward it, the teacher may realistically expect success. Suppose, however, that the teacher has not put the expectation into perspective and finds that the student does not share the goal, or will not accept the teacher's approach. The teacher's expectation may then not come about; a very disappointing experience. For example, if the teacher expects all students to raise their grades because the teacher has tried to match learning styles, then the absence of immediate progress may cause the teacher to question the students or the concept of style!

Finally, if we take the third interpretation—to consider duty bound to occur—the teacher may link the outcome of expectations to his/her success or failure as a teacher, or to the worth of the students. For example, if the teacher expects orderly and organized students, who is to blame if they are not? Or, if a student does very well in a competitive exam, is the teacher or the student responsible for the development of the student's ability?

In summary, the kinds of expectations we hold govern the kinds of subjective demands we place on students.

Objectives

Expectations

Values

Attitudes

All place demands on the learner's mind.

What values do you bring to the classroom? How do they create subjective and adaptation demands? Webster equates value with worth—"value, worth: the quality of being useful, important or excellent." Let us make a finer distinction between the two words in this way:

Worth: what is intrinsically or enduringly excellent, meritorious or desirable.

Value: immediate estimation of the worth of something to an individual or in a particular situation.

When we consider our classroom values, do we attempt to give an "immediate estimation" of thoughts and actions that are "intrinsically or enduringly excellent, meritorious or desirable"? In valuing certain ideas and actions, do we value the students who exhibit them? Who are your favorite students—the ones who make it all worthwhile? Why do they have this privileged status with you? Do they represent something you value? For example, what types of students do you value most?

What types of ideas do you value in discussions?

• Here-and-now, practical discussions?

• Discussions about ideas and debates?

• Discussions about feelings?

• What if, or futuristic, discussions?

Can you define your attitude toward teaching? Webster defines *attitude* as the position of something in relation to a frame of reference. Where is teaching in the frame of reference of your life? Is teaching your source of pleasure, pain, money, power, autonomy, independence, accountability, creativity? Asked about their attitude toward teaching and why they became teachers, some teachers replied

> *"Ultimately, in teaching, I'd like to think I will be better equipped to foster the real person that each child was meant to be."*

> *"I became a teacher to make schools safe for CRs and others who do not seem to fit well."*

> *"I am a teacher because I wanted to stop kid crunching."*

> *"I came to teaching to help children collect any parts which may have been chopped off along their path of schooling."*

> *"I want to help children maximize their potential."*

Is teaching just a job? Is it your mental stimulation? How do you convey your attitude toward teaching to students? What do you think about how you convey content to students? The following story, written by Ralph A. Raimi, professor of mathematics at the University of Rochester, reveals one teacher's attitude, how he placed his role in perspective to his students and his subject matter.

The Law of Cosines

Sometimes I find it necessary to tell a class something most of them have already been taught somewhere else. I cannot go on without first being absolutely sure they all know it, but I do not wish to bore or insult the majority who, not being teachers themselves, like Joubert and me, might object to learning twice. In such cases, I often begin like this: "Many of you already know what I am about to tell you, but some of you do not. Those who do know —please be patient; there is no need to be bored or insulted. Look on it please as a performance. My subject is beautiful, even if it is familiar; I hope I can deliver it in appropriate style. You do not complain, when you attend a concert, that you have heard Beethoven's Seventh Symphony before, do you? Well, the Law of Cosines is just as lovely a monument to the human spirit.

"You may complain if I give a bad performance, sure; but if I do it competently, this repetition of a thing of beauty should be a pleasure to you, even more than to those of your classmates who, not having your experience behind them, will have to strain their powers to follow me this first time around." And then, I go on with it, hoping to make the performance one of concert quality, to be sure, but not entirely for the reason advertised. I know from experience, you see, that precious few of those students actually do understand the Law of Cosines. Many think so, having heard the words before, and would therefore mistakenly tune out my exposition, did I not first give them a second self-respecting reason for listening. Sure, one can always clobber them with exams, but as the Preacher saith, wisdom is better than weapons of war.

SPECIFIC ADAPTATION DEMANDS

Every teacher makes adaptation demands of students in the classroom through specific means—rules, scheduling procedures—as well as through invisible means—objectives, expectations. Students must use adaptation energy or risk some form of difficulty in the class.

Every teacher has "rules" in the classroom. These may range from restrictive to loose and unenforced. Children who prefer order and structure easily meet the demands of an exacting but fair teacher. On the other hand, children who work best on their own or in a relatively informal environment may find it uphill work to behave satisfactorily for such a teacher.

Extremely random children who thrive under the less-structured conditions may find themselves continually called to task in a very structured class in ways that they do not understand. Many parents have heard their child say, "But, I didn't do anything wrong!" or "I don't know why she yelled at me!" or "Mr. Wing is so mean!" And many parents also attest that one child, a random, had troubles with a teacher but that a highly sequential sibling sailed right through with the same teacher. On the opposite side of the coin, a teacher who provides fewer rules may frustrate children who learn best within well-organized environments. Whether a teacher organizes the classroom with firm rules or under flexible arrangements, all children must use their natural abilities or adapt.

The disciplinary measures taken by different types of teachers also place demands on students. Art Combs offers this definition of *discipline*: (13)

> *Discipline is a consequence of fundamental beliefs about self and others, about human rights and responsibilities and about cooperative efforts and willingness to carry one's full share in an interacting world.*

In the classroom, the teacher produces his/her disciples by guiding students to understand fundamental beliefs and vision of rights and responsibilities. Students who easily understand or adapt to the discipline of the teacher work well with the teacher.

In some classrooms, the teacher states the discipline code with explicit words, such as, "In my class, we will...." For other teachers, discipline may revolve around the students' and the teacher's value decision about right and wrong in the classroom: "How do you feel when another student disrupts you?" In this case an understanding of values and feelings plays a shaping role in the discipline structure. For still other teachers, discipline may center on utilitarian or traditional approaches: "We will all write a ten-page term paper." In this case, custom and methodological approaches determine the structure. Teachers may also base discipline on a shared set of standards: "How should we organize this project?" In this case the students decide on the discipline structure that will be useful to them.

None of these procedures is necessarily better than any others. Some teachers depend on only one of the structures, others blend structures, depending on students and subject matter. However, every structure places demands on students to use their natural abilities or adapt.

We often equate discipline with punishment. But, if we regard discipline as the means by which the teacher creates "disciples," and as a code of behavior that is constantly in effect in the classroom, then punishment must take a different approach. Combs defines *punishment* as

> *a precision tool, applicable to highly specific circumstance. (14)*

Teachers inflict punishment for a severe infraction of the discipline code. A teacher who routinely assigns extra homework for students who talk in class enforces discipline. A teacher who frequently rewards students for good behavior with a popcorn party enforces discipline. And a teacher who routinely handles all behavior problems in the classroom enforces a discipline code, but when such a teacher sends a student to the office for misbehavior, the teacher is punishing the student.

Students expend natural and adaptation energy to meet formal curricular demands, as we shall see in coming chapters. Learners use both kinds of energy throughout the school day to meet the demands of the informal curriculum: rules, reward criteria, the routes to leadership, reactions of the teachers to assignments, and the like.

The ways in which teachers understand and interpret learning styles, reject certain behaviors, argue against some students, unknowingly or silently sabotage some efforts—all these and other aspects place demands on children. For example, a dominant concrete random teacher may interpret a dominant concrete sequential child as a dependent, uncreative learner, a non-CR mind. (CR characteristics: originally creative, independent.) This teacher has failed to see that the natural CS child creates in technical ways within his/her own preorganized structure, and thus makes strong adaptation demands of the child.

Some teachers, in rejecting certain behaviors ("You may not ask other students for directions"), make strong adaptation demands of students who need to talk over work before doing it. Some teachers argue against behaviors: "You cannot use the paint in this way." Other teachers sabotage students, leading them to believe they are correct, only to make them redo their products in the end. If you doubt a teacher's power to place adaptation demands on a student, I recommend that you listen to a song by the late Harry Chapin, "Flowers Are Red." His story of a young boy who wants to use "all the colors in the rainbow" captures the subtlety of adaptation demands with perceptive irony.

Teachers also place adaptation demands on students in the way they reward or reject certain behaviors. For example, one teacher praised creative children in class but discouraged interpersonally skillful children by reprimanding them for any peer contact during class. Teachers may reward neat papers with stars or they may depreciate the value of neatness with comments like "Don't waste your time copying over that paper."

The ways in which teachers define *respect* place energy demands on students. For example, some teachers want students to show their respect through polite manners or unquestioning acceptance of the teacher's decisions. Other teachers want students to treat the teacher as a valued friend. Other teachers equate respect for them with the students' respect for their content area: "A student eager to study math from me has respect for me." And still others believe they have their students' respect when the students work in the same way the teacher works without direction.

Teachers place adaptation demands on the students by valuing certain types of students. To illustrate, some teachers value students who do their work on time, appear neat, follow directions, and have task-commitment. Some value students with interpersonal skills and a sociable personality, and who add humor to the day. Some teachers like students who prefer academics; others, students who are divergent thinkers, like to experiment, and want an action-oriented class. Although most teachers attempt to treat all students evenhandedly, it is almost inescapably human—subtly, unconsciously, or privately—to favor certain kinds of students. We must accept that our "robes of justice" can hide "feet of clay."

AN INSTRUMENT

I have discussed at length the idea that the teacher is an instrument of thought in the classroom. The teacher's being and the teacher's bearing, in addition to the teacher's content knowledge and methodological expertise, all influence the course of the class. Teachers may create students who are problem learners, unruly in class, or unable to master material because the teachers themselves place adaptation demands on students that cannot be met. Classroom problems created because of the nature of the teacher are not solved by changing the students. The teacher must change.

One administrator divides his teachers into two groups: because-of-me teachers and in-spite-of-me teachers. Because-of-me teachers help children to succeed when they recognize the demands they make of students and by helping students to meet the demands. In-spite-of-me teachers may or may not recognize the demands they make but in any event do little to help students meet the demands.

In short, **every teacher is an instrument of thought in the classroom and every teacher places demands on students.** Teachers can aid others to meet demands through flexibility in teaching, gaining the sensitivity to change teaching attitude and action patterns in a purposeful way.

CHAPTER 5

FOUR TEACHING STYLES

*The greatest educational experiences in my life, the
ones that taught me the most....Then, it would be
those that taught me what kind of person I was; the
experiences that drew me out, strengthened me, made
me taller and stronger.*

—Abraham Maslow

Each of the four learning styles—concrete sequential, abstract sequential, abstract random, and concrete random—has a set of characteristics that distinguishes it within teachers. We can identify the dominant styles of teachers by their attitudes and behaviors toward the learner, the curriculum, the classroom, and the educational process in general.

Some teachers reveal a dominant teaching style, identified quickly by other teachers and by students. Some teachers have a dominant teaching style but consistently style flex into the four learning styles. Observers find it more difficult to identify a predominant teaching style for such teachers. And, still other teachers have a true balance in both their learning and teaching styles.

The purposes of identifying teaching style are

• to assess the similarities and differences between one's teaching and learning styles;

• to assess the impact on the teacher if learning and teaching styles are dissimilar;

• to distinguish between a teacher's natural style and his/her style flex-abilities;

• to evaluate the impact of a teacher's style on different types of students;

• to find ways to broaden a teacher's style in order to meet the needs of a range of students; and

• to determine the point at which a teacher does not have the ability to meet the stylistic needs of students.

As we look at each of the four styles of teaching, we will stereotype their differences in order to differentiate among them. However, no one has a "pure" style of teaching any more than a "pure" style of learning. For each style of teaching, we will consider several factors, including style characteristics, classroom behaviors, a variety of curricular issues, and supervision preferences.

Other researchers have also provided ways to describe teaching style. However, you will find the last category—descriptions, interpretations, and stress symptoms—unique among teaching-style assessments. Rather than simply providing a description of behavior, such as "the teacher organizes sequentially," I will examine the effective, ineffective, and stress behaviors of each style's characteristic. That is, a teacher who organizes sequentially can do so in an effective way, in an ineffective way, or in a way that reveals stress. Teaching style, then, is not just behavior, but meaning applied to behavior—the phenomenological approach once again.

Effective teaching behaviors and characteristics in each style help to create the physical, social, emotional, intellectual, and/or spiritual growth and development of students. Ineffective behaviors and characteristics do not directly aid in the growth and development of students or teachers, and may, indeed, create significant harm.

Stressed teaching behaviors are symptoms of stress within a teacher. Teachers in each style experience stress differently. According to noted authority Hans Selye, "Stress is the way our mind and body respond to a stressor." For example, symptoms of stress are tension and anxiety. Causes of stress are such things as unresolved style mismatch between administrator and teacher. For our purposes, we will make note of the signs of stress, a way to stay alert and attune to its potential causes.

Please bear in mind that the guidelines for analyzing each teaching style describe general indicators. Teachers are people, all different and deserving of respect due to all individuals.

The Concrete Sequential Teaching Style

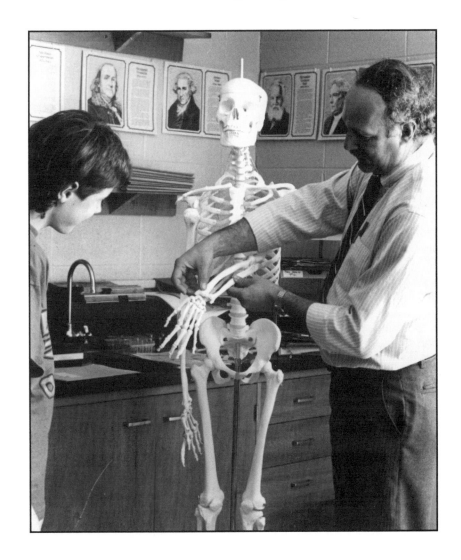

A fourth-grade, concrete sequential student's reply when asked to describe his teacher, Mrs. M.

"She helps you when you get an answer wrong. She explains why you got it wrong. She doesn't leave you alone to figure it out for yourself. She has a good sense of humor."

—Mike

Concrete Sequential Teachers

Adult Style Traits		Teacher Style Traits
Relate best to the concrete, physical, hands-on world	◄──►	Emphasize practical learning; use hands-on materials; take field trips
Prefer order that is sequential, structured, and step by step	◄──►	Provide structured assignments with exacting directions
Use the five senses to explore	◄──►	Use hands-on learning experiences
Require specific, clear cut data, exact directions, specific answers, detail	◄──►	Value specific, detailed work; like to use worksheets and skill-builders
Think in ways that are methodical, ordered, predictable	◄──►	Want practical learning; like concise formats; build physical products
Strive for perfection, precision, and organization	◄──►	Demand perfection; want realistic products that look good
Prepare to create in a mechanical or technological way; achieve a purposeful objective through practical approaches; create a tangible product	◄──►	Foster creativity through prototypes and replicas; are action-oriented; cover content in detail; develop learning centers
Operate in a tried-and-true pattern, within a hierarchical structure, according to conventionally correct procedures	◄──►	Rely on traditional procedures and patterns; expect the class to be teacher-directed; tend not to change prepared lesson plans
Expect to provide a detailed answer or product; take things at face value; want to be rewarded for efforts	◄──►	Are task-oriented; work with small instruction-based groups for skills; value practical knowledge; reward with grades
Prefer quiet, controlled environments and value efficient use of time	◄──►	Run an orderly classroom; finish work on time; do not look for change without cause

A PROFILE: THE CONCRETE SEQUENTIAL TEACHING STYLE

Educational Objectives

Concrete sequential teachers favor behavioral objectives that have measurable outcomes, and immediate and specific application for students. A typical objective for the CS teacher of a fourth-grade nutrition class states: students will plan, organize, and produce snacks for the class according to their knowledge of the four food groups.

Concrete sequential teachers work with a time schedule in mind. For example, the CS teacher would provide a clear structure, sequencing the students through the food groups in systematic and efficient fashion. This teacher may begin with a prepared chart, or demonstration of the four food groups, check for understanding with a short quiz, and then assign students to bring foods representative of each group. To create an informational display, the students would label foods according to groups.

Materials

Concrete sequential teachers rely on concrete, hands-on materials such as artifacts, replicas, working models, displays, touch-displays, learning centers, and mechanical apparatus, as well as factual and realistic illustrations.

Their classrooms contain many different types of hands-on materials, systematically located in designated, labeled places for functional use. Books provide sources of how-to information, factual reference, and back-up evidence. CS teachers like to use a variety of hands-on teaching aids and to assign worksheets in order to reinforce learning.

Course Design

Concrete sequential teachers organize the class so that students move efficiently from one activity to another. CS teachers help students learn to organize their time, finish projects, and apply knowledge in practical ways. To accomplish these goals, CS teachers arrange the day around short lessons that have clear starting and stopping points, utilizing such strategies as

- *self-paced, individualized lessons*
- *programmed instruction*
- *specialized training sessions*
- *informational lectures*
- *primary resources*
- *performance contracts*
- *mastery learning*
- *demonstration teaching*
- *field trips*
- *apprenticeships*

**Dominant
Teaching Techniques**

The concrete sequential learning style functions best by moving from specific details or facts to the larger picture, or more general conclusion. Accordingly, concrete sequential teachers tend to provide materials and techniques that encourage students to think from the specific to the general. For example, they teach vowel sounds for the purpose of building word sounds. The practical and realistic CS teacher also uses techniques that foster immediate, observable, and measurable achievement and evaluation.

CS teachers like learning to fall on target the first time around, and want students to correct their mistakes promptly and move on. They have a tendency to apply rather than discuss, to see detail rather than generalize, to work at a steady pace from one stage to the next, and to require right answers rather than favor process outcomes. CS teachers use techniques that allow for these tendencies, such as

- *practical, specific, and concrete examples*
- *opportunities to practice teacher-demonstrated techniques*
- *problem solving that follows specific rules*
- *step-by-step learning procedures*
- *immediate and correction-oriented feedback: quizzes, question-and-answer periods, measurable checkpoints , application worksheets*
- *memorization*
- *reinforcement homework*

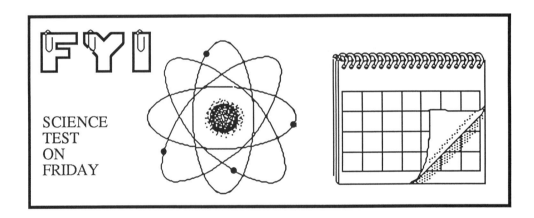

Teaching Aids

Because concrete sequential teachers operate in the physical, action-oriented world of task-oriented achievement, they use many physical aids to demonstrate concepts, points, or structure and to help students have contact with content. Concrete sequential types of aids are

maps	*charts*	*pamphlets*
flowcharts	*outlines*	*flipcharts*
computer programs	*bulletin boards*	*diagrams*
workbooks	*manuals*	*prototypes*
overheads	*fact sheets*	*checklists*
guides	*models*	*exhibits*

Learning and Teaching Style: In Theory and Practice

*Interpersonal
Environment*

Concrete sequential teachers want results achieved efficiently, but they also value physical and active involvement for students with their assignments. To this end, they arrange

- *task-oriented committees*

- *individualized work stations*

- *tutorial approaches*

- *group work with behavioral objectives; limited social group work.*

Bridging Techniques

Teachers with concrete sequential preferences use bridging techniques to develop concrete sequential thinking patterns in all styles of students, to aid CS students who must learn to use non-CS techniques, and to help non-CS students work in CS ways

- *outlines of key points*

- *focusing questions*

- *procedural steps*

- *written summaries of main points*

- *anticipation questions*

- *checklists of points and vocabulary*

Curricular Style

Concrete sequential teachers prefer a curricular style that favors behavioral objectives and material organized in a step-by-step approach with factual content. They work easily with curriculum kits and structured programs that have lesson plans and guidebooks.

*Supervision
and
Evaluation Preferences*

Concrete sequential teachers respond best to supervisory and evaluation procedures that respect their style's natural preference for order, predictability, realism, objectivity, and accuracy. Such procedures

- *state the time of the administrator's visit;*

- *provide the teacher with sufficient time to prepare the lesson in the way the teacher desires;*

- *permit the administrator to stay for the full length of the lesson;*

- *provide an immediate follow-up conference with a checklist of observations;*

- *provide direct positive and negative comments, with sound recommendations for improvement, if necessary;*

- *allow the administrator to visit a specified number of times according to contract, or tradition.*

DESCRIPTIONS AND INTERPRETATIONS

Effective concrete sequential teachers offer students an action-oriented curriculum that allows them to learn a practical, organized, tangible content in a positive, useful, and caring way. Ineffective CS teachers confine students to a narrow definition of the CS world. CS teachers under stress behave in ways that may prevent them from using their abilities and capacities to advantage. Teachers should work to investigate and eliminate the causes of stress, or at least place them in perspective.

Concrete

Effective: show students how to understand and work within the hands-on world.

Ineffective: confine learning to the concrete.

Under stress: cannot translate the concrete into meaningful ideas.

Sequential

Effective: value order, structure, and linear thought.

Ineffective: insist on everyone's expressing feelings, ideas, and products in a linear way.

Under stress: ignore the situation or problem if they do not know how to handle it.

Action Oriented

Effective: operate as "doing" teachers in order to complete objective.

Ineffective: lose sight of the purpose of their activities.

Under stress: forget the feelings of others in order to produce results.

Practical

Effective: provide useful, reliable, and organized information and approaches.

Ineffective: disregard ideas, feelings, options, and changes because they interfere with the practical.

Under stress: lose sight of an activity's value if practicality is missing.

Organized

Effective: organize naturally.

Ineffective: insist everyone apply their organizational approaches.

Under stress: apply an organizational pattern or plan of action without thought.

Factual

Effective: enjoy facts, respect the wealth of factual information, and regard facts as the foundation for a larger body of knowledge.

Ineffective: anchor in facts, refusing to acknowledge the forest for the trees; stop discussions that do not relate to precise facts.

Under stress: need an unusually large set of facts to make a decision.

Accurate

Effective: work accurately with ease, using their ability to check for detail, and provide completeness.

Ineffective: insist on pinpoint information even when a theme or generalization gives more appropriate results.

Under stress: overreact to minor errors.

Efficient

Effective: work well within time limits.

Ineffective: demand everyone work within their time frame.

Under stress: become short-tempered when time seems misused.

Consistent

Effective: use tried-and-true patterns to achieve their objectives.

Ineffective: refuse to change or try new approaches.

Under stress: pretend not to care about change.

Task Oriented

Effective: keep a steady pace to get the job done.

Ineffective: place the task above everything else, or take over from others just to get the job done.

Under stress: move nonstop, losing perspective on the real time needed to finish the job.

Steady

Effective: are predictable, reliable, and dependable.

Ineffective: take one approach and never vary, i.e., use only worksheets and Dittos.

Under stress: blame others for mistakes, problems, or unfinished work.

Hierarchically Directed

Effective: like well-defined roles in which people can function smoothly.

Ineffective: overcontrol, act bossy, and behave in authoritarian ways.

Under stress: equate disagreement with disloyalty or laziness.

Application

Schools tend to foster concrete sequential approaches to their organization and evaluation. Every teacher must use some concrete sequential abilities in order to

- *meet the organizational demands of school and classroom*

- *meet standardized evaluation demands*

- *address the needs of CS students*

- *teach all students how to work in CS ways*

- *provide hands-on experiences for students*

- *put theory into practice*

- *collect a variety of resources*

- *provide actual experiences for students and individualized learning*

- *maintain a core of basic skills*

How, when, and why do you teach in the spirit of the concrete sequential approach?

The Abstract Sequential Teaching Style

A fourth-grade, abstract sequential student's reply when asked to describe his teacher, Mrs. M.

"She's smart. She has a sense of humor. She teaches great. She lets us have a second recess."

—Nick

Abstract Sequential Teachers

Adult Style Traits		**Teacher Style Traits**
Relate best to the abstract world of ideas	⟷	Emphasize ideas, concepts, and theories
Prefer order that is sequential, structured, and logical	⟷	Consider the relationship of the whole to its parts; analyze and evaluate
Use intellect to explore	⟷	Rely almost exclusively on logical reasoning; develop and prove theories
Require exact, well-researched, documentation and content expertise	⟷	Teach through lecture; use extensive reading, want students to have a bank of knowledge
Think in ways that are intellectual, analytical, and evaluative	⟷	Want students to be curious about great ideas, to be motivated by "why?"
Strive for conceptualization, knowledge, scope, and sequence	⟷	Want students to devote energy to difficult assignments for the intellectual reward of learning for its own sake
Prepare to create a theoretical model; validate ideas and analyze data; develop, extend ideas	⟷	Organize problem solving around evaluation of ideas; provide students with critical reviews of subjects
Operate within a logic system, with collegial relationships, according to tradition	⟷	Have consistent and reliable rules and procedures; expect respect for the professorial role; do not involve emotions in decision making
Expect to gather existing knowledge, analyze new knowledge, achieve content expertise	⟷	Emphasize subject matter and resources; want to challenge students intellectually; expect perfection
Prefer quiet, intellectual environments, large blocks of time, and the traditional roles of academe	⟷	Like libraries, traditional classrooms; need time to think through ideas, organize materials, and plan approaches; like long-term projects; enjoy the professor-student relationship

A PROFILE: THE ABSTRACT SEQUENTIAL
TEACHING STYLE

**Educational
Objectives**

Abstract sequential teachers favor conceptual objectives with outcomes that indicate the student's ability to analyze, theorize, and evaluate ideas. The AS teacher favors the classics and wants students to have both depth and breadth of subject matter. An objective of the analytical and theoretical AS teacher of an English class states: students will read four novels by one author and analyze theme and characterization.

Because abstract sequential teachers value depth of knowledge, they need blocks of time available to them. They would rather cover a few topics in depth than several superficially. Thus, an abstract sequential has no difficulty spending six weeks reading, analyzing, and hypothesizing about one of Shakespeare's plays.

Materials

Abstract sequential teachers rely on ideas presented in a sequential way, usually through lecture and extensive reading.   Books and other printed works are the major materials evident in their classroom. Abstract sequential teachers require completion of a daily homework assignment and usually review it the next day.

Course Design

Abstract sequential teachers organize their classes around the expert, the teacher, and with reference sources. Teaching strategies encourage students to be

- *recipients of information, through lectures and extensive reading*

- *contributors to the forum of ideas, through debates, seminars, panel discussions, roundtables*

- *producers of documented evidence, through oral reports and presentations, and research and term papers*

- *developers of hypothetical models, by conducting research studies and by developing hypothetical solutions to problems*

- *critical thinkers who analyze and interpret data; interview experts; develop philosophical positions; defend their ideas*

**Dominant
Teaching Techniques**

The abstract sequential learning style functions best by considering the "big picture." Accordingly, AS teachers tend to provide materials and techniques that encourage students to use this approach. Intellectual and systematic abstract sequential teachers also encourage long-term research, evaluated according to the quantity and quality of information provided. As a result, AS teachers use techniques that demand

- extensive reading:
  __ to gather facts
  __ to compare theories
  __ to collect research findings

- extensive research:
  __ to have hard evidence for conclusions
  __ to build on the "shoulders of giants"
  __ to avoid speculation

- expert information
  __ to gain breadth and depth in a subject
  __ to know opinions and biases of specialists

- intellectual processing
  __ to conceptualize
  __ to analyze information
  __ to hypothesize about new information
  __ to evaluate new and existing information
  __ to draw conclusions by synthesizing ideas

- memorization and comprehension
  __ to be able to use facts to prove a point
  __ to draw conclusions from facts

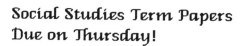

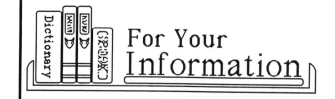

Social Studies Term Papers
Due on Thursday!

For Your
Information

Teaching Aids

Because abstract sequential teachers operate primarily in the world of logical ideas, their teaching aids are

- publications

- information briefs

- texts

- reference reading

- optional reading

- audiotapes

- conceptual pictures

Interpersonal Environment

Abstract sequential teachers want students to employ their own intellectual powers. As reference-based teachers, they ask students to research, listen to experts, and use critical thinking skills— analysis, hypothesis, synthesis, and evaluation. To this end, AS teachers stress

- *formal classroom structure*

- *high-content-centered style of teaching*

- *collegial relationship between teachers and students*

- *"meeting-of-the-minds" atmosphere*

- *intellectually competitive group work*

- *standard rules of behavior and procedure*

- *respect for organization, time, procedure, and tradition*

Bridging Techniques

Abstract sequential teachers use these types of bridging techniques to develop abstract sequential thinking patterns in all styles, to assist AS learners who must learn using non-AS techniques, and to help non-AS learners work in AS ways:

- *provide bibliographies, references, or library work*

- *encourage "research" opportunities*

- *minimize workbook assignments and tasks*

- *open opportunities to analyze, hypothesize, and evaluate ideas*

Curricular Style

Abstract sequential teachers prefer a curricular style emphasizing theoretical objectives that address a scope and sequence content. They systematically plan courses in advance, and organized around specific topics. They accept curriculum guides as overall frameworks but use their own expertise, knowledge, or research ability to provide the specific content. When preparing to teach a new subject, AS teachers become students of the subject. AS teachers enjoy writing courses on specialized topics and build a store of materials for each course over the years.

Supervision and Evaluation Preferences

Abstract sequential teachers prefer a supervisory and evaluation procedure that respects their style's natural preferences for logic, content expertise, conceptualization, and academic excellence. Such procedures

- *state the time of administrator's visit*

- *limit administrative visits in frequency and length*

- *provide an administrator who has expertise in the teacher's field*

- *plan for immediate follow-up*

- *limit criticism, and respect the teacher's own evaluation*

- *praise the teacher's subject-matter orientation*

- *provide an essay-type evaluation form*

- *allow reasonable visits from a qualified administrator*

DESCRIPTIONS AND INTERPRETATIONS

Effective abstract sequential teachers can provide students with an academic curriculum that stresses academic excellence, self-pacing, organized study habits, and in-depth knowledge of the subject matter. Ineffective abstract sequential teachers defeat these purposes or confine students to a narrow definition of the AS world. However, teachers can also experience stress, preventing them from using their abilities and capacities effectively.

Abstract

Effective: thrive in the world of ideas.

Ineffective: cannot translate ideas into concrete forms.

Under stress: continue to generate more and more ideas, convinced they do not have enough data to make a correct conclusion.

Sequential

Effective: provide a logical sequence to the curriculum, organize and schedule lesson plans, and run predictable day.

Ineffective: bore students with an unvarying routine and tight rules.

Under stress: become overly cautious about creating change or making mistakes.

Academic

Effective: model the role of the professor.

Ineffective: attend only to academically strong students.

Under stress: feel unworthy, insecure, or unable to do justice to their subject.

Intellectual

Effective: help students to develop their intellectual capacities in a positive way.

Ineffective: look down upon students who do not excel as high intellectual achievers.

Under stress: doubt their own abilities.

Studious

Effective: role model the ability to "love my subject."

Ineffective: allow no humor, practical application, or divergent thinking.

Under stress: forget about the therapeutic value of "play"; always do "the right thing."

Learning and Teaching Style: In Theory and Practice

Debating

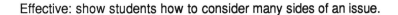

Effective: show students how to consider many sides of an issue.

Ineffective: argue easily.

Under stress: support only one position.

Evaluative

Effective: apply critical thinking skills to arrive at a conclusion.

Ineffective: judge others according to one standard.

Under stress: forget about alternative approaches in an effort to get the right answer.

Critical

Effective: play the devil's advocate to arouse debate.

Ineffective: criticize to hurt or demean.

Under stress: forget other's feelings in order to point out right from wrong.

Award Excellance

Effective: give high grades as the reward for scholarly work.

Ineffective: make high grades almost unachievable, attainable in only the teacher's way, or as a bribe to gain student compliance.

Under stress: cannot understand how to work with other types of students.

Conceptual

Effective: research and write curriculum guides for content-area courses.

Ineffective: never change the course content once settled with comfortable ideas.

Under stress: show discomfort with rapid change as well as unproven theories or new approaches to ideas and content.

Vicarious

Effective: can make ideas, people, and places come alive through symbols, images, and the written and spoken word.

Ineffective: refuse to use concrete learning opportunities such as field trips.

Under stress: gloss over concrete experiences as nice but superficial.

Product Oriented

Effective: aid students to master large amounts of content.

Ineffective: take pride in themselves as tough teachers who give the most work.

Under stress: forget the process of learning out of desire for results.

APPLICATION

Schools tend to favor abstract sequential approaches to content and to teaching methods by supporting the textbook as the primary student material and the teacher as the major conveyor of information through lecture.   Every teacher must use some abstract sequential abilities in order to

- *meet the scope and sequence demands of the curriculum*

- *utilize the text resources provided to students*

- *address the needs of students with abstract sequential styles*

- *teach concepts*

- *help students learn to work in abstract sequential ways*

- *relate the content to theories of learning and to the subject*

- *have referential knowledge of a subject*

- *choose from among different philosophies of education*

- *search for new knowledge*

- *understand developmental stages of children*

How, when, and why do you teach in the spirit of an abstract sequential approach?

The Abstract Random Teaching Style

A fourth-grade, abstract random student's reply when asked to describe her teacher, Mrs. M.

"She tells a lot of jokes and is real funny. She's nicer than my other teachers. She helps us out more. She gives us more activities and movies. She teaches us more so most of us learn in a day or week."

—Kim

Abstract Random Teachers

Adult Style Traits	**Teacher Style Traits**
Relate best to the abstract world of emotions, spirituality	Emphasize development of positive student self-concepts and growth
Prefer order that is nonlinear, harmonious, not traditional	Develop content through cultural, artistic, aesthetic, and literary media; encourage self-expression and imagination
Use an emotional base to explore	Rely on personalization
Require personalized experiences, positive relationships, support	Emphasize high morale, cooperative learning; give praise generously
Think in ways that are interpretive, perceptive, imaginative, psychic	Value the creative, imaginative, and humorous in student products, even if basic skills are missing
Strive for an understanding of human nature, communication	Build curriculum around the needs of students; promote a sharing attitude; help students develop coping skills
Prepare to create in interpretive ways; work on many projects at once	Participate enthusiastically in school and classroom life; enjoy change; rarely follow structured plans or write lesson plans; look for variety
Operate on an inner signal system; work within broad guidelines; value trust and loyalty	Thrive under student responsiveness; develop the curriculum on an as-needed basis
Expect to use holistic approaches, pursue goals in their own way	Want to develop sensitive, interpersonally effective people
Prefer aesthetically pleasing and informal environments; seek friendly and equity-based relations with others; value cooperative environments; use own timetable	Create unstructured classrooms and include plants, furniture, artwork; hold person-to person conferences; set own schedule as much as possible

A PROFILE: THE ABSTRACT RANDOM TEACHING STYLE

Educational Objectives

Abstract random teachers write global objectives. Outcomes show the students' understanding, appreciation, and interpretation of the subject matter as well as of themselves. AR teachers expect aesthetic, interpretative, and reflective products; flexibility in thought; open and active communication of feelings, content, ideas; ability to listen to, learn from, and respond to other students; reactions to environmental stimulation, including color, mood, and sound. A typical objective for the emotion-based AR teacher of a seventh-grade social studies class states: students will appreciate the role of France in the Revolutionary War.

Abstract random teachers do not work naturally within others' time schedules. They tend to "flow" with the moment, capitalizing on student interest and enthusiasm rather than adhering to the sequence of a schedule.

Materials

Abstract random teachers use their personal rapport with students to interest and encourage them to learn. They may have a variety of materials in the room for students to use if they wish, or they may devote considerable time to class and small-group discussion about feelings, interpretation of ideas, or attitudes about a subject. Books serve as a connecting link between the student and the outside world—a way for the student to visit other minds.

Course Design

Abstract random teachers organize their classrooms so that students have many opportunities to work together, to learn from each other, to share with and help one another. These teachers use such strategies as

- *group-based study projects and investigations*
- *teaching/learning teams*
- *discussion groups*
- *lecture/discussion groups*
- *short reading assignments followed by group discussion*
- *classroom meeting format*
- *cooperative learning*

The abstract random style learns by considering the holistic nature of learning and subject matter. Accordingly, AR teachers tend to use techniques that ask students to consider the whole rather than specific parts of a subject. For example, they might ask how pesticides affect aquatic life rather than how DDT affects fish in rivers versus in lakes. Sensitive and interpretative AR teachers also use techniques that require students to personalize learning, to use their emotions, and to relate to others. In discussing the early colonists' move from England, this teacher might ask if any students in the class had ever moved to a new community, or how the students would feel if their parents told them today to pack for a move to New Zealand.

AR teachers concern themselves more with the process of learning than with the products. For these teachers, the quality of classroom interaction determines successful teaching and learning. AR teachers place the highest premium on cooperation, consensus, trust, and personal enthusiasm for involved learning. Therefore, they do not plan for the sake of time, detail, or specific content coverage. They structure their classes for student involvement and self-expression, weaving content and detail into the curriculum.

As a result, they use such teaching techniques as

• *group discussion*

• *values clarification*

• *group problem solving on social and personal issues*

• *media: movies, filmstrips, television*

• *arts: music, art, drama, art activities*

• *imagination games: guided fantasy, role play*

• *literary interpretations: metaphors, similes, stories*

• *cooperative learning*

• *personalized interpretations*
  ~ how would you feel if...
  ~ becoming an inanimate object
  ~ take the viewpoint of...

• *personal reflection—journals, letters to the teacher*

• *aesthetic connections: photographs, posters, designs that elicit the mood, beauty, or force of a topic*

• *reading concerned with people, cultures, feelings, personal experiences, the human condition*

• *transpersonal exercises: trust walks, sharing games, cooperative games, self-realization exercises, activities to learn empathy, sympathy*

Teaching Aids   Because abstract random teachers operate in the world of feelings, relationships, and a personal interpretation, their teaching aids serve to develop these areas. They use

- *posters*
- *comfortable environment*
- *nonverbal activities*
- *grading options*
- *multimedia*
- *testing options*

- *discussion starters*
- *music*
- *art*
- *optional work places*
- *high-impact materials*

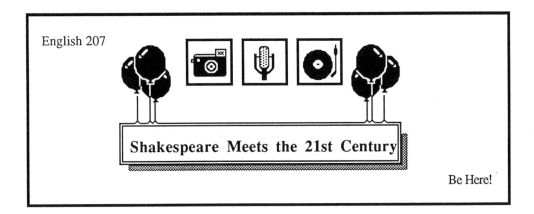

English 207

Shakespeare Meets the 21st Century

Be Here!

Interpersonal Environment   Abstract random teachers want students to experience the process of learning through cooperative experiences. They arrange

- *group dynamics, informal and flexible group assignments*
- *team learning requiring high group cohesion and trust*
- *socializing times as rewards*
- *open channels of communication with the teacher*
- *peer tutoring, peer teaching*

Bridging Techniques   Abstract random teachers use bridging techniques to develop abstract random thinking patterns in all styles, to aid AR learners who must learn using non-AR techniques, and to help non-AR learners work in AR ways

- *optional opportunities for group work*
- *flexible time limits with options for negotiation*
- *"down time" with the teacher*
- *learning related to empathetic, aesthetic, or emotionally based qualities*
- *freedom of movement and expression*
- *"open-door" policy for students to talk to teachers*
- *options for activities and testing*
- *personalized feedback and listening for understanding*

Curricular Style   Abstract random teachers prefer a curriculum that involves values, self-expression, communication, people, feelings, and aesthetic appreciation. They work easily with multimedia, group activities, and interpretative materials.

*Supervision
and
Evaluation Preferences*   Dominant abstract random teachers prefer a supervisor style with evaluation procedures that respect this style's natural preference for personalized experiences, emotions, interpretation, relationships, and acceptance. They are most comfortable with procedures that

    • *have a supportive administrator who visits often;*

    • *require no official or formal preparation;*

    • *give the administrator freedom to "drop in" on classes;*

    • *provide suggestions for improvements but accept that these teachers may be very sensitive to criticism;*

    • *have a lengthy, discussion-oriented postconference session;*

    • *allow time to think about and react to evaluation before signing it.*

DESCRIPTIONS AND INTERPRETATIONS

Effective abstract random teachers can offer students personalized attention to their social, emotional, and psychological developmental needs in a learning climate that fosters imagination, personal growth, and creativity within the academic curriculum. AR teachers use these abilities ineffectively when they defeat these purposes or confine students to a narrow definition of AR. Under stress, AR teachers do not fully use their abilities and capacities.

Abstract

Effective: thrive in the world of feelings.

Ineffective: allow emotions to control their lives.

Under stress: react in an overly emotional way, cry, or anger easily.

Random

Effective: provide options for students on time, content, interpretation.

Ineffective: disregard time, students achieve no common content, anything goes.

Under stress: turn flexibility into chaos, and compensate by overstructuring time and tasks.

Personal

Effective: relate to students based on personal concern, knowledge, and enjoyment.

Ineffective: become a student again.

Under stress: become emotionally involved with students' lives, impairing teaching effectiveness.

Sensitive

Effective: tune in to class mood, student needs, and student issues.

Ineffective: cannot evaluate negatively for fear students will dislike them.

Under stress: carry a grudge long after they have settled an issue.

Imaginative

Effective: provide interesting and unusual ways of working with content.

Ineffective: let arts, aesthetics, and imagination games become the curriculum.

Under stress: become overly involved with using imagination, forcing it on all students.

Accepting

Effective: appreciate many different kinds of students, attempt to find and develop their best qualities.

Ineffective: accept or ignore all types of behavior regardless of impact or consequences.

Under stress: feel crushed when others do not reciprocate their friendship.

Flexible

Effective: can productively change plans to accommodate the situation.

Ineffective: can "flow with the tide" but lose productivity.

Under stress: let others manipulate their time.

Emotional

Effective: express love, anger, and other emotions appropriately.

Ineffective: are volatile, unpredictable, impulsive, overreactive.

Under stress: filter their decisions exclusively through their emotions.

Interpretative

Effective: are perceptive; can sense mood and quality of student behavior.

Ineffective: interpret everyone through their AR point of view.

Under stress: excuse negative behavior.

Feeling Oriented

Effective: listen to, nurture, and support students.

Ineffective: ignore students who do not tune into their feelings.

Under stress: think in totally subjective ways.

Understanding

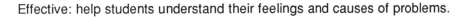

Effective: help students understand their feelings and causes of problems.

Ineffective: sympathize with students, encourage them to feel sorry for themselves.

Under stress: take on students' problems as their own.

Social

Effective: combine fun and humor with students, understand the therapeutic value of play.

Ineffective: equate socializing with quality teaching.

Under stress: cannot enjoy a serious class of students.

Sentimental

Effective: keep fond memories and gifts of students as inspiration.

Ineffective: romanticize the past, forgetting to deal with present reality.

Under stress: keep physical and emotional "relics" as a crutch for dealing with today.

APPLICATION

Schools favor abstract random approaches to counseling and the arts—literary, visual, performing—and in establishing school spirit. Every teacher must use abstract random abilities in order to

- *facilitate group discussion*
- *develop cooperative learning*
- *work with feelings and emotions of students*
- *aid interpersonal relations*
- *have flexibility*
- *meet the needs of AR students*
- *aid other students to work in AR ways*
- *maintain a warm, open classroom atmosphere*
- *involve students in planning and carrying out work*
- *have emotional stability*
- *offer a variety of imaginative and interpretative experiences*
- *recognize and understand personal problems*
- *understand and work with emotional needs of individual students*

Chapter 5: Four Teaching Styles - The Abstract Random

- *understand and work with emotional needs of individual students*

- *establish rapport with students and parents*

- *have a sense of humor*

- *build student self-awareness*

- *encourage understanding in students*

How, when, and why do you teach in the spirit an abstract random approach?

The
Concrete
Random
Teaching Style

A fourth-grade, concrete random student's reply when asked to
describe his teacher, Mrs. M.

*"She is different from most teachers. She isn't so picky. She is
a fair teacher and often gives-in to kids. We get our way to do things.
She is not always so serious. I can't stand teachers who are always
so serious."*

—Shane

Concrete Random Teachers

Adult Style Traits

Relate best to the concrete world of experience

Prefer order that is nonlinear, multifaceted and uses broad guidelines

Use experiences to explore

Require problems, open-ended solutions, competition

Think in ways that are intuitive, divergent, investigative

Strive for independence, creativity, alternatives, and originality

Prepare to produce original creations and solutions; provide options; assume a leadership role

Operate as a risk-taker and experimentally

Expect to instigate beneficial change; search for possibilities

Prefer a busy environment, many types of people; enjoy the role of mentor, guide, or seer

Teacher Style Traits

Emphasize investigation and exploration of possibilities

Work with umbrella ideas; use no standard structure or format; play the role of guide or facilitator

Use many, varied, and unusual activities in the classroom to provide content

Challenge students to move beyond given knowledge

Value students with insight and divergent thinking; develop enthusiasm for exploring

Want students to think for themselves and make sound judgments; value and foster original forms of expression; use brainstorming easily and frequently

Model creativity by continually providing new resources, products, and activities; work for student self-responsibility and leadership

Encourage investigation, independent study and diverse ways of learning

Provide opportunities for students to develop fluency, flexibility, originality; interested in futuristics and discovery learning

Like to try many types of activities with students; encourage students to value, work with, and learn from many kinds of people

A PROFILE: THE CONCRETE RANDOM TEACHING STYLE

Educational Objectives

Concrete random teachers favor global objectives that encourage students to raise questions, delineate problems, generate alternatives, and propose solutions. A typical objective for the experiential and divergent senior high concrete random science teacher states: to investigate the history and development of metallurgy and to apply its principles.

CR teachers work within general time frames rather than with specific deadlines. They plan the topics and principles of the course, letting the specific lessons develop according to students' use and direction of interest. Thus, a lesson on metallurgy may lead to study on how coins are made or study of the history or process of counterfeiting.

Materials

Concrete random teachers rely on many, varied, and unusual resources. Their classes may contain machinery, art materials, inventions, discarded "junque," kitchen appliances, and any other commodities that arouse students' curiosity to investigate, experiment, or explore. CR teachers consider the world, or at least the locale, their classroom. They have students "on assignment" outside the school as easily as in the classroom because they value students' experiencing as rich and varied a curriculum as possible. They do not limit content to books or the classroom materials.

Course Design

Concrete random teachers organize their classes so that students can operate independently or cooperatively. CR teachers strive for diversity in the classroom environment, open choices for students, and interest-arousing activities to stimulate thinking. CR teachers utilize such strategies as

- *independent study projects*

- *inquiry learning assignments*

- *lecture/discussion/application*

- *experiments*

- *games and simulations*

- *case studies*

**Dominant
Teaching Techniques**

Concrete randoms learn by experience. Such learners like to frame out the whole picture, then let others fill in the details. As a result, teachers of this style tend to provide materials and techniques that encourage students to consider broad implications and applications. CR teachers like to generate many different interpretations and outcomes, and regard the process of learning as more valuable than the final product. CR teachers have a high tolerance for ambiguity and for unstructured experiences. They frequently use techniques such as

- *brainstorming*

- *creative problem solving*

- *developing and testing alternative solutions*

- *investigative activities*

- *inquiry approaches*

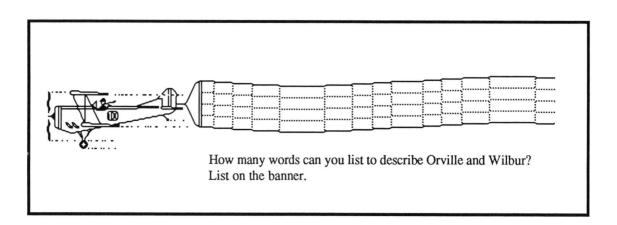

How many words can you list to describe Orville and Wilbur?
List on the banner.

Teaching Aids

Because concrete random teachers operate in the real, physical world with an investigative, experimental, and divergent attitude, they use teaching aids that encourage students to probe, discover, and create new ideas and products. Teaching aids for concrete random teachers can range from the field outside the classroom window to the parking meters on the street, from the school to the city hall. Concrete random teachers use almost any item, place, or idea to encourage open-ended learning. To that end they use aids such as

- *investigative kits*   - *hands-on materials*

- *unusual or undefined artifacts*   - *art materials*

- *usual items used in unusual ways*   - *exploratory materials*

- *exploratory situations*

Interpersonal Environment

Concrete random teachers want their students to work independently as well as cooperatively. They cultivate an environment so that students can:

- *work with many types of students*

- *use teacher guidelines, not teacher structure*

- *have a sense of freedom to experiment*

- *keep a flexible attitude*

- *know how to choose from among options*

- *have a mentoring relationship with an adult, not necessarily the teacher*

Bridging Techniques

Teachers with strong concrete random abilities use these bridging techniques to develop concrete random thinking patterns in all styles, to aid CR learners who must learn to use non-CR techniques, and to help non-CR learners to work in CR ways:

- *state learning objectives as problems*

- *encourage student-designed reports or projects*

- *encourage original and creative additions to mandatory work*

- *solicit unusual and diverse ideas*

Curricular Style

Concrete random teachers prefer a curricular style that favors creative and investigative problem solving. They model the scientific method (hypothesis, solution, test) in their day-to-day curriculum. They want students to experiment with ideas and materials through application and to solve problems with limited amounts of given information. They do not like directions on what or how to teach but willingly join a curriculum team to determine the guidelines for content.

The dominant concrete random teacher prefers a supervisory style with evaluation procedures that respect this style's natural preference for divergent thinking, experiential learning, risk taking, change, and flexibility. They appreciate procedures through which

- *the teacher maintains an open-door policy;*

- *the administrator appears in the school, halls, and classrooms;*

- *the administrator communicates personally rather than by memo;*

- *the administrator evaluates based on personal knowledge of the teacher and the students in each classroom;*

- *the administrator gives critical feedback but gives the teacher the option of creating a solution to the problem;*

- *the administrator has referential, supervisory, or personal credentials in the teacher's eyes;*

- *the evaluation conference has both written comments and an informal discussion.*

DESCRIPTIONS AND INTERPRETATIONS

Effective concrete random teachers can offer students an experiential curriculum that allows them to learn by exploration, investigation, problem solving, and independent projects. The CR teacher encourages creative expression, divergent thinking, and applications for important concerns: moral, social, political, scientific. Ineffective CR teachers frustrate students' opportunities to achieve these means and ends. CR teachers use their abilities and capacities ineffectively when they confine students to a narrow definition of the CR world. Under stress, CR teachers have difficulty using their abilities and capacities effectively.

Concrete

Effective: offer students a chance to understand and affect the world in which they live.

Ineffective: do not look beyond physical world to emotions and ideas.

Under stress: cannot translate concrete to emotional world.

Random

Effective: provide time, content, and interpersonal options for students.

Ineffective: disregard time, plans, and needs of others.

Under stress: become overly organized and cautious.

Questioning

Effective: show the value of questioning.

Ineffective: never accept the ideas of others.

Under stress: doubt themselves as well as others.

Divergent

Effective: see many, varied, and unusual interpretations.

Ineffective: do not attempt to implement a plan from start to finish.

Under stress: see faults in every solution.

Independent

Effective: lead naturally and take pride in appearing different from others.

Ineffective: will do anything to be different.

Under stress: withdraw into themselves.

Inventive

Effective: look for new and unusual solutions to problems.

Ineffective: concern themselves only with possibilities.

Under stress: use any means to solve a problem.

Experiential

Effective: provide real-world experiences for students as a base for learning.

Ineffective: allow experiences to take precedence over all else.

Under stress: cannot evaluate the quality of experiences.

Problem Solving

Effective: teach students the scientific method: observe, hypothesize, experiment, and conclude with correction.

Ineffective: refuse to give credit to others, insisting on their own originality.

Under stress: forget the ideas of others deserve credit.

Change Agents

Effective: can bring about systemic change: put a new curriculum in place.

Ineffective: will do anything just to change.

Under stress: have no interest in new things.

Original

Effective: turn the creative process into original and unique products

Ineffective: refuse to give credit to others, insisting on their own originality

Under stress: forget that the ideas of others deserve credit and are not their own.

Learning and Teaching Style: In Theory and Practice

Application   Schools favor a concrete random approach to their open education
programs, team-taught classes, community and experiential programs,
mentoring programs, and science fairs. Every teacher must use CR abilities in
the classroom in order to

- *meet the needs of CR students*

- *aid other students to work in CR ways*

- *establish the importance of the experimental attitude*

- *help students work comfortably in CR ways*

- *encourage divergent thinking and risk taking*

- *help students work comfortably with open-ended problems*

- *link the importance of experimental finding to research*

- *foster creative expression*

- *vary instructional approaches*

- *provide a multitude of educational experiences and a variety of
  meaningful experiences*

- *encourage independence, self-direction, self-discovery*

- *search for new alternatives*

How, when, and why do you teach in the spirit of concrete random
approach?

In Part II we looked at the characteristics of four types of teachers, based on Gregorc's theory and model of learning style. We considered how the teacher serves as an instrument of thought in the classroom. We established that a teacher's style's goes beyond a set of outward behaviors that we recognize and catalogue. And we defined teaching style as a set of attitudes and actions that place demands on the teacher and the students.

This chapter was designed to help you distinguish your teaching behaviors, their relation to your natural style, and the implications of your style for you. But, as the Chinese proverb states: "We can study until old age...And still not finish." As you assess your teaching style, consider your natural mediation abilities and your flex-ability to meet others' styles. Watch out for accommodating others' styles in name only, mechanically using techniques in all styles but keeping a dominant style approach.

With mechanical accommodation, teachers can unknowingly fail to address different learning styles because they do not understand or know how to flex into other styles. They assume that they need all styles because they use the recommended teaching techniques for each style. However, they merely use the techniques without stepping out of their own style.

With style flex, teachers find new ways to approach existing material. Without style flex, teachers can continually use new materials without varying their style demands for students. Teachers who style flex with limited strategies, but value them, help students far more than the teacher who uses several approaches but values only one. For example, many teachers use movies as a teaching tool. However, some teachers believe movies are strictly for fun, and discuss them superficially, if at all; they never hold students accountable for information or interpretation; they do not teach students how to learn from, or reflect upon a film, and they never evaluate the importance of the film for student learning by any means, whether by test, essay, creative writing assignment, or project. In effect, they use movies mechanically, not as a true abstract random technique.

Worse yet, some teachers regard techniques that are not in their style or that they do not understand as gimmicks, diversions for students, or entertainment. These teachers cannot distinguish qualitative differences in learning style and see only the most superficial aspects of styles other than their own.

In other circumstances, some teachers cannot use their natural abilities effectively in the classroom. They have difficulty style flexing to meet the needs of students because their personal lives and goals are in turmoil. Once they settle and redefine their personal lives, they regain their style flex-ability. For example, one teacher commented:

> *I asked substitutes, other teachers, personnel, and parents who have been in my classroom to describe its ambience and my ability to meet the needs of all learners....I must admit I like the images others had of my classroom. I feel much more comfortable in my classroom this year. It is sad to say that I don't believe some years ago these things would have been said about my classroom. Then again, my own life at that time was a turmoil of unhappiness....But now I have external pressures which I can handle one day at a time, whereas before I had to live*

*with negative pressures internally, minute by minute. I
didn't like ME inside or outside of the classroom at that
time. Now I feel that I am evolving.*

As a teacher, you bring your own qualities and style to the position. You can maximize yourself in your work by using your own natural qualities and by refining your style flex-abilities to meet multiple types of people and circumstances. Make your goals, perceptions, and expectations of yourself congruent with your view of the goals, expectations of your job, and those who evaluate you.

Some teachers style flex well to the requirements placed on them, or to their perceptions of requirements. However, when you perfect your style flex-abilities you may fail to use your natural qualities to any great degree. You may develop your style flex-abilities to the detriment of your truest talents.

If the way you would like to operate as a teacher is very different from your perceptions of how you are expected to operate as a teacher, how do you react?

- *Do you ignore what you do not wish to consider?*

- *Do you attempt to be true to yourself yet meet the demands of others?*

- *Do you question yourself? Your perceptions? Others' expectations?*

- *Do you assume you ought to operate as expected?*

- *Do you just operate as expected?*

- *Do any of these responses cause you stress?*

- *How do you recognize and deal with your stressors?*

- *How can you identify and reconcile differences between your perceptions of yourself, your vision of your teaching role, your perceptions of environmental demands, and the actual demands?*

People have a goal-oriented "vision" of what is best for them. We have a style that favors select approaches. As a result, it is impossible to think in truly objective ways. We never can step completely out of our picture. We always exist in relation to others. If we accept this, then our mental health as teachers can only improve. When our perception of our personal goals, qualities, and style aligns with our expectations of others, we experience less stress and feel more worthy.

As you learn more about teaching style, you will identify your dominant teaching assumptions, attitudes, and patterns. With this information, you may choose to

- *refine your natural talents and become a "master teacher" in certain styles or circumstances;*

- *cultivate your natural talents to full capacity;*

- *develop natural capacities previously untapped;*

- *broaden your style flex-abilities and teaching options;*

- *add teaching techniques to your repertoire of skills;*

- *open the opportunity for students to work in their own style by not only providing options but also aiding them to understand how to create their own options;*

- *stretch as far as possible to uncover unused or unrecognized skills.*

Teachers use their natural qualities to offer qualitatively unique and positive learning experiences for students in many different ways. On the one hand, they may help students by frequently style flexing and providing options in attitude or activity.

On the other hand, they also can teach students how to style flex by role modeling the positive qualities of their natural style. In this way, students learn to style flex in order to develop their own skills, not to meet the unmovable demands of the teacher. And they learn to understand that they must meet the legitimate needs of others. Both teachers and students develop flex-ability when they learn to replace their limitations with an effective alternative.

Style flex is a sophisticated concept. According to Gregorc, dynamic style flex is

> "the application of will to align appropriate mediation channels with environmental demands." (15)

Style flex can occur only through appreciation, understanding, and knowledge of other styles. It requires an in-depth analysis of the demands of our own style as well as the demands of the other styles. Style flex does not give superficial accommodation to another. Style flex does not "water down" the curriculum to a simpler level. Style flex does not diminish the quality of the response or product, nor provide mechanical adjustment to an instructional activity.

What style flex does do is cause an active response by one person to the legitimate needs of others. In style flex, we step into another's style in order to align, or we withdraw our own style demands so that others may respond in their own way.

According to Gregorc, the step beyond style flex is a

> TRANSCENDENT MEDIATION ABILITY ...
> the ability to function fluidly and powerfully through all
> channels in accord with constitutional capacities. This
> ability also permits the individual to gain an overview
> perspective of multiple realities and to compound channel
> qualities to address complex environmental demands. (16)

Regrettably, some teachers misuse the style information to meet their own ends because they understand style only at its most superficial level. Barriers to the effective use of style occur if

- *teachers use only one style with no regard for the consequences on student learning;*

- *teachers mechanically attend to style by providing activity options with little or no understanding of the qualitative differences demanded by the options;*

- *teachers cannot work with styles because they do not understand qualitative differences;*

- *teachers refuse to style flex;*

- *teachers use style as a smokescreen for lack of content expertise or understanding of teaching methods;*

- *teachers regard style as nothing more than teaching techniques.*

Clearly, effective application of the concepts of learning style and teaching style requires more than learning how to match style or mechanically following a style formula.

Part III

Student Style
In Focus

The child needs a framework within which to find himself [herself]; otherwise, he [she] is an egg without a shell.

—Theresa Ross, teacher

PART III

STUDENT STYLE—IN FOCUS

*You know, it's of little wonder that you are tired and
sometimes frustrated at the complexity of the
education process. But remember—you are not alone.
I can do many things for myself and can help myself
quite naturally. All I need are people who care and
who recognize me for who and what I am. And, most
of all, I need educators who lovingly wish to guide
me and other future world citizens because of a
spiritual need deep within them.*

Signed,
A Future World Citizen

—Anthony F. Gregorc

    Any search for one's inner self—strengths and weaknesses—poses
difficulties and challenges, sometimes creates resistance, but always
fascinates. My research found clearly that children, from very young through
pre-adult, have stages of style development and levels of awareness about
their own natural styles. Their personal and educational experiences expand,
condition, or modify their natural styles.

    For two reasons it is not an easy task to assess the learning styles of
children by using a psychological mindstyle approach. First, the Gregorc
approach to style requires a sophisticated understanding of style before it can
be applied for assessment purposes. Second, children experience conditions
that may help or hinder their use of a natural style. The person with an
untrained eye, or the researcher who does not use a phenomenological
approach, may easily misinterpret a child's learning style, or miss it completely.

    With this concern, can we interpret a young child's or adolescent's style at
all? Yes, but only after we have considered the range of influences on style so
that we base decisions about style on complete and accurate information, not
just on superficial behaviors.

    According to Gregorc, learning style emerges from mind qualities:
mindstyles. To use learning style variables effectively, we have to work from
their source, the individual mind. Our purpose in assessing the style of
children parallels that for adults: to aid them in the lifelong process of

self-realization and eventually self-actualization.

In Part III, we will highlight critical factors connected to student learning style and discuss the pros and cons of matching and mismatching students' learning styles. We will also profile the behaviors of each style in depth.

CHAPTER 6

LEARNING STYLE IN THE CONTEXT OF A CHILD'S LIFE

*The marvelous thing about learning style is that every
teacher can help to provide a warm prevailing breeze
to lift all those "kites" and help them soar.
Sometimes the strings may get tangled up, but now
we can understand how a little more dimension and
space can keep them free and flying.*

—Emilie Piper, teacher

Many conditions influence the way children behave, and thus the way we interpret their styles. Strong elements impact children's lives: their physical, emotional, intellectual, and developmental stages of growth; the influence of parents and home environment; the expectations and learning demands of teachers; and the influence of peers.

DEVELOPMENTAL CONNECTIONS

Developmental Stages

Developmental stages of growth may temporarily inhibit or override typical style behavior until a child completes a particular stage. Consider seven-year-old Sarah. Her parents and teachers see her as a characteristic AR/AS style: emotional, sensitive, with many friends (AR), an "A" student and avid reader (AS) who has little interest in hands-on projects or structured work (CS) or in investigative or experimental learning (CR). For a six-month period, the normally affectionate and gregarious Sarah insisted that no one liked her anymore. She judged herself a failure. She seemed to have changed overnight into an insecure, grade-conscious, withdrawn child. Several months later, she returned to her old self. Upon study of Sarah, home demands, teachers, and peers, it became apparent that developmental insecurities overrode her naturally positive style.

In a child with dominant CS strengths, the seven-year-old's developmental insecurities might have manifested themselves differently. For example, CS children who organize easily, follow directions, and work with projects may question their own ability to follow directions, worry about arriving late for school, and seek approval at every turn. On the other hand, the usually dominant CR child may change from an independent and imaginative child to one who threatens to run away from home, or to one whose active imagination conjures real nighttime fears.

By the time seven-year-olds blend into eight-year-olds, their natural, positive style usually returns. Keep in mind that developmental stages occur within a six-to-nine-month range. Thus, preadolescent children of any age may potentially vary nine months apart in developmental issues from their peers.

Parents have recounted tales of their twins who simultaneously experienced age-related developmental stages in entirely different ways. Take Kate and Marie, twins who had just turned six.

Marie, a CS/AS type, turned her life into a matter of possessions: everything belonged to her, resulting in constant fighting with Kate. The usual AR/CR Kate began to alternate between telling her mother she loved and hated her, and continuously threatened to abuse Marie!

According to Gesell Institute research, a breakup in personality equilibrium characterizes the six-year-old stage; children desire new things to excess, insist on everything their own way, and find it impossible to adapt. The Institute attributes six-year-old behavior to these **developmental causes**:

> Behavior at this time is in many ways reminiscent of that which we have described as typifying the two-and-a half-year-old. The child is, to begin with, violently emotional. And in his emotions, he functions at opposite extremes. He loves one minute, hates the next....What has happened is that Mother is no longer the center of his world. Now, he wants to be the center of his world, even though he hasn't yet developed a secure sense of himself. He wants to come first, to be loved best, to have the most of everything....Six...is very demanding of others and very rigid in his demands. He has to have things just so. He cannot adapt. It is the others who must do the

adapting....He tends to be extremely negative in his response to others. That he has been asked to do something is sufficient reason for refusing to do it....It is most difficult for him to choose between any alternative, because he wants both. It is also more difficult for him to accept criticism, blame, punishment. He has to be right. He has to be praised. He has to win. He is as rigid and as unadaptable in his relations with others....Things have to be done in his way. The others have to give in to him. If he is winning, everything is fine. If the others win, tears and accusations that the others are cheating abound. (17)

Thus, sometimes developmental changes in children have a single cause—for example, the six-year-old's breakup in equilibrium. But, the natural style of the child will often determine how the child will act out in any one stage.

Young children seem not only to move through the ups and downs of developmental stages but to do so through positive and negative apects of their own natural styles. Or they may "try on" altogether different styles, in response to developmental changes. I can only marvel at the fortitude of the elementary school teacher who has some students entering a developmental stage, others leaving it, and some in full swing of a stage, in one or more of four styles, positive or negative in tone all at the same time!

Adolescence, too, has its developmental needs for identity made easier or more difficult because of stylistic differences. For example, an eighth-grader exclaimed during an interview about her dominant abstract sequential style, "That's just what I didn't want to be!" At this point in her development, she wanted to reject her natural intellectual abilities for a more socially accepted image. But another AS eighth-grade student said of her AS style, "I feel bad at times because I want to contribute a neat idea to Mrs. R.'s lecture, but the kids who don't know me well just think I am trying to make points with her."

During adolescence, naturally positive abstract random students may have the easiest time socializing with peers, or they may become painfully shy, have a difficult time giving attention to school, or may not be able to resist the excess of peer activities. And some need to use the adolescent time to throw off the sequential cloak others imposed on them during their elementary years. For adolescents in search of a style identity as well as a developmental identity, this stage is extremely turbulent.

During adolescence naturally dominant concrete random students, who often meet with little cooperation for their style from some teachers, may turn their experimental nature away from studies. They may become discipline problems; grow disaffected with school in general, and experiment in any way—positive or negative—in order to give release to their developmental needs within their own style.

Recognizing Preferences

As a researcher, I have observed that younger children do not usually recognize distinct style preferences, or necessarily have the same style characteristics as adults with the same style. For example, first-grade children of all styles say they love to learn from movies, from books, and from games. They love worksheets and think their teachers are wonderful as long as they are kind and fair. Young children rarely know how they learn best. They do not recognize that a teacher organizes a structured or unstructured class, even though they may have great difficulty in meeting the teacher's demands.

Young children who have a dominant style, however, show definite tendencies in the basic perception field—concrete or abstract—and the basic ordering field—sequential or random. However, because of their lack of life experience and their developmental immaturity, we usually cannot identify young children according to the behaviors shown by adults, adolescents, or preteenagers. We can understand the behaviors—style—of young children better if we consider the context of their world and the needs of developmental stages. Picture David, a kindergarten child, intensely engaged in coloring —tongue clenched between his teeth—furious when another child knocks his elbow and causes his crayon to mark across the page. He smashes the paper into the wastebasket and calls it quits. Yet, Josh, another child with the very same coloring pose, also "victimized" by the same fast walker, simply gets another paper and starts again. Both boys are concrete sequential, yet each has a different way of showing his style.

Children experience developmental changes in many stylistic ways.

At certain ages some abstract random children keep their bedrooms in perfect order because they want to please Mom. Sometimes even the most concrete sequential children have much too much to do to bother with cleaning their bedrooms. Most adolescents are peer centered, but this does not necessarily mean that most have an abstract random style. However, abstract random types often seem to use their style most freely as teenagers!

Developmental stages in children and young adults influence the way they reveal their style. In addition, different age groups also have their own social, cultural, and environmental norms. For example, the "in" phrase for twelve-to-fourteen-year-olds of any style may be "that's excellent!" But, the same phrase may signal an abstract sequential style in adults.

As children grow, develop, and mature in physical, psychological, emotional, intellectual, and spiritual ways, they understand, and use, their abilities and capacities in more sophisticated ways. Style, as representative of a person's mediation abilities and capacities—abstraction and concreteness, and sequence and randomness—is present in all people, but the behaviors that distinguish the kinds of style may be different for age groups, cultures, and socioeconomic classes, and in different environments.

Matching Style and Developmental Stages

Young children undergo rapid developmental changes, have few life experiences, and identify quickly with the comments made about them by parents and teachers. Given these conditions, young children should encounter a rich school curriculum that permits their experiencing all four styles of learning, not one matched strictly to their learning style. Children should work with teachers of all four styles who have a positive and effective teaching style, who understand all student learning styles, and who style flex with ease. It is useless for children to work with negative and ineffective teachers, regardless of their style.

Young children need the opportunity to use their own style as well as to learn how to "stretch" into other styles. However, some teachers attempt to use this approach of purposeful, guided match and mismatch of learning style as a way to force children to abandon a predominant style in favor of the teacher's style "for their own good." This is NOT a correct interpretation!

Thus, young children ought to have an opportunity to experience many styles in a loving, safe environment. In this way, they can use their own style yet learn how to work in other styles. Young children suffer when placed in a totally mismatched situation. Further, we must not force them to use only one style, whether their own or the teacher's. Continuous mismatch—a subject we will address shortly—is destructive at any age but especially devastating to the psychologically immature child who cannot understand why he or she has so much difficulty.

When students reach the middle school years, they no longer define worth and self from adults and begin instead to look inward. If they do not find a sense of self there, peers quickly take over as the support system. In these years of young (ages ten - twelve) and middle (ages twelve - fourteen) adolescence, children benefit from style as a tool to help them see themselves in relation to others and the world. Learning about style provides the opportunity for them to consider their unique abilities, capacities, and preferences in a safe way—no style is right or wrong.

At this time of self-discovery and intense affective desire, style provides a tool to meet an especially strong need for understanding and acceptance in the adolescent. It is appropriate to include discovery of self and style in a style-differentiated curriculum at the high school and junior high or middle school levels. But, **until the adolescent years children do not have the abstract cognitive ability to understand the *significance* of style.** Youngsters who are in transition developmentally toward more formal operations and abstract thought, gain more from a study of style than those who have not yet left the concrete stage. Most young, gifted adolescents and high school students are ready to study style. Some junior high school students do not have the maturity or readiness to address style but others receive much needed validation from style. Learning disabled students in junior and senior high especially appreciate information about style. Once students begin to study style, they need caring teachers trained to understand learning style as a theory and practical approach to learning.

As adolescents mature, style can aid them to validate themselves, and can serve as a communication vehicle and a means to identify strengths, weaknesses, and causes of stress. Teachers who understand style can help counselors and counsel students themselves in explanations of career education, and in any program that requires students to base their work on knowledge of themselves. Needless to say, a recognition of style can help children of most ages to work more effectively with others and their curriculum.

PARENTS

Parental influence and home environment directly shape or alter a child's naturally dominant style. Parents help develop their children's natural, positive style and aid their journey to mentally healthy, self-confident adults.

Parents of children with special gifts face a dilemma. Do they nurture the gift or insist on a variety of experiences to develop the whole child? A recent study found that adults who had excelled in one area —for example, in performing musically—virtually devoted their lives from a very early age to the development of this natural gift to the exclusion of other experiences.

Parents who do not guide their children to understand the positive and negative sides of their natural style may foster the "social brat." Parents like this believe, mistakenly, that children are free to be themselves under these conditions. Other parents understand the meaning of natural style so poorly that they have no idea how to shape it, nor care about doing so.

The environment cultivates a child's natural style by encouraging style's positive expression, simultaneously exposing the child to experiences that broaden stylistic options, adaptive abilities, and coping mechanisms. For example, the abstract random child develops a positive sense of self when parents respect the child's sensitivity, admire interpersonal skills, and help him/her understand the power of emotions. But the child also gains when parents insist, for example, that an AR child develop useful organizational skills and try experimental and problem solving methods. In effect, they encourage their child to broaden his/her selection of stylistic options yet not diminish natural style.

If parents can help their children to understand natural abilities, as well as to learn additional stylistic skills, the chances improve that children will develop healthy self-concepts and learn to recognize and adapt to school demands. On the other hand, when the environment, home or school, forces children to give up their natural dominant styles, they lose their sense of self and, possibly, trust in others.

Certain environments—home or school—ignore or denigrate a naturally dominant style to the point where a child hides it. For example, parents who see only weakness instead of sensitivity, might criticize a gentle abstract random child. Negative outlooks like this create children who are ashamed of their own talents or who become inhibited emotionally.

The environment can also suggest that children replace one natural style with another. For example, parents who want to create a child in their image, to have a son or daughter step into the family profession or business, to attend the family alma mater, or otherwise fit the family mold—"All the Bateses become lawyers"—often guide a child in a certain style. In such cases the parents try to make their children live up to preconceived ideas.

Learning and Teaching Style: In Theory and Practice

Some parents, unhappy with themselves, resist any indication of "like father, like son." The result: the parent attempts to restructure the child. Teachers may not be able to influence such factors. But, our awareness of these influencing factors will help prevent simplistic diagnoses.

TEACHER EXPECTATIONS

Teacher expectations also play a role in students' freedom to use their natural styles. We often see children so motivated to perform well as good students that they adapt intuitively to the demands of the teacher, submerging their own style. For example, Sam was in the sixth grade before he had a teacher who would address his abstract random style. By then he had so mastered the concrete sequential and abstract sequential behaviors, which are usually stressed in schools, that he appeared to be a CS/AS child. His parents knew better; they felt Sam's lack of enthusiasm for school and recognized his adaptation to a very sequential system.

Sam seemed to have a reprieve in sixth grade: his teacher was an understanding abstract random. In reality, everyone agonized. Why? Sam's teacher sought AR behaviors, learning, and products. She encouraged peer learning, group discussions, creative writing, personal expression, and use of imagination. Sam fought her approach with sequential techniques, acquired under sequential teachers. The more open-ended the assignments, the more Sam demanded structure. Encouraged by his parents, his teacher continued to offer the AR choices. By midwinter Sam began to realize he did not have to be so sequential, ordered, and structured to succeed. Sam felt a light dawn. He wrote poems and stories, created role-play scenarios of learning topics, wrote the script for a slide show on local geography, and "discovered" he liked to learn. For the first time, Sam's parents saw a naturally vibrant boy who no longer equated school with forced labor.

A burst of sun or a shower of rain can frequently come from the same source.

Teaching style can affect children in different ways.

Still other teachers see only the lack of their own style in their students. For example, a concrete random teacher may see concrete sequential children as noncreative instead of well structured. Abstract sequential teachers may view concrete random children as undisciplined and as nonreaders rather than as experimental and problem oriented. The concrete sequential teacher may judge some abstract random children as disorganized rather than notice the AR flexibility, imagination, or interpretative abilities. CS teachers may cultivate and praise the student who always hands in assignments on time. AR teachers may not set store by deadlines, so they may subtly convey to the CS student that they do not value one of that student's strongest points: meeting a due date.

PEER INFLUENCE

Friends and alliances continue to play a major role in the way children see themselves. This, in turn, affects how they use their natural style. To illustrate, a student may suddenly take advanced science because all his/her friends are taking it. Or a CS student who requires quiet and long hours of study may join a gregarious study group because he wants to date a girl in the group. When given choices, adolescents, in particular, may follow the crowd instead of their own style, especially if they have little understanding of the importance of style. Therefore, teachers cannot expect to address student learning style based solely on the student behaviors they observe during short periods. They must also put the behaviors into the context of the students' lives.

DEGREES

Every child has a style, but some are more developed than others. In chapter 2 we discussed the six levels of style development. We will apply them now to understand student style development.

Developed

Children with a strongly **developed** style have a clearly distinguished stylistic pattern that accurately reflects their natural abilities, capacities, and preferences. We can easily identify their stylistic type. Usually, learners with a strongly developed style are comfortable with themselves and at ease within their stylistically matched learning areas. Adults who truly know them agree on their strengths and weaknesses. And the children fully recognize themselves within a stylistic pattern. When students understand their style, they are usually successful with style-matched materials. Likewise, these students will accept opportunities to learn skills in order to "stretch" their style.

Emergent

Students with an **emergent** style do not have a clearly distinguished style that reflects natural abilities and capacities. They attempt to confirm abilities and capacities that they have not previously recognized. For example, children controlled and contained at home may find a new side of themselves in a concrete random's kindergarten class that stresses open-ended exploration. When parents and teachers observe how a child changes under certain conditions and environments, they see how the emergent style of learner begins to take shape.

Experimental

Students with an **experimental** style do not have a clearly defined style that reflects natural abilities and capacities. They search for conditions to bring out their style and try many different style approaches to learning, never really sure which "fit" is best. Unlike students who are equally proficient in all four styles, these students do not recognize a "natural" area and may operate differently in different classes, depending on the teacher. Students at an experimental level do not know their strengths and weaknesses, and may not excel in any one style of learning. At some time, opportunities and experiences may point toward a particular set of abilities and capacities. But students at the experimental level may also continue "trying out" what comes along, without ever really knowing, or caring, about their own style.

Adaptive

Students with **adaptive** styles may or may not have a set of abilities and capacities that stand out sharply as style. However, they do know how to adapt to environments and people, and operate differently depending on the teacher and the class. On the one hand, they may work well under all kinds of conditions. Or, they may acquiesce to the demands of the situation and produce "acceptable" rather than "excellent" work. These students may have the art of "reading the environment" without sacrificing individual talents, or they may adapt so much that they always "give in" to others, submerging their unique abilities. While we may admire adaptation skills in a student, overuse can cause the student's natural abilities and capacities to atrophy.

Masked

Students with **masked** styles may or may not know about their natural abilities and capacities. They pretend to have certain abilities and act as if they are a particular style. Students mask style for many reasons. They may want to court the favor of a teacher, a parent, or another child. They may have little self-confidence, or no self-acceptance, or they may sense little respect from others. They may believe they should act in certain ways, either through direct messages ("Good students write neatly") or through indirect messages ("I just don't know what's wrong with you"). Students may mask to receive an "A" grade or to earn parental approval. They may learn to "overinflate" an average ability, "deflate" a strength, or "moderate" a gift either for reward or to neutralize criticism and avoid punishment.

Whereas adaptive behavior may cause the loss or repression of natural abilities, masked behavior often replaces natural abilities with other abilities. The student may ultimately equate masked behavior with his/her actual abilities. When under pressure to perform, masked behavior usually falls apart. The student can become defensive or hostile, or crumble under a feeling of failure. Masked behavior is dangerous. Although it temporarily fulfills a need, it exacts a price in the end.

Hidden

Students with **hidden** styles do not know their natural abilities and capacities. Usually, these students face many forces that prevent one's ability to recognize a natural style. Children hide their true selves when they face physical or emotional abuse, serious life adjustment (divorce, death), an alcoholic family life, physical or emotional poverty. For any number of personal reasons, some children cannot reveal their true style.

> ## The Range of Student Styles
>
> *Developed*
>   *Emergent*
>   *Experimental*
>   *Adaptive*
>   *Masked*
>   *Hidden*

Many factors influence how style develops, how we can see style, and how we can attend to style. In summary, let's review some key points in thinking about student styles.

- *Several conditions may modify the appearance of a student's natural style, camouflaging its actual nature.*

- *If the teacher understands the complex forces working with and against the expression of a student's natural style, then he/she has greater chances of success in meeting the learner's real needs. This requires individual effort.*

- *Teachers offer more to students when they address the natural style needs of the students rather than ones conditioned by the environment. This begins through choice in the classroom.*

- *A teacher can recognize learning style more easily if he/she*
  - ~ *has full understanding of his/her own mind's style;*
  - ~ *watches student behavior in unguarded moments rather than in controlled environments;*
  - ~ *works with students to understand their perceptions, seeks assistance in resolving mismatch, and provides many options for learning.*

- *Learning preferences based on student self-reports may or may not be accurate because students*
  - ~ *expect sequential approaches to school;*
  - ~ *lack knowledge and experience with a variety of learning strategies;*
  - ~ *distrust teacher motives and give "what the teacher wants to hear."*

- *Learning style approaches that reinforce learned preferences rather than operate from natural abilities and capacities may serve to narrow learning options rather than broaden student understanding of options.*

- *Learning style information is used appropriately for assessment purposes rather than for diagnosis and prescription.*

Learning style is not a panacea for education's ills. It is a sophisticated approach to understanding and respecting the individual qualities and needs of teachers and students. Style encourages people to accept their strengths, to face their limitations, and to grow and develop toward self-actualization. Teachers play a vital role in creating the reality to make this process open to all students. Goethe captured the power and potential of style as teachers work with boys and girls, and young men and women. He advised:

> **If you will treat an individual as he is, he will stay as he is, but if you treat him as if he were what he ought to be, he will become what he ought to be and could be.**

CHAPTER 7

THE PRIORITIES, POWER AND POTENTIAL OF LEARNING STYLE

A small stone upturned can be the start of an avalanche.

—Silver Chord, teacher

Five priorities direct the application of style for students. First, we help students realize their natural abilities and capacities as part of the lifelong process toward self-actualization. Second, we aid students to increase learning achievement. Third, we assist students in recognizing and appreciating others' abilities. Fourth, we aid students in meeting the legitimate needs of others by teaching style-flex strategies and style-adaptation skills. Fifth, we provide students with ways to survive demands of others by teaching them how to recognize and use coping skills.

STYLE: A VEHICLE

Learning style provides an excellent communication vehicle to explain individual differences of students and teachers to students. When teachers recognize, accept, and value different learning styles, they validate the worth of all students, and open the doors to cultivate the beauty of different styles. When student have a common language—CS, AR, AS, and CR— teachers give them a means to voice, straightforwardly, agreement and disagreement with others and with learning methods.

But we must teach about style in a careful, knowing way that builds understanding. I can guarantee that you gain nothing by adapting adult instruments to children's levels, and cause more potential harm than good. You develop little of lasting value by giving students a one-shot explanation of style. You experience considerable frustration in giving simplistic behavioral descriptions, e.g., sequentials are neat, randoms lose things. You misuse style by equating it with personality or brain behavior. You create a dangerous tool for others to use, e.g., "I can't do this assignment. It's not my style."

My research shows clearly that students gain immensely from a carefully developed understanding of style differences, style demands, style flex, and style mismatch. Teachers who invest time and energy to unravel the complexity of style with adolescents and young adults report significant results in student self-understanding, communication between teacher and student, and the student's ability to make better decisions about the way he/she views a teacher or an assignment. (18)

Further, a style approach allows teachers to place perspective on competition. If teachers provide options rather than force all students to take the same approach to learning, students have a greater chance to succeed in their own way. Teachers release social pressure on students to conform to an academic or peer-group image when options help all students learn effectively. Consistent use of style-based approaches in counseling students and in classroom activities significantly increases the mental health quotient of a classroom. Student self-esteem and self-concept rises when psychologically safe ways permit students to accept differences in themselves and others.

As a tool for career education, style provides a perspective on the demands of the workplace. For example, Sally knows she does not want to become a lab technician but does not know why. Marcia wants to enter business but does not know in what capacity or area she can best use her strengths. Students need to know that some occupations carry very strong style demands but that others call for the strengths of the person, and not conformity to the job. As a tool for career education, style can open students' eyes to particular careers and aid them to assess style demands of the work. Students and teachers, however, need to resist the temptation to dismiss a career consideration simply because the style demands appear mismatched to the student. Students will find it more productive to identify how they can use their mindstyle strengths as well as minimize their limitations in meeting job expectations.

LABELING

By using labels for different styles, we have a basis for shared understanding. We can use labels to take pride in differences or we can use labels to box in students and narrow the richness of their character. Labels can also prevent people from dealing with a problem—"How can anyone teach that boy, he's a random!" Labels can provide an excuse for behavior—"I need you to do exactly as I say. You know I am a sequential." On the other hand, labels present positive opportunities for assessment. But labels work effectively only when used with discretion, vigilance, and caution. As we discussed in chapter 3, labeling carries with it a responsibility for awareness of its potential uses and abuses.

If you introduce students to the concept of learning style and the typology of four styles, then you must communicate clearly their responsibility to use labels to value rather than restrict themselves and others. It takes care to teach students that they cannot reduce the human spirit and mind to a set of four styles but may use the concept of four styles as a source for acceptance and appreciation of others. They should understand, too, that their peers may accept or reject them based on style if they value one style more than others, or they misunderstand the meaning of a style. And they must realize, too, that they have only a general initial exposure to style, not a degree in psychology.

Many parents express their approval and desire for their children to hear about learning style concepts. They also reveal deep concern about the misuse of labels by some teachers. What do these fears say about our profession and parental trust in it? With a subject as sensitive and powerful as learning style, parents have a right to feel assured that teachers treat their children as unique individuals, regardless of their preferred styles of learning.

**STYLE IN
THE CLASSROOM**

In the classroom students face demands from the teacher's style, from the curriculum, from the daily activities, from social groups, and from their own style. Students have various levels of abilities to adapt and to meet the demands of others. They may adapt mechanically—turning in a twenty-page term paper, painfully processed. Or they may adapt qualitatively— learning how to understand and work with the demands of a twenty-page term paper. Teachers can instruct students how to respond appropriately, but for some students all the instruction in the world may never "take" if it does not link into the way their minds function.

Students need choices so that they can work in their own styles, but they also need to try new approaches and entertain new ideas. Teachers who never demand that students experience different styles may never see all the style range of particular students. Students need to experience many ways to know and to think about themselves. But students will not venture into uncomfortable styles if teachers do not validate their natural style first. **When students spend their energy in defense of their own styles, they have little left over for stretching those styles. Unless a student feels psychologically safe, the teacher has little chance to broaden the student's style.**

**MATCHING
AND
MISMATCHING**

Several arguments support both matching and mismatching of student style with teacher and curricular style. The evidence for matching style is strong: (1) student achievement increases; (2) student self-concept improves; and (3) student learning takes place with greater ease, maximum energy flow, and most efficient results. A student who learns in his/her naturally dominant style is more likely to earn high grades, which can result in an "I'm okay" feeling. Matching can aid students to validate themselves by allowing them to discover, accept, or utilize their naturally dominant abilities, creating an "I'm special, too" feeling. And, matching style can promote mental health by helping students to learn with the least stress, to get maximum results from the time invested, and to enjoy a sense of control over their own learning processes. We've all seen the glee in the child who says, "I can do that—it's easy!"

Several arguments also exist against matching. Critics cite the disadvantages of mismatch: (1) it precludes learning in other styles; (2) it discourages experiments with new ways of learning; and (3) it blocks personal growth and development by confining each student to one correct approach.

If students rely on learning experiences solely within their preferred range of learning style, they limit ways of learning, start to expect others to conform to their ways, and narrow their thinking to view nonconformers as wrong or deviant. By always working from a matched position, students may never have the opportunity to see the gifts, abilities, and differences in others. They may stereotype those different from themselves, or they may refuse to socialize with people of divergent styles. I wonder how often someone labels a child "weird," or some other derogatory term currently in vogue, simply because he/she does not meet the closed style of the group.

On the opposite side of the coin, we can see the advantages for mismatching learning style. Through mismatch, students can gain new insights and, possibly, new skills. Through mismatch, students learn to work in a minor area. They may discover a previously untested or unexplored field in which they have significant ability or interest. Or, they may discover more about themselves, noticing areas they should avoid or that require assistance or extensive practice before they can use the style effectively. If teachers help students to realize that their own limitations are the strengths and aptitudes of others, learners may come to appreciate others without having to discount themselves. How many students, I wonder, have suffered at the hands of name-callers who ridiculed them for pursuing what others did not. Through guided and purposeful mismatch students increase their own style flex-abilities by entering strange waters, or Robert Frost's "road not taken." And they may also follow the advice of Thoreau more easily in judging those different from us:

> *If a man does not keep with his companions, perhaps it is because he hears a different drummer. Let him step to the music which he hears, however measured or far away.*

Continuous mismatch of style is more detrimental to the mental and physical health of the student than continuous matching. If severe mismatch persists over long periods, students risk serious consequences. First, they may find they have to use an inordinate amount of energy to achieve goals—a dominant random student probably must devote considerably more time to learn highly sequential chemistry material than an equally intelligent sequential learner.

When students make such comments as "Why do we have to study?" what do they mean? From some, the question means, "What does this have to do with me?" From others, the question relates the message, "I don't understand this." And for some, the question hides their real point, "I have a better way to learn this."

Further, serious and prolonged mismatch between student style and the style demands of the material prevents students from learning material, but also impacts upon self-concept. No one feels good about himself/herself in the face of failure.

According to Gregorc, prolonged and extreme mismatch can result in physical and mental stress, such as stomachaches, headaches, and allergies, caused by misdirected and unused energy. It can also produce physical and mental "dis-eases," such as alienation, resentment, anger, withdrawal, and drug and alcohol abuse, as well as suicide.

Sadly, some of the adolescent suicide attempters and completers achieve high grades and succeed by everyone's standards. Their notes, poetry, writing, and conversations reveal a painful message, "I played your academic game, but no one cared about the real me." These children tell us through their words and actions that we praised their academic performance, enjoyed their abilities, and encouraged their conformity to our values. But, in our eagerness to promote their success, we forgot about their spirit.

Extended mismatch can exact a powerful price. It does not always wreak visible havoc on the student, but it will erode the core of a child, slowly removing precious vitality.

EDUCATION?

Of all God's creations on this good earth
I know the most wonderful comes from the birth
Of a child.

When a child is born he is one of a kind
With a unique body and an inquisitive mind,
To expand.

From the cradle to walking his time is spent
Being stimulated and taught by his environment,
Learning.

He learns to be loving or he may learn fear
He learns to laugh and to shed a tear,
When hurt.

He grows and heads out into a world unknown
For the school environment he trades his home
And security.

Under the influence of teachers to whom he is sent
The most formative years of his life will be spent
Learning.

He comes with excitement his eyes all aglow
With hundreds of questions just wanting to know,
Why?

This child with the inquisitive mind like clay
Is shaped and molded and taught each day,
To conform.

He rebels against the system that seems so mundane
He is threatened with failure, his eyes now show pain,
Then nothing.

With other children in the same situation
He learns to conform and consume information,
He obeys.

Instead of expanding his mind will shrink
He is taught information but not how to think,
For himself.

He is tested to see how much he consumed
He is praised for proficiency but his mind is doomed,
To mediocrity.

The system must be changed at any cost
It is not education when a mind is lost
Forever.

                                        —Bob Wilkerson, 1981

Chapter 7: The Priorities, Power, and Potential of Learning Style   127

CHAPTER 8

FOUR LEARNING STYLES:
AN IN-DEPTH LOOK

Don't you see my rainbow, teacher?
Don't you see all the colors?
I know that you're mad at me.
I know that you said to color
the cherries red and the leaves green.
I guess I shouldn't have done it backwards.
But, teacher, don't you see my rainbow?
Don't you see all the colors?
Don't you see me?

—Albert Cullum

This chapter provides an in-depth profile of the four learning styles as they are seen in student attitudes and actions. The profile of each style is a composite of characteristics and behaviors. Each profile is categorized stereotypically as the extreme and well-developed dominant style. For example, the profile of the concrete sequential represents a student who operates from a CS style exclusively. In reality, no one appears, or operates, solely from one style.

It is crucial to note that not all students operate from a well-developed or mature style. For example, the third-grade student with poor fine-motor coordination may avoid the CS trait of "hands-on building" because his/her physical development overrides this possibility. The student, however, may still be a dominant concrete sequential in mental ability. Or, a high school student who has a difficult home life may avoid the AR traits of "tying to emotions" because emotions are too painful to address. This person may be in tremendous need to be understood as an AR.

However, the words of one teacher must ring in our ears when we work with student style. She warned, "People should realize that amateur psychology on a student can be equivalent to a nuclear holocaust for that person." I fully agree. Style information used to define and "treat" students is style information misused.

We study student behaviors not to diagnose and prescribe but to gain the ability to look more closely, listen more carefully, and question more effectively when we work with students. We seek to broaden our views about the way people think and to develop our own awareness of differences. This can happen only if we know how to observe and how to question.

We cannot forget, too, that students do not live in a vacuum of style. As children grow and develop from infancy to young adulthood, there are individual goals, needs, developmental tasks, and experiences that shape their lives. Within these conditions, teachers and parents are in the most influential position to affirm personal worth and unique capability, to redirect or rechannel negative and destructive behaviors, and, most important, to create space for personal mental abilities and driving forces to be recognized and exercised by the individual child.

By better understanding the mind of each style in theory, we are in a better position to understand individual differences and needs in reality. If we can recognize patterns of behavior and their causes, we can increase the possibility that we will recognize all students as individuals rather than attempt to understand them from our way of thinking.

In this chapter student styles will be described from the view of the well-developed, dominant style. The teacher, then, has the opportunity to apply this information responsibly for the growth and development of students. The checklist in each style indicates major traits and characteristics, primarily positive, demonstrated by students at all grade levels. The lists provide a synopsis of behaviors and describe only the general, commonly observed characteristics of students who have a well-developed, dominant style that is used with ease and effectiveness.

Students who are under stress, frustrated by mismatch, facing a learning disability, or experiencing significant self-concept problems will not necessarily be identified by the behaviors on this list without personalized assessment. Students under stress often act out, withdraw, or otherwise engage in behavior that reveals few positive style clues. Students cannot show their style in the classroom if their style is not allowed or encouraged, if there is mismatch. If a teacher imposes one style—no matter how kindly—students simply do not have the confidence, personal resources, or established self-concept to reveal their own style. Often the teacher sees rebellion or other negative behavior, the recourse of choice for many a mismatched student. Students damaged by years—or sometimes just months—of mismatch and failure do nothing in the class rather than continue to put energy into failure. Teachers of learning disabled students express their amazement at how little of the child the regular classroom teacher can see when mismatch takes place. Often, the resource teacher, not the classroom teacher, sees the true style because in the resource room more style matching occurs. Only in-depth study identifies such students with accuracy.

A checklist is not a diagnostic instrument that is definitive and prescriptive. A checklist indicates only how one person sees another; in this instance how the teacher sees the student. Assessment is only as effective as the assessor!

Used properly, checklists are useful for indicating patterns of behavior, namely, how students deal with their world; types of preferences, ways by which students attempt to learn; and kinds of attitudes, clues to how students may interpret themselves, others, and the environment.

With checklist information, a teacher has the opportunity to assess and work with a child from a particular point of understanding. It is the teacher's responsibility to use checklist information with discretion, vigilance, and caution. Such checklist information should never be used to label students, or to confine their experiences. Nor should it be used to box students into one style.

With this information, you may be better equipped to recognize styles of behaviors, preferences, and needs, and feel more free to accommodate different needs. You are not expected to diagnose and prescribe to individual styles. Rather, I hope you will use your knowledge to relate better to students, to prevent learning trouble and difficulties before they become insurmountable obstacles, and to offer a greater variety of learning and interpersonal experiences for your students.

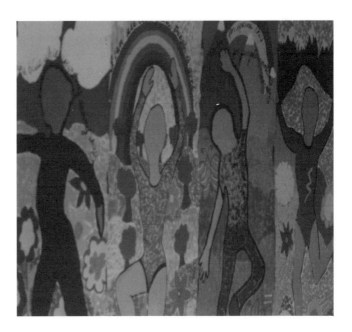

The Concrete Sequential Student Style

" If I could tell my teacher about me in order to help me be a better student, I would ask for specific instructions and exact procedures. I would ask for more individual activities and less groupwork because I work better on my own. I would also like exact due dates so I could know when to start and have my project finished on time."

—Holly

UNDERSTANDING THE CONCRETE SEQUENTIAL LEARNING STYLE OF STUDENTS

Concrete sequential learners have special abilities to learn about the world in an orderly and step-by-step way. They show their finest abilities when learning focuses on information, detail, facts, and eventual right answers that are useful to their lives and way of thinking. They perform at their best using one or more of their physical senses. For example, many CS types demonstrate their gift of touch in their preference for hands-on activity. They would rather work on a group project than read about a project. They prefer to join work on a community project than to join a group to discuss an idea. CS learners work in top form in a class with set procedures and limits that are understood by students and enforced by the teacher. CS learners organize well and behave like on-the-job workers. They keep themselves busy and involved in specific projects, tasks, and activities. They also prepare in advance for things that really matter to them.

CONCRETE: RELATE BEST TO THE PHYSICAL, HANDS-ON WORLD.

- [ ] Have hands-on hobbies, such as building models, collecting stamps, using computers.
- [ ] Need specific, real examples. Have a "show-me" attitude.
- [ ] Show creativity by making or remaking realistic products and exact replicas.
- [ ] Accept things at face value—what you see is what you get.
- [ ] Enjoy all types of hands-on experiences, such as crafts, fixing things, electronics.

SEQUENTIAL: ORDER THE WORLD IN A STEP-BY-STEP FASHION.

- [ ] Like to organize and run things, arrange things just so, and work from patterns.
- [ ] Can't change their minds easily once they have made a decision.
- [ ] Work easily with the step by step of the computer.
- [ ] Collect, organize, arrange, classify, list, categorize, and order.
- [ ] Need and enjoy structured situations, e.g., assigned seats and an organized teacher; do not tolerate rearrangement of their things.

THOROUGH: COMPLETE WORK WITH ACCURACY.

- [ ] Take thorough notes; copy details with precision.
- [ ] Like to finish one thing at a time and pursue projects to the end.
- [ ] Draw conclusions only after all the facts have been gathered.
- [ ] Pay attention to detail, specific information, directions, and time.
- [ ] Want the teacher to verify the accuracy of their work.

FACTUAL: MAKE DECISIONS BASED ON THE FACTS THEY OBSERVE.

- [ ] Enjoy reading for specific detail and information.
- [ ] Base opinions on what they see, feel, and observe.
- [ ] Look for specific answers, not generalizations or interpretations.
- [ ] Learn quickly through demonstration and guided practice.
- [ ] Avoid group work.

PREDICTABLE: DO WHAT THEY SAY THEY WILL DO.

- [ ] See things through to the end.

- [ ] Prefer to get things done themselves.

- [ ] Can be counted on to follow directions.

- [ ] Expect others to follow their procedures.

- [ ] Work well with learning contracts.

PRACTICAL: WANT USEFUL LEARNING AND ACTIVITIES.

- [ ] Use reliable approaches to get things done.

- [ ] Look for useful solutions to problems.

- [ ] Want results immediately.

- [ ] Ask and show how things work in real life.

- [ ] Find lectures boring and prefer physical activity with learning; are get- to- the point learners.

HARD WORKING: GIVE MUCH TIME AND ENERGY TO FINISH THINGS.

- [ ] Like to get going and keep things going.

- [ ] Put effort into their work.

- [ ] Want results at the end of efforts—payoff.

- [ ] Equate schoolwork with a job.

- [ ] Need to be "busy" and involved with practical tasks.

EFFICIENT: KNOW HOW TO COMPLETE WORK ON TIME.

- [ ] Give particular value to time and to being on time.

- [ ] Pay attention to deadlines.

- [ ] Ask for exact directions to avoid wasting time.

- [ ] Become angry when others misuse their time.

- [ ] Described by others as students who spend time on task.

Frustration   Circumstances that violate or deny the CS natural need for hands-on activity and structure frustrate this mind. Typical situations are

- *General discussions that lead to no specific point.*
- *Continuous reading and lecturing.*
- *Problems without clear directions.*
- *Time with no activities to fill it.*
- *People who ignore, miss, or do not care about details.*
- *People who always change their minds.*
- *People who expect the concrete sequential person to change the ways that work well for him/her.*
- *People who impose their way without searching for a more practical or efficient approach to a problem.*

" I know I have trouble with metaphor. Now I know why."

" It's tough trying to follow you day after day. You relate one subject to another...for example, human territory traits to bee dancing!"

" I like problems to solve that have some real basis in fact."

"I enjoy learning most when I can do something hands-on and there is competition involved. I like to win."

Stress Behaviors   Concrete sequential learners impose stress on themselves and receive stress from others. The CS self-stressors result from a need for perfection, detail, correct answers and immediate solutions to problems, and a drive to bring work to closure as quickly as possible. CS minds receive stressors from others who misuse their time, change directions, alter plans, become emotional, or restructure their things.

When students experience stress, they act out in ways that show their need for structure and realistic and practical solutions, and discomfort with emotions, abstraction, and open-ended situations. Representative CS stress behaviors include

- *A short-temper and bossy attitude.*
- *A pretense not to care, and acting out in order to hide confusion.*
- *An inability to get along with others until the stressor is removed.*
- *Denial of, or disregard for, a problem because they do not know how to handle it.*

- *Blame placed on others but little assessment of how they fit into a problem.*
- *Acceptance of others' authority when unsure of themselves.*

Negative Traits

The traits and characteristics that diminish the concrete sequential learner's potential have roots in the CS qualities of structure, realism, authority, and direction. CS learners benefit from "stretching their style" in order to find more enhancing responses. Typical CS traits that show negative tendencies:

- *Limited willingness to try new things.*
- *No "tolerance for ambiguity."*
- *Inattention to others' needs in order to finish a task.*
- *Resistance to possible alternatives in favor of immediate solutions.*
- *Preference to work with things to the detriment of ideas, people, or emotions.*
- *Tendencies to create face-to-face arguments over right and wrong.*
- *Need to dive headfirst into activities rather than listen to explanations.*
- *Willingness to speed through an assignment just to finish.*
- *Criticism of others who can't or won't organize and work in the CS way.*
- *Disapproval of another's style with no regard for feelings.*
- *Acceptance of legitimate authority figures without question.*
- *Need to hold a grudge rather than to forgive and forget.*
- *A need always to have "the" answer.*
- *Unwillingness to give new situations a chance to succeed.*
- *Tendencies to act "bossy," and insist on own way.*

TEACHING THE CONCRETE SEQUENTIAL LEARNER

Concrete sequentials produce their best, natural work by using approaches that allow them to use their strengths. They learn especially well using the physical senses: sight, sound, touch, taste, and smell. They enjoy activities that allow for hands-on learning with specific directions that lead to practical conclusions. They do well with traditional classroom work that includes structured work, such as outlines, computer work, specific worksheets, classifications and categorizations, charts, dioramas.

Potential Difficulties

The concrete sequential learner may have difficulty with techniques, activities, and materials that require use of random abilities, especially of the polar opposite style, the abstract random. Concrete sequential learners *may* need assistance with such areas as

group discussions	*quotations*	*poetry*
expression	*abstract questions*	*complex logic games*
sitting still	*finding the main point*	*open-ended creativity*
interpretation	*imagination topics*	*abstract ideas*
problem solving	*what-if questions*	
waiting	*listening for long periods*	

Key Bridging Techniques

Bridging techniques are helping attitudes and helping activities that address some aspect of the learner's style to achieve an objective. Teacher attitudes and actions that help the concrete sequential learner:

- *State objectives as behavioral expectations.*

- *Define: the topic, how students will achieve objectives, expectations from students, anticipated student outcomes from instruction.*

- *Outline the key points and content coverage.*

- *Provide clear organizational procedures for notes, preparations, and due dates in a concise manner.*

- *Follow exact directions and established rules.*

- *Give practical, specific examples and concrete illustrations to explain abstract ideas.*

- *Use specific checks to test for understanding and provide immediate progress reports.*

- *Show appreciation for detail, structure, and physical products.*

- *Use a task-oriented, hands-on approach that allows physical movement.*

- *Organize groups that have individualized assignments or are task-oriented.*

RATIONALE

If the CS person thinks in "methodical and deliberate" ways, then instruction must be structured.

If the CS person thinks in "linear and literal" ways, then instruction must be clear, with exact directions.

If the CS person thinks "within the physical world," then instruction must be practical and hands-on.

The concrete sequential learner must include study approaches that facilitate and activate his/her CS mind. Successful concrete sequential learners study within their own style before flexing into the styles of others. Techniques especially helpful for concrete sequential students allow them to use their own strengths. When teaching study skills courses, introduce the concept of learning differences and provide these types of suggestions for students who have a strong CS preference.

Build on your organizational strengths.

- Don't start your studying until you are sure of the task.
- Pace yourself. Plan out what you need to spend extra time on.
- Double check directions.
- Organize your time realistically.

Provide yourself with details.

- Keep an assignment book.
- Observe the specific steps in a demonstration so that you can replicate them.
- Overlearn technical and new vocabulary.
- Make an outline before writing an assignment.

Use a study system that has specific steps.

- Use the SQ3R (survey, question, read, recite, review).
- Pay attention to the way your text chapters provide study clues (bold face, boxes, charts).
- Make study charts of information and applications.

Check with a person who has demonstrated accuracy and attention to detail.

- Ask teachers for specific examples. Be sure you understand the material.
- Find one or two friends with whom you can always check your notes and assignments.

Set up a quiet environment.

- Know what interferes with your concentration and eliminate it. (You may not strangle your younger brother!)
- Arrange a study corner and work there consistently.
- Find a quiet place to work— free from television, people, music, and other distractions.

Use your learning strengths.

- Ignore a teacher's personality; concentrate on content.
- Use charts, lists, notes, review sheets, chapter checks— any specific information that helps.
- Use your physical senses, study out loud, vary your activities.

Using these techniques can also help other styles of students become more concrete sequential in their study process. But students who have very little concrete sequential ability have great difficulty with these skills and often reject them along with the study process. Because much of schoolwork requires students to produce in a CS way---for example, a multiple-choice test---techniques that foster this approach help the receptive student who can flex to do well. Students who cannot flex easily into this style must learn reasonable and effective techniques for coping with the CS approach.

The Abstract Sequential Student Style

"If I could tell my teacher about me in order to help me be a better student, I would suggest that she explain things very clearly and add visuals with the data to back it up. Assign us the chapter to read, but abandon those chapter questions. Finish class discussions with a summary at the end of class. I hate to be left hanging."

—Shelley

UNDERSTANDING THE
ABSTRACT SEQUENTIAL
LEARNING STYLE OF STUDENTS

Abstract sequential learners have the special ability to learn about the world from extensive reading and working with ideas. These student exhibit their finest talents when they focus learning on ideas, intellectual discussion, and theories, and when teachers require logical analysis. They are at their optimum when challenged with ideas. AS learners would rather read about ideas and problems than work on hands-on projects, discuss feelings and viewpoints, or test solutions to problems. AS learners give their best in classes that require content knowledge, discussions of theories, research papers, and learning from lectures. AS types tend to see the "big picture," to provide overviews of the content. They are able to write about concepts like "freedom" without difficulty. They do their work with logical, systematic progress, keep detailed and accurate notes, and read all assignments to prepare for tests. They are very grade conscious and tolerate few errors in themselves or from others. They get their rewards when their intellectual abilities are recognized by the teachers they respect and admire.

ABSTRACT: RELATE TO THE WORLD THROUGH IDEAS AND CONCEPTS.

- [ ] Like to talk about ideas rather than detailed points.
- [ ] Like to debate and match wits with others.
- [ ] Are consumers of information.
- [ ] Read for the love of reading.
- [ ] Have a large vocabulary for their age.

SEQUENTIAL: ORDER THE WORLD IN A LOGICAL, STRUCTURED WAY.

- [ ] Are consistent and predictable; immerse themselves in study.
- [ ] Need blocks of time to complete work, and want to develop assignments thoroughly.
- [ ] Like a quiet environment in which to think and work; dislike group work.
- [ ] Appreciate rules and laws as a means to give everyone controlled freedom.
- [ ] See themselves as "keepers of the law," and responsible for living within it.

THINKER: APPRECIATE INTELLECT AND IDEAS.

- [ ] Appear smartest in book knowledge; need to be respected for their intelligence.
- [ ] Would rather think through an idea than work on a project.
- [ ] Gravitate to book reports and research projects.
- [ ] Challenge teachers who are not expert in content.
- [ ] Are motivated by conceptual problems, e.g., the potential for nuclear war.

STUDIOUS: LIKE TO LEARN AND STUDY FROM BOOKS.

- [ ] Like learning just to learn.
- [ ] Have inquisitive minds.
- [ ] Learn well from lecture and thorough reading.
- [ ] Want quality courses of study; are impatient with work beneath their ability.
- [ ] Consider reading a hobby.

REASONING: FIND ANSWERS BY MAKING LOGICAL ARGUMENTS.

☐ Want enough time to gather ideas and reach conclusions.

☐ Are good lesson learners.

☐ Usually choose book reports or reading over other choices of assignments.

☐ May be accused of "thinking too much."

☐ Enjoy a guided independent study.

CRITICAL: LIKE TO JUDGE THE VALUE OF THINGS.

☐ Can be intellectual diplomats, or argumentative debaters.

☐ Exclude feelings in making judgments.

☐ Examine evidence closely.

☐ Choose to have a few select friends who value intellectual approaches.

☐ Need reasons before they will change; have difficulty initiating change.

ANALYTICAL: LIKE TO CONSIDER THE WHOLE AND ITS PARTS.

☐ Want to understand how and why things are as they are.

☐ May appear to be "lost in thought" as they analyze pieces of ideas.

☐ May "read" too much into a question, or make a problem bigger than it really is.

☐ Create new ideas and hypotheses rather than concrete products.

☐ Need extensive amounts of information before they analyze.

EXCELLENCE: SEEK TO ACHIEVE IN ACADEMIC PERFORMANCE.

☐ Hold themselves to very high standards.

☐ Tolerate few mistakes.

☐ Accept only "A's" for themselves.

☐ Value grades as a measure of excellence.

☐ Perceive criticism as a questioning of their intelligence.

Frustrations   Circumstances that violate or deny the AS natural need for logic, ideas, analysis, and intellect frustrate this mind. Typical situations are

- *Assignments to work with disinterested others.*
- *Too little time to learn a subject thoroughly for an "A" grade.*
- *Those who laugh at intellectual people.*
- *Those who believe intellectual people have no feelings.*
- *Teachers and students who "fool around" in class.*
- *Physical activities in which they fear for their safety (e.g., gym)*
- *Questions in class when preparation time has not been given.*
- *Open-ended activities in which they must create from nothing.*
- *Assignments to copy material over.*
- *Hands-on or "messy projects."*

> *" I love to read novels, long ones, mainly non-action. Jane Austin is my favorite author."*
>
> *" When I work in groups I'll volunteer to do almost anything, as long as it doesn't require working with the rest of the group."*
>
> *" If I have to work on a long project, I like to spend my time thinking about it and doing research until nearly the deadline. Then I clear the boards and concentrate solely on that until the task is done."*

Stress   Abstract sequential learners impose stress on themselves and receive
Behaviors   stress from others. The AS self-stressors result from a need use their intellectual abilities and to analyze completely. AS stressors result from others who use imagination, divergent thinking, and intuition rather than logic, and who prefer personalized and group work rather than independent work, as well as from situations that prevent content coverage.

When abstract sequential students experience stress, they act out in ways that show their need for logic and intellect, and their discomfort with emotions and open-ended thinking or lack of analysis. Representative AS stress behaviors include

- *An overly cautious, overly studious attitude.*
- *Panic about grades.*
- *Doubts suddenly about their own ability.*
- *Lack of attention to schoolwork.*
- *Derogatory comments about schoolwork.*

Negative Traits

The traits and characteristics that diminish the abstract sequential learner's potential have roots in the AS qualities of logic, intellect, and conceptual ability. AS learners benefit from "stretching their style" in order to find more enhancing responses. Typical AS traits that show negative tendencies:

- *Belief that they are the smartest, without respect for other's intelligences.*

- *Willingness to follow rules just because they are a tradition.*

- *Disregard or disrespect for students whose grades are lower.*

- *Inattention to the feelings of others.*

- *Taking over discussions with their own "right" view.*

- *Use of arguments to prove their intellectual superiority.*

- *Criticism of others; intolerance of criticism by others.*

- *Concern with perfection.*

- *Behavior as a "teacher pleaser."*

- *Acceptance of everything they read without question.*

- *Resentment over situations that prevent them from getting a high grade.*

- *Envy of others who get higher grades.*

TEACHING THE ABSTRACT SEQUENTIAL LEARNER

Abstract sequential learners produce their best, natural work by using approaches that require extensive amounts of reading, development of ideas and information, finding out what the "experts" say, analyzing and evaluating the causes, problems, and results of events, actions, and ideas. They learn especially well using reason and logic. They form an answer, using all the parts of their information to create a new hypothesis.

POTENTIAL DIFFICULTIES

The abstract sequential learner may have difficulty with techniques, activities, and materials that require use of random abilities, especially of the polar opposite style, the concrete random. Abstract sequential learners may need assistance with such areas as

- *Writing creatively, using imagination as a resource.*

- *Working on competitive drills.*

- *Taking surprise tests.*

- *Playing games and simulations.*

- *Getting and giving overly critical comments.*

- *Gaining group discussions skills; avoiding group arguments.*

- *Giving a practical answer to an open-ended, concrete problem.*

Because the AS style connects best to ideas, logic, and content, we can provide bridges that address these strengths. Several examples are listed below.

- *State objectives as conceptual problems.*

- *Provide general structure to objectives.*

- *Give clear organization of process and product expectations.*

- *Use a content-centered approach.*

- *Provide a syllabus for independent reading and research.*

- *Organize group work for a meeting of the minds; include debate.*

- *Allow blocks of time for students to think, organize, and finish work.*

- *Minimize hands-on activities and extremely structured work.*

- *Translate the meaning of concrete, hands-on activities into an idea, principle, or conceptual point.*

RATIONALE

If the AS person thinks "with intellect and logic," then instruction must require analysis as well as evaluation from the student.

If the AS person thinks in "traditional" ways, then instruction must incorporate traditional classroom structure and lecture.

If the AS person thinks in ways "concerned with subject-matter expertise," then instruction must refer to a body of research.

AS STUDY STYLES

The abstract sequential learner must include study approaches that facilitate and activate his/her AS mind. Successful abstract sequential learners have a natural approach to studying. They rarely need outside assistance. If so, the following suggestions to AS learners may help them focus.

Read

- Reread highlighted material.
- Use note-shrinking skills: "shrink" notes into the margins of your notebook.
- Highlight the key concepts.
- Devise logic problems to solve from your reading assignments.

Listen

- If the teacher lectures, take notes according to the teacher's style of lecturing.
- Listen during a lecture for repetition of important ideas and key points.

Plan

- Decide on the topics the teacher could ask about. Plan out answers.
- Spend a few minutes before writing to make an outline of the points you can discuss in an essay.
- Gather as much information as you can on a topic.
- Plan sufficient time to cover all the material. Do not overlearn the early sections and run out of time for later sections.

Write

- Use context clues in objective tests.
- Summarize your notes.
- Write a self-check quiz and answer it.

Techniques like these help students who do not have a strong abstract sequential style to gain some of the AS skills, especially if the teacher or the content demands an AS approach. Many study skills programs are biased in favor of this style of study. When teaching these techniques to students who have a minimal AS preference, explain the style demand and emphasize the value of gaining these strategies as coping techniques. Be sure to include study techniques from other styles and to value style approaches equally.

The Abstract Random Student Style

" If I could tell my teacher about me in order to help me be a better student, I would tell her that I like a partner to work with who enjoyed working with me. I'd like to take part in group discussions. I like my opinion heard. I'm not conceited. I just like others to know my my feelings on a subject."

—Bruce

UNDERSTANDING THE
ABSTRACT RANDOM
LEARNING STYLE OF STUDENTS

Abstract random learners have special abilities to learn about the world by working with others, in group discussions, and with material that allows them to give their impressions and feelings. These students show their finest abilities when their learning focuses on themes, ideas, people, and feelings, and in situations that do not require them to follow exact rules or directions. They are at their best when personally involved with what they are learning. They would rather have a discussion about a topic than work on a project, or read about it. They would rather deal with problems involving people than with more general problems. AR learners give their best in a class when the teacher emphasizes a cooperative group approach, personal interaction, and open communication between students and teachers. AR learners enjoy the visual and performing arts, and the humanities, as well as interpretative reading and writing, expressions of feelings, and the relationship of subjects to people.

ABSTRACT: RELATE BEST THROUGH FEELINGS.

☐ Filter the world through emotions.

☐ Need free time to reflect and to consider feelings.

☐ Cry easily over sentimental issues and sensitive experiences.

☐ Tune into the mood of their surroundings.

☐ Avoid competition.

RANDOM: ORDER THE WORLD IN A NONLINEAR WAY.

☐ Are flexible and adaptable, but need quiet time to recharge.

☐ Take pride in ability to adjust to changes easily.

☐ Need flexible time schedules.

☐ Miss or forget directions; have difficulty with extremely structured assignments.

☐ May not know how to translate imaginative ideas into structured, physical products.

SENSITIVE: ARE TUNED TO THEIR OWN FEELINGS AND TO OTHERS.

☐ Work best with teachers with whom they can be open.

☐ Work to please others, and to create and develop special relationships with them.

☐ May be secretive, especially if very shy.

☐ Worry when disciplined by teachers and parents.

☐ Show concern over discipline by asking, "What will they think of me?"

INTERPRETATIVE: GIVE MEANING TO IDEAS IN A PERSONAL WAY.

☐ Personalize or decorate bookcovers, papers, or room.

☐ Keep things for beauty and personal meaning rather than practical use.

☐ Prefer interpretations and explanations rather than exact answers.

☐ Appreciate music, poetry, art, literature, and drama.

☐ May have great difficulty separating things into clear-cut categories.

IMAGINATIVE: USE IMAGINATION TO CREATE NEW IDEAS.

- [ ] Can be colorful personalities.
- [ ] Need "down" time to restore a creative spark.
- [ ] Enjoy fantasy and pretending.
- [ ] May have an overactive imagination, according to non-ARs.
- [ ] Have real fears that seem imagined to non-ARs.

EXPRESSIVE: SHOW EMOTIONS AND EXPRESS FEELINGS OPENLY.

- [ ] Have emotional faces and wear their hearts on their sleeves.
- [ ] Like an audience and attention, especially if personally outgoing.
- [ ] Are spontaneous and excitable; need emotional energy to create.
- [ ] Can supply the "life-of-the-class" spirit.
- [ ] Take punishment with resentment if not allowed to explain it personally.

PEOPLE-PERSON: NEED TO HAVE SPECIAL RELATIONSHIPS.

- [ ] Are at emotional best with a true friend, and focus attention on friendships.
- [ ] Unable to concentrate if upset with a special person.
- [ ] Resist control by others but give in easily to trusted friends.
- [ ] Organize time around others and the opportunity to be with others.
- [ ] Are easily hurt by remarks, unkind words, and being excluded.

UNDERSTANDING: ARE ABLE TO GRASP OTHERS' POINTS OF VIEW.

- [ ] Are sympathetic and warm-hearted, and want others to act that way with them.
- [ ] Are good listeners and supporters.
- [ ] Like to share experiences.
- [ ] May leave their own work undone to help others out of concern.
- [ ] Are sensitive to the feelings of others, and respond best to teachers who are sensitive to them.

Frustrations
Circumstances that violate or deny the AR's natural need for emotion, personalization, interpretation, and harmony frustrate this mind. Typical situations are

- *Explanations of feelings to those who cannot see the random viewpoint.*

- *Orders to "toe the line," "shape-up," or meet deadlines.*

- *Separation from friends as punishment.*

- *No time to be themselves.*

- *Requirements to compete with others for the sake of competition.*

- *People who do not understand random explanations.*

- *People who laugh at their sensitivity.*

- *People who "set them up" for hurt feelings or emotional reactions.*

- *Demands to put ideas and answers into a finished product once they have been mentally completed.*

"I have the most difficult time with material that is programmed without graphics, or descriptive (heavy use of words or numbers) without dialogue or action."

"I love to read novels, inspirational philosophy, psychology and humorous books."

"When I work in groups, I am the one who usually relieves the tension with humor unless I feel threatened by a strong personality in the group."

Stress
Abstract random learners impose stress on themselves and receive stress from others. The AR self-stressors result from a need for strong relationships, a tendency to respond emotionally and be easily hurt, and a need for acceptance from others. AR stressors result from others who disregard emotion, are abrupt in relationships, impose sequential order, and insist on competition.

When abstract random students experience stress, they act out in ways that show their need for personal and interpersonal relationships, emotional stability, and self-acceptance. Representative AR stress behaviors include

- *Crying for no apparent reason; experiencing emotional extremes.*

- *Lashing out at others to vent anger; excessive worry.*

- *Feeling worthless, body language that reveals emotional hurt.*

- *Retreating from relationships.*

Negative Traits

The traits and characteristics that diminish the abstract random learner's potential have roots in the AR's qualitites of nonlinearity, emotion, personalization, and noncompetitiveness. AR learners benefit from "stretching their style" in order to find more enhancing responses than their negative ones. Typical AR traits that show negative tendencies are

- *Losing things, missing appointments, and forgetting agreements.*

- *Insistence on their way regardless of circumstances.*

- *Inattention to details, assignments, and promises.*

- *An unpredictable attitude and moodiness.*

- *Attention to every emotional whim.*

- *Concern about treatment from others, to the extreme.*

- *Jealousy and dominance in relationships.*

- *An attitude of the disruptive class clown.*

- *Indecision for fear of hurting the feelings of others.*

- *Holding a grudge against persons who have hurt him/her.*

- *Refusal to be leaders so that they will not offend anyone.*

- *Inattention to responsibilities.*

- *Reliance on emotions as their sole decision-maker.*

- *Taking punishment with resentment, anger, or hurt.*

- *Willingness to act out when hurt or disturbed.*

TEACHING THE ABSTRACT RANDOM LEARNERS

Abstract randoms produce their best, natural work by using approaches that require interpretations and explanations rather than exact answers; communication through artistic media; reading for emotional enjoyment; personalized meaning; and opportunities to work with others. AR learners interpret the world through their emotions, which allows them to understand ideas, people, places, and things in a personalized and interpretative way. This special ability lets them be artists (visual, performing, or writing) and support humanitarian causes.

Potential Difficulties

The AR learner may have difficulty with techniques, activities, and materials that require use of sequential abilities, especially of the polar opposite style, the concrete sequential. Abstract random learners may need assistance with such areas as

- *Leadership roles in which the rules are more important than the people.*

- *Working alone for long periods of time.*

- *Highly structured assignments; sticking to the point in such assignments.*

- *Tight rules and regulations, and heavy-handed discipline.*

- *Understanding exactly what the teacher expects.*

- *Knowing the sequential steps in a sequential task; recognizing CS tasks.*

- *Finishing work within given time limits.*

- *Completing hands-on projects to perfection.*

Bridging techniques are helping attitudes and helping activities that address some aspect of the learner's style to achieve the objective. Teacher attitudes and actions that help the abstract random learner:

- *State objectives in terms of personal understanding.*

- *Provide open-ended structure with personal timetables.*

- *Organize learning to include personal, artistic, aesthetic, emotional, or people-oriented activities.*

- *Develop a class atmosphere that is interpersonal, and has open and inviting channels of communication between peers and adults.*

- *Be appreciative of personal sensitivity.*

- *Offer interpretative and imaginative activities.*

- *Minimize competition.*

- *Have students express their personal reactions in a journal or letter.*

- *Emphasize group trust and cohesion.*

- *Provide options.*

RATIONALE

If the AR person thinks "thematically," then instructional strategies must be flexible and open.

If the AR person "experiences emotionally," then instructional strategies must explore feelings and personal reactions.

If the AR person tunes "to inner patterns," then instructional strategies must allow time for personal ideas and beliefs.

The abstract random learner must include study approaches that facilitate and activate his/her AR mind. Because tests usually favor the CS and AS styles, the AR learner must develop the ability to achieve many sequential outcomes (facts, data, analysis) but do so with recognition of his/her own style strengths. When you are working with students who have a strong abstract random ability, offer these study hints.

Use your natural ability to learn with others.

- Form a productive study group of three people. Agree on your study process.
- Get a study-buddy.
- Allow time with personal friends to recharge your battery as a reward for work done.
- Ask people to give you deadlines, and check in with people throughout the task.
- Listen carefully to class discussions and participate in group work.

Recognize how strongly emotions influence your concentration.

- Take time to develop a good relationship with your teachers.
- Settle personal concerns and problems that prevent concentration.
- Talk with your teachers, especially if you feel they are not on your side.
- Get help from adults who care about you personally.
- Avoid negative people.
- Separate your interests in a course from your responsibilities in a course.
- Be aware of the ways in which your environment influences your emotions.

Build on your strength to learn by association.

- Learn to remember detail through visualization and verbal association.
- Use stories, metaphors, and creative expression to convey ideas.
- Suggest alternative ways of interpreting things.
- Use television as a way to gather some types of information.
- Gather information from as many sources as you can (people, books, media).
- Be creative, silly, imaginative—anything that works to help you associate information.
- Use visuals in your notes to capture ideas. Ask teachers to help you learn graphic organizers.

Use a whole-picture approach to gather details.

- Learn to make colored mindmaps before you outline.
- Work with themes and large concepts in a mindmap, then fill in the details.
- Work at home on large sheets of newsprint and organize information with color-coded pens.
- Check notes with a study buddy. Fill in missing notes in a color pen so you don't miss them.
- Create a study system notebook: one side for notes, the other side for a visual or graphic.

Watch your time.

- Stick to a task as long as you are able; take a break; do a different task; return to the first.
- Be flexible but get your work done.
- Don't underestimate the amount of time needed to finish an assignment. Set artificial deadlines.

Color code

- Color code a large monthly calendar with school information only: test dates, due dates, meetings.
- Color code the cover of your texts with the color of your notebooks.
- Use highlighter pens in different colors to code concepts, details, questions and answers.

The Concrete Random Student Style

" If I could tell my teacher about me in order to help me be a better student, I would like her to know that I am smart, daring, a leader (in a way). I like to use games to learn, math games especially. I'd like her to know that I get bored with my routine school work and I wish we could do more projects."

—Jack

UNDERSTANDING THE CONCRETE RANDOM LEARNING STYLE OF STUDENTS

Concrete random learners have special abilities to learn about the world by working with few rules, by using a problem-solving approach, and by experimenting with different ideas and products. These students demonstrate their finest talents when they focus on problems, interesting investigations, "why" questions, and discovery learning. They are at their sharpest when trying out their ideas, and applying what they have learned. They have extraordinary abilities to brainstorm and to suggest alternative ways of considering ideas and problems. They are real-world learners who would rather test to see if something works by actually trying it out than wait for a sure answer that it works. CR learners give their best in a class that uses many types of resources, encourages active investigations, and promotes problem-solving approaches. They prefer to change things rather than repeat what they have already tried. They look for different and unusual ways of learning, working, and creating. CR learners test our traditional assumptions about the world.

CONCRETE: RELATE BEST TO REAL UNSOLVED PROBLEMS.

- [ ] Are motivated by the process of discovering answers to problems.
- [ ] Prefer strategy problems; do not need many details to problem solve.
- [ ] Enjoy simulations and games that present problems.
- [ ] Need to have their answers valued, not just their ability to find a teacher's answer.
- [ ] Will create their own problems if meaningful activities are missing.

RANDOM: ORDER THE WORLD IN A NONLINEAR WAY.

- [ ] Have many different ideas and interests.
- [ ] Put ideas together according to their own system of logic.
- [ ] Are flexible.
- [ ] Look for options and possibilities.
- [ ] Have several projects or activities in the works at the same time.

INDEPENDENT: RELY ON THEMSELVES.

- [ ] Are willing to be different from others to keep their independence.
- [ ] Like to be the leader and set the course.
- [ ] Are not controlled easily by others; have the attitude "don't fence me in."
- [ ] Like a "fair fight"—want competition to be a real challenge with those of equal ability.
- [ ] Compete with themselves as well as with others.

CREATIVE: DEVELOP NEW IDEAS AND MAKE NEW PRODUCTS.

- [ ] Like to find out-of-the-ordinary answers; like to discover what could be.
- [ ] Have unusual interests and many ways of doing things.
- [ ] Create original projects and products.
- [ ] Are energized by opportunities to create or to do what has not been done.
- [ ] Take pride in creating immediate solutions to problems that others find difficult.

Learning and Teaching Style: In Theory and Practice

EXPERIMENTAL: LIKE TO SEE WHAT WOULD HAPPEN IF...

- [ ] Want to probe and examine on their own.

- [ ] Try many different kinds of things.

- [ ] Work within general guidelines, not exact rules.

- [ ] Enjoy hands-on experimenting.

- [ ] Are willing to ignore social convention in order to find out about people and their ideas.

INVESTIGATIVE: LIKE TO FIND OUT CAUSES.

- [ ] Like to explore; must be actively involved with their own learning.

- [ ] Are curious about subjects and problems with no specific answers.

- [ ] Are willing to risk or disregard danger to pursue an answer or opportunity.

- [ ] Will test others and situations to find out about people and their ideas.

- [ ] Are fascinated by the nonordinary.

INTUITIVE: KNOW THE ANSWER WITHOUT UNDERSTANDING HOW.

- [ ] Find solutions to problems without following a given procedure.

- [ ] Create answers by trying different solutions.

- [ ] Skip the detail for detail's sake aspects of a project.

- [ ] Use insight and intuition effectively in problem solving.

- [ ] Work well with trial and error approaches that rely on a hunch of what will work.

CHANGING: LIKE VARIETY, CHOICES, AND FREQUENT CHANGE.

- [ ] Change often during the course of a project as they get newer ideas.

- [ ] Find the process of working on a project as important as the finished product itself.

- [ ] Value the option to revise a project that is in process.

- [ ] Are driven to find out, "What would happen if I changed...?"

- [ ] Can take an ordinary idea and restructure it—"Look what I can do if I...!"

Frustrations

Circumstances that violate or deny the CR's natural need for change, options, problem-solving, and investigation frustrate this mind. Typical situations are

- *Restrictions and limitations, such as demands to sit still for long periods.*

- *Requirements to do things exactly as someone else wants them done.*

- *The necessity to find the answers someone else is looking for.*

- *No space to "mess around."*

- *Formal reports.*

- *Time schedules.*

- *Routines.*

- *Redoing a project.*

- *Continuing on a project when there is no interest in it.*

"For me, following specific and exact directions is frustrating unless I can follow them in my own time and manner."

"When I have to work my way through a problem without direction, I spend a lot of time thinking and letting it gel until the solution miraculously appears."

"The most enjoyable way to me to gather information is in a broad scope, taking many ideas from people, reading parts of many articles, and then putting materials together in my own way."

Stress Behaviors

Concrete random learners impose stress on themselves and receive stress from others. The CR self-stressors result from a need to have minimal restrictions on time and energy, and to have opportunity for change and new ideas. CR stressors result from others who impose their viewpoint or ways of learning, and who confine the concrete random mind to one view.

When concrete random students experience stress, they act out in ways that reveal their need for personal challenge and independence. Representative behaviors include

- *Becoming uptight and cautious.*

- *Getting very organized and orderly, and to-the-point.*

- *Having no interest in new things.*

- *Withdrawing into themselves.*

- *Acting out in negative ways.*

- *Challenging others on unimportant issues.*

- *Listening to sequential opinions instead of trusting their intuition.*

Negative Traits   The traits and characteristics that diminish the concrete random learner's potential have roots in the CR qualities of nonlinear thinking, ability to change frequently and quickly, need for personal independence, and desire for challenge. CR learners benefit from "stretching their style" in order to find more productive responses than their negative ones. Typical CR traits that show negative tendencies are

> * *Using disruptive, aggressive, violent behavior as a means of breaking out of a situation.*
>
> * *Doing anything, just to be different.*
>
> * *Starting many projects but never finishing them.*
>
> * *Forgetting what is not right at hand.*
>
> * *Being concerned only with what might be, and forgetting practicality.*
>
> * *Getting angry with others who cannot keep up.*
>
> * *Having to explain each step of the way.*
>
> * *Jumping to conclusions without any reason.*

TEACHING THE CONCRETE RANDOM   Concrete randoms use their intuitive abilities to explore the possibilities in any field of study. They are most effective when they are able to experiment with ideas they develop after mental, spoken, or written brainstorming. Concrete randoms produce their best, natural work by using approaches that require problem solving, open-ended options, different ways to arrive at answers, and independent work.

Potential Difficulties   Concrete random learners may have difficulty and need assistance with sequential and abstract materials, such as

> * *Completing a project when inspired by a new idea.*
>
> * *Accepting that the rules in their minds may not be the rules that others accept or are willing to follow.*
>
> * *Choosing one answer on a standardized test when they can can prove two correct answers.*
>
> * *Keeping a detailed record.*
>
> * *Doing structured lessons with no room for a different idea.*
>
> * *Doing formal reports.*
>
> * *Working with teachers who grade only the answers, not the process.*
>
> * *Finishing timed tests, on time.*
>
> * *Reading extensively when the material could be summarized in a chapter.*
>
> * *Spending large amounts of time on ideas that have no usefulness, or cannot be applied.*

Because the CR style connects best to the world of action and problems in a multifaceted and open-ended way, we can provide bridges that address these strengths.

- *State objectives as problems.*

- *Establish guidelines, not rules, to complete objectives.*

- *Offer choices and options within assignments.*

- *Suggest the alternatives to be investigated within a topic.*

- *Value diversity in thinking.*

- *Encourage self-designed and informal projects.*

- *Use a process rather than product approach.*

- *Present an investigative attitude.*

- *Organize diverse work groups.*

- *Use comparison and contrast statements between content and real situations.*

It is difficult to provide specific style bridges for CR learners because their minds are attracted to what is unknown, not suggested, different, and experimental. In fact, if too many options are listed for CR learners, they may have a difficult time finding something to do that is not on someone's list! They are more likely to provide their own style bridges when given the opportunity, multiple resources, time, and trust of the teacher. As problem solvers and divergent thinkers, they prefer to have guidelines and suggestions to start the flow of ideas. They do not repond well to mandated activities, no matter how open ended they are. If the teacher can be open and accepting of CR learners within the bounds of responsible action, they can often provide their own style bridges. However, it is also vitally important that the teacher evaluate CR activities for their own merit rather than against another style's standards.

RATIONALE

If the CR person is "concerned with problems and possibilities,
then instruction must use inquiry, discovery, and exploration.

If the CR person thinks with "insight and penetration," then,
instructional styles must take a problem-solving approach.

If the CR person thinks "beyond logic and convention," then
instructional styles must seek creativity and originality.

CR STUDY STYLES

The concrete random learner must use study approaches that facilitate and activate his/her CR mind. CR learners who have difficulty with homework and tests often attempt to study in a CS way, but find it too time-consuming as well as unchallenging. In order for CR learners to absorb CS and AS information yet stay productive, they need to work with their own natural tendencies in a systematic way. The following techniques help CR learners to use their own style, as well as meet the sequential demands so frequently found in the school curriculum.

Use your natural ability to think divergently.
- Believe that good thinkers see things from more than one view.
- Offer teachers alternative ideas; the worst they can do is say no.
- Do not accept stereotypical views but look for other values.
- Use humor and cartoons when you take notes.
- Create ideas rather than judge them.
- Keep a questioning attitude.
- Be a brainstormer—"what are the many ways I could...."
- Learn mindmapping and webbing techniques.

Set up problems
- Volunteer for problem projects rather than research projects when possible.
- Write your own study problems and solve them.
- Think about problems from many points of view.

Check your time
- Ask people for deadlines.
- Recognize when you have almost finished a product and finish it! Assess whether you have the time to change things at the final minute if the change or the product is not personally important to you.

Accept your need for change.
- Make changes in the things that you can control so as to satisfy your need for change. (For example, study one week in the basement, then move to another room the following week.)
- Give yourself enough time to "sleep on an idea," for your first idea is bound to change.

Find support
- Seek out supportive people of all ages who value and reward divergent thinking.
- Raise questions with your teacher before or after class that help you think about the material in an interesting or creative way.

Part IV

Style Differentiated Instruction
In Focus

*Grow, move forward, with measured pace
checking yourself all along the way.*

—I Ching
The Book of Changes

Part IV

STYLE DIFFERENTIATED INSTRUCTION—IN FOCUS

This research on (learning) style strongly supports Marshall McLuhan's position that the "medium is a message and a massage." And it causes me to pause and reflect upon how haphazard, naive, and selfish some educators are in their selection of instructional means, methods, and environmental conditions.

—Anthony F. Gregorc

Many concerned and dedicated teachers inevitably ask how they can incorporate the principles of learning and teaching style into instruction for the benefit of their students. Style Differentiated Instruction (SDI) provides a process for teachers to do so.

Teachers have appropriate background to apply Style Differentiated Instruction when they

- **Know Their Personal Learning Style**—dominant mediation abilities and capacities.

- **Know Their Teaching Style**—attitudes, actions, activities, and adaptation demands.

- **Know Their Students**—student style signals and the range of students' style flex-abilities.

Once teachers have this knowledge in hand, the SDI approach can help teachers to

- **Evaluate Curriculum**—assess content, objectives, and stylistic demands.

- **Apply Style Differentiated Instruction**—intentionally vary options and opportunities among and within styles.

- **Serve the Needs of Students**—provide match and guided mismatch experiences.

To develop a systemwide curriculum around a Style Differentiated

Instruction approach requires a sophisticated understanding of style as a concept. As with many ideas, we can actualize it to its full implication when we appreciate its complexity. We can reduce it to a simplistic level by if we do not thoroughly understand it.

SDI   Style Differentiated Instruction, **as a concept**, is the process of selecting the most appropriate style response for the learning situation. The teacher intentionally matches or mismatches the learner's style—through attitudes or activities—in order to develop the learner or achieve worthy learning goals.

Style Differentiated Instruction, **as a model for instruction**, is the set of formal guidelines designed to implement this concept. These guidelines include explanations of

- *Bridging techniques: the process of helping a learner overcome mismatch in order to achieve an objective.*

- *Instructional techniques: the techniques that match the learning preferences of different styles.*

- *Instructional demands: the style demands of activities.*

- *Levels of thinking: the ways in which styles applies to Bloom's Taxonomy.*

- *Approaches to instruction: organizational techniques to provide style differentiated activities.*

- *Modality connections: modality preferences of different styles.*

- *Lesson Design: a formal structure for developing concepts.*

My goals for Style Differentiated Instruction do not limit themselves to concerns for academic achievement. Rather, they reflect my own philosophical beliefs about teaching and the role of education in the development of the child. I wish for SDI to act first as a vehicle for the development of students' natural gifts and abilities—both in mind and spirit. Learners deserve to leave the cocoon-like microcosm of school with a belief in their intrinsic worth formed from learning experiences that found their strengths and taught them to manage their limitations.

Second, I strongly acknowledge the value of quality academic content. We know that attention to style improves academic achievement, and for many students enriches their learning far beyond the traditional approach. We know, too, that students must develop a style-flex repertoire, learn adaptation techniques, and gain coping skills in order to meet the legitimate academic demands and interpersonal needs of others. However, we find very strong evidence that students do not flex well without belief in their own strengths first.

Third, I value the importance of higher-level thinking abilities. Our approach aims to give all students the skills to gather knowledge and gain comprehension in all styles. We also see that many students learn to apply or analyze extremely well in ways that require their style strengths. And, we find it essential to provide learning bridges if we wish them to become skillful in using the critical thinking attributes of other styles. We see that students develop creative abilities when they have choices for self-expression within their style.

Finally, we can foster a healthy self-concept in our learners if we give them opportunity to achieve success in legitimate ways, not in a watered-down curriculum. When learners can take pride in their accomplishments and feel the ownership of work well done, then they believe in themselves. No adult words of praise can ever ensure a strong self-concept for students in the way that personally felt success can generate.

Part IV will offer guidelines for Style Differentiated Instruction. The guidelines offer suggestions, not formulas, to meet student learning style preferences and needs.

I have not provided one definitive formula because learners and teachers have unique and individual minds. My extensive research indicates that people learn not only through different media but also in their own sequence. Careful attention to children's and adults' achievement suggests that people do not learn in a given sequence of styles. Rather, they uniquely achieve quality learning, and individually produce quality products.

If we expect teachers to attend to style, we must provide them with a variety of ways to understand and approach style. These ways and approaches must allow the teacher to sustain and develop his/her own personal teaching style and academic content, and meet situational demands. Yet, they must also extend the teacher's repertoire to meet the needs of the learner. In short, teachers need the tools to meet styles under a variety of circumstances whether they teach spelling, develop a particular thinking skill, explain a sophisticated concept, guide project development, write a curricular unit, counsel a student, or work in any learning situation.

No teacher can or will meet every learner's style all the time. But given knowledge of a variety of ways to address styles—from simple to sophisticated—teachers can choose an approach or two that they can manage.

As you deepen your knowledge of style, and gain confidence in your ability to understand and to accommodate other styles, you will integrate your own approach to style into your content area and teaching needs. The principles of SDI can serve only as guides for you. You must apply them in your own creative teaching way.

I have not found it easy to apply a psychological approach to style. The significance and importance of style application to teaching, however, seem paramount. British educator David Fontana writes on the subject of psychology and teaching in this way:

> It would be wrong to suggest that
> modern psychology has final answers to
> all the questions that face us in
> education. Children (and teachers) are
> individuals, and often must be studied as
> individuals before detailed guidance on
> particular problems can be given....Human
> behaviour is very complex and its
> measurement and assessment fraught with
> many difficulties....But psychology helps
> the teacher recognize the factors that
> influence child behaviour and learning
> and assists him in developing strategies

*to cope with the tasks that face him in
the classroom. Furthermore, it helps him
examine his own general professional
behaviour, and to identify areas where
this behaviour may itself have
contributed towards particular problems
that may have arisen....Psychology shows
us that no child's behaviour can be fully
understood unless we study also the
behaviour of others—teachers, parents,
school friends—toward him. Each
individual stands at the center of a
complex matrix of inter-related
influences, each of which must be taken
into account if we are to comprehend
why he lives his life as he does. (19)*

CHAPTER 9

STYLE DIFFERENTIATED INSTRUCTION: BRIDGING TO THE LEARNER

I will act as if what I do makes a difference.

—William James

The effective application of Style Differentiated Instruction requires teachers to know, accept, and work with many styles in a personal as well as academic way. As Arthur Jersild comments in *In Search of Self*:

> *Every teacher is in his own way a psychologist. Everything he does, says, or teaches has or could have a psychological impact. What he offers helps children to discover their resources and their limitations. He is the central figure in countless situations which can help the learner to realize and accept himself or which may bring humiliation, shame, rejection, and self-disparagement.*

In Jersild's reality, the teacher combines self into a dynamic with students through his/her attitude toward students in working with them and through his/her way of helping students work with instructional activities. In SDI terms, we call this dynamic process "bridging."

DEFINITION OF BRIDGING

Bridging is the technique of addressing a student's basic style need within a learning situation, most frequently in a stressful or mismatched situation. We can bridge to the learner in attitude and through action. We apply attitudinal bridging when we recognize the perceptions of others and reach out to them as individuals. We use activity bridging when we offer suggestions to students to help them through a learning difficulty or a style mismatch for which they have no alternative but to accomplish the task. Like the stepping-stones we find to cross a stream, or the bridge across a river, learning-style bridges help the learner overcome obstacles that prevent him/her from achieving an objective. A learning-style bridge may be nothing more than a loving arm around the child whose facial expression betrays confusion, or may be as simple as using visuals to explain a concept in addition to a written definition.

Students need learning bridges under three circumstances in particular:

- *when the task requires a learning style the student cannot meet through his/her natural style or through style flex-abilities;*

- *when the student has minimal motivation to flex;*

- *when the student needs extra attention to be most productive.*

For example, in most classrooms, teachers make the Friday spelling test a routine event. Most students have little difficulty if they take the time to practice and memorize the words. But in every class a few refuse to bother or have little motivation to do another routine sequential task. A close look at these students often reveals children with a strong random learning need or preference.

The wise teacher does not leave the solution to the student, does not nag the learner, and refuses to watch boredom mushroom into underachievement. Instead, the teacher bridges to these learners and offers a way for them to use some aspect of their personal learning style as they achieve the final objective, learning to spell. Perhaps the teacher reminds the whole class that a computer game offers fun while learning, and then specifically talks to Joyce about giving it a try. Maybe this teacher spends a few minutes with the whole class developing visual images and association clues for difficult words, then challenges Peter to develop some creative clues for several words for the class the next day.

Importance

It is most important to note that bridging does not change the student's responsibility to meet the learning objective, and bridging does not excuse the student from completing the assignment. Bridging does help the learner achieve the objective or complete the activity.

In the following example, students practice vocabulary words—a sequential task—with style bridges. Notice that all students are responsible for the same assignment: to know the meaning of the words. But the teacher has provided a bridge to random learners to help them accomplish the task. Rather than asking students to memorize vocabulary words or simply use them in a paragraph, she has added the opportunity to learn by association, humor, and personal interest. We know that most sequential learners will learn the vocabulary words without these techniques, but that most random learners will struggle needlessly without them.

A Bridging Example

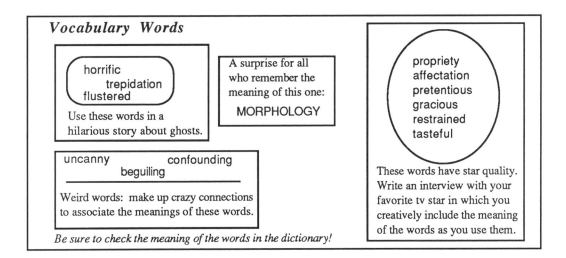

Vocabulary Words

horrific
trepidation
flustered

Use these words in a
hilarious story about ghosts.

A surprise for all
who remember the
meaning of this one:
MORPHOLOGY

uncanny   confounding
        beguiling

Weird words: make up crazy connections
to associate the meanings of these words.

Be sure to check the meaning of the words in the dictionary!

propriety
affectation
pretentious
gracious
restrained
tasteful

These words have star quality.
Write an interview with your
favorite tv star in which you
creatively include the meaning
of the words as you use them.

You can bridge easily, as in the above example, if you provide an additional way for a student to process information, as in the computer suggestion for the spelling example. You can bridge if you reinforce the learner's self-confidence by encouraging him/her to use a personal strong point as in the request to Peter. You can bridge if you set up a comfortable psychological environment, as did the teacher whose classroom bulletin board read, "Success is being the best YOU can be." You can bridge by setting up a comfortable physical environment, as does the teacher who simultaneously allows quiet work with partners as well as individual student work.

Remember, however, bridging does not substantially change the nature of the learning objective. Rather, students use some aspect of their own style to achieve that objective. Bridging works bests, as you might suspect, with students who are still willing to learn but are having difficulty doing their best. Bridging is less effective with students who are at-risk learners or who have lost motivation for learning. These types of students need their styles matched directly.

Bridging techniques do not involve
complex changes but basic style
adjustments, explanations, or alternatives
within an assignment or activity in order to
help a student learn and achieve success.

ATTITUDINAL BRIDGES   A teacher's first link with the learner's style begins with attitudinal bridging: the willingness to support the learner as a person, and to offer that support with a style understanding. Remember the day in which you could not cover the content of the science lesson but then you saw Dana was eager to learn? Did you make it a point to tell her you realized her disappointment and to remind her that the work would be first on the agenda tomorrow? If so, you provided the bridge she needed to hear. Have you ever felt the pain of embarrassment for a child like sensitive Jason who had difficulty with a peer? Did you find the time to talk about it with him? If so, you provided the bridge he needed to feel.

As you can see, attitudinal bridging follows effective interpersonal techniques and sensitive attention to the learner with a style understanding. Some of the time, you will look at a learner and know you must do something to reach out to him or her with a style understanding. But more often than not, you will not have time to plan your bridging interventions. The need occurs on the spot.

Attitudinal Bridging
Characteristics

As I observe teachers who bridge effectively through attitude toward their learners, I have found several characteristics in common. These teachers maintain open communication in the classroom. They encourage learners to share their feelings and explain their difficulties, and they see questions as a means to understand the learner, not as a threat to their authority. Teachers who bridge have a warm interpersonal environment. They often tack up posters with comments, like "If life gives you lemons, make lemonade." They enjoy shared conversations with students and take an interest in their concerns. Their classrooms reflects a place where people work together.

Teachers who bridge check the perceptions of their students rather than project their own views. To check perceptions, you might ask students to write a personal evaluation of the class. You might devote the last Friday of every month to a class meeting. You may just stand in the hall and check informally for problems. Teachers who bridge try to recognize the concerns of their students with attention to style. By checking for perceptions, you may hear a concrete sequential student's concern for better directions or an abstract random student's need to have more time to finish a project. By checking perceptions, a teacher listens to the ways in which various styles interpret the class.

Teachers who bridge go out of their way to value all points of view, to encourage diversity, and to make it psychologically safe to risk giving an alternative viewpoint in the classroom. You can value all points of view by praising specific style behaviors: a concrete sequential's ability to organize a group for a task or an abstract sequential's ability to find information no one else noticed. You can encourage diversity by praising questions and out-of-the-mainstream responses. You can make it safe to risk giving an unusual answer yourself, by displaying posters that praise creativity, by using quotes that challenge the norm, and by valuing originality. Not many students will risk the diversity of their own thought if sneers, laughter, or even friendly chuckles follow their different-from-the-norm thinking.

Along the same lines, teachers who bridge can do more than tolerate style. They can actively appreciate it. From my viewpoint, tolerance of style means only that I recognize a style and may even allow it but I surely do not respect it. On the other hand, a teacher who appreciates style acknowledges, "That's not my way, but I like what you bring that is so different from me."

Teachers who bridge have a positive attitude, a willingness to see the cup half full, a sense that a problem can be solved if we look hard enough for a solution. A positive teacher can see the benefits many styles bring to a class and literally sets the tone for belief in oneself.

Teachers who bridge respect feelings, and even seek them out. They willingly apologize when wrong, without a defensive attitude, and they don't lose face easily. They seek out the feelings of their students and respond to their students' authentic concerns. They don't laugh at students' feelings but do laugh with them. Teachers like this can put a hand on a student's shoulder to reveal understanding as easily as they can laugh at their own mistakes in class.

Teachers who bridge find ways to praise a learner for himself/herself, not just for the behaviors expected in a classroom. For example, a teacher like this might praise an abstract random learner's attention to details that the learner previously missed. But this teacher will also make it a point to value this learner's sense of humor, or creative writing talent, or whatever seems to be the special quality of the person.

No teacher can be all things to all students. But without a doubt, setting a tone in your class by following guidelines like these gives you a better chance to know your learners, to hear and see their styles, to understand learning from the learner's point of view.

ACTIVITY BRIDGES

Activity bridges are instructional techniques, processes, or strategies that help the learner achieve an objective. Activity bridges take on special importance when all students work on the same activity, when a student has difficulty achieving the objective, or when the student engages with a style-mismatched, higher-level thinking activity.

Let's look at an example of bridging through an activity for each of the four styles.

Bridging to the Abstract Random

As an example of bridging through an activity, consider how you might handle students when you ask them to role play characters from the Constitutional Convention. You know that several students with strong random styles would enjoy writing an original dialogue and would learn from portraying an imaginary conversation among the delegates.

But you also know that some students with a strong sequential preference experience considerable discomfort in such activities. Rather than require all students to be "actors," you suggest for the benefit of the abstract and concrete sequential students that some reenact a formal debate between delegates Roger Sherman and James Madison; for this they could write a brief, authentic, and predictable script. As part of this lesson, you could also help students think about their own enjoyment, or lack thereof, in this type of activity, and their own learning style. You could help them see the various ways they could handle themselves in the future, if put into this position with a teacher who does not know about style preferences.

What have you accomplished by giving students two ways to participate? On the one hand, you have valued different processing styles. On the other, you have given students a reasonable way to achieve the objective without compromising the intent of the objective. You have helped students complete the assignment, absorb the content, and it is likely, retain motivation for learning.

Bridging to the Concrete Sequential

Concrete sequential learners need explicit directions, an example or model and a factual reference, not because they have weak minds but because they want to do their work "the right way the first time." We need to be definite about our expectations with CS learners. Once they have finished their work, concrete sequential learners have little desire to return to the project for elaboration—they want it done and over with!

What happends if your expectations were clear in your mind but are not clear in theirs? You invite considerable distress when you tell concrete sequential learners they did not do the task correctly, or need to redo their work. For example, imagine the concrete sequential student's reaction to this assignment: "Conduct an interview with a person who has died. Find out if he/she would like a second chance to live, and why." Given this assignment, a conscientious seventh-grade CS learner wrote a *factual* "who, what, why, where, and when" report about his grandmother's life. Already concerned that his abstract random teacher didn't value his viewpoint, he went out of his way to make the product physically correct. He typed the inteview on a computer, used various type faces, added a graphic, and printed it on bright blue paper. If we want a learner like this to move beyond the mechanically correct product, we must provide the coaching-and-practice bridge for "point-of-view" writing. Otherwise, this learner creates the assignment in his/her own mindset: factual and practical, not heartfelt and personal.

Bridging to the Abstract Sequential

Picture the very young abstract sequential learner who does not want to participate in the kindergarten circus. Why not? In part, this learner needs recognition of his/her intellect: this does not happen if one role plays the clown. In addition, this learner experiences great discomfort in unpredictable situations that do not require a cerebral answer. How could the teacher involve this type of student in the circus? She helped him/her find a worthy AS part—the ringmaster who is the mastermind, expert, overseer of the circus. This teacher gained the confidence of the learner who realized that the teacher would not put him/her in an embarrassing role. She built the bridge to this learner's participation.

Bridging to the Concrete Random

CR learners need problems. One math teacher explained that his CR student completed math homework only five minutes before class but always knew the material. Without style knowledge, the teacher would have considered the student unprepared for class. With style knowledge, the teacher realized the student's need for a problem. The student did not find a problem in the homework assignment; he created his own problem: can I get the work done before class starts? Rather than chastise the student for last-minute work, the teacher said nothing as long as the student understood his work.

CR students value independence. Instead of challenging a student to defy you by not doing the assignment, could you challenge the student to find a different approach, to extend the investigation, to try his/her method? Mark's enthusiasm for science soared in fifth grade because his teacher valued his divergent thinking and allowed him to include his own experiment. For example, when the teacher told the class to find the correct way to connect a light bulb, battery, and wire together to light the bulb, Mark tried to see how many stacked batteries it would take to burn out the bulb! Rather than recite the litany of off-task criticism of Mark, the teacher asked him to discuss the thought process that led to the experiment. She built the bridge to thinking and learning.

IN SUMMARY

As you can see, teachers bridge to learners during instructional activities in planned as well as spontaneous ways. In the example above, you could plan to bridge the role play to sequential students. At other times, you might not even realize a student needs a bridge until you see or hear the student's response. For example, you might not expect a certain student to have difficulty with an art activity until you see his/her inability to begin the project.

In the next few pages, you will find a summary of some common bridging techniques to the minds of different styles, as well as some bridging techniques that help you bridge to learners when they work outside their own styles.

Bridges to
The Concrete Sequential Mind

BRIDGES TO THE CS MIND

- Provide fail-proof directions and a model or example.

- Include physical activity or opportunity to move around.

- Check student's work within a few minutes of starting work.

- Teach advance organizers, such as Venn diagrams, charts.

- Make display centers of concrete illustrations of a concept.

- Include tactile materials as learning tools for free time.

- Organize memorization teams for memory requirements.

- Keep a written reference of procedures in a consistent place.

- Avoid cluttering the CS desk and mind with too many directional handouts.

- Maintain a few, practical rules that never bend.

- Praise this learner's strengths.

- Do what you say you will do, and minimize last-minute changes.

- Tie new learning objectives to students' real-life interests.

Bridging to CS Learners in Concrete Random Activities

- Be definite about your expectations if you expect a product.

- Work personally with students when you want them to elaborate on a paper or project. Bridge to the fact that in the CS student's mind, "done is done" and elaboration is painful.

- Help students accept change by presenting ways for them to bring about the needed change.

- Reward attempts at new ways of doing things.

- Ask for CR behavior, one step at a time.

- Demonstrate and practice using no-fail examples.

- Respond to questions with definitive answers rather than "what-do-you-think" responses when the CS learner is too frustrated to continue without direction.

- Recognize students' need for perfection as you encourage less perfection when not needed.

Bridging to CS Learners in Abstract Sequential Activities

- Divide long assignments into smaller assignments that you check upon completion.

- Intersperse long lecture with application activities.

- Use specific, concrete illustrations, demonstrations, or real things to explain abstract points.

- Use a structured chart to teach main idea and supporting details in writing analytical answers.

- Review key lecture points for students to check their notes.

- Use charts, diagrams, and other structured visuals to show the conclusion of "big picture" ideas.

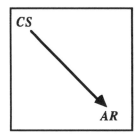

In the polar opposite style:
Bridging to CS Learners in Abstract Random Activities

- Provide practice-time after directions.

- Keep activities short.

- Use concrete illustrations.

- Reward risk-taking.

- Keep group work in small groups—three students.

- Provide frequent feedback and monitoring.

- Provide a time-out spot, quiet corner, or opportunity for the CS student to check thinking or work during the course of the activity.

- Watch for frustrations, aggravation, and hostility; intervene, if necessary.

- Provide a discussion guide.

- Bring closure to AR activities with a summary or wrap-up in a factual way.

Bridges to
The Abstract Sequential Mind

BRIDGES TO THE AS MIND

- Voice your understanding of AS academic orientation.

- Place AS students in positions of responsibility for intellectual tasks.

- Allow AS students to be the "experts."

- Value written reports and oral presentation of ideas.

- Provide opportunities for library-research checks.

- Help AS students enjoy the role of "excellent student" without a put-down from others as a bookworm or teacher's pet.

- Make readings and bibliographies available.

- Incorporate research into optional assignments.

- Show value for AS analytical questions.

- Show recognition of AS students' intellectual interests by asking for their ideas on a subject.

- Appreciate AS students' thirst for more knowledge.

- Give AS students a grade.

- Understand that completion of a long project provides an intrinsic value. Let AS students savor the sense of their own work by talking about the project with them individually.

Bridging to AS Learners in Concrete Sequential Activities

- Pair AS students with a knowledgeable CS peer.

- Provide explicit directions.

- Allow notes or a report to accompany a hands-on product.

- Minimize workbook, drill/skill, and overly detailed assignments.

- Provide reading assignments that explain the purposes and possibilities of activities, such as lab experiments.

- Give AS students resources to check.

Bridging to AS Learners in Abstract Random Activities

- Explain why you are using AR techniques.

- Minimize students' need to participate in extremely personalized activities that openly require emotional involvement.

- Provide, or ask students to find, background about the originators of AR techniques, such as for guided imagery, if that is a technique used in class.

- Analyze the value of AR thinking, such as interpretive writing and imagination, in areas such as the arts, literature, or human relations.

- Respect the AS need to work alone rather than in a group on important projects.

- Acknowledge AS students' discomfort with group work, if necessary.

- Praise successful attempts at working effectively in a group.

- Gain closure by bringing discussions to a logical conclusion.

- Steer AS students away from monopolizing group discussions with their views.

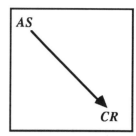

In the polar opposite style:
Bridging to AS Learners in Concrete Random Activities

- Make sure AS learners know the purpose of their activity.

- Help AS learners to focus on a topic from among several choices by analyzing their interest in the topic.

- After brainstorming activities, ask AS students to rank the value of the ideas and provide a reason for their ranking.

- After a simulation, ask AS students to analyze or evaluate how the simulation illustrated an idea or a story.

- During problem solving, provide specific strategies for different problems with reasons that they work.

- Reward trial-and-error attempts at problem solving.

- Focus independent study projects so that AS students are not lost in the possibilities.

- Schedule several teacher-student conferences for independent study projects.

- Avoid change-for-the-sake-of-change experiences.

- Offer a reading reference that relates discovery activities to a concept.

- Accept that AS students want time to think about an idea before going on to the next one.

Bridges to
The Abstract Random Mind

BRIDGES TO THE AR MIND

- Provide frequent positive, personal praise for work well done.

- Value socializing time as a benefit of work accomplished.

- Encourage peer learning and cooperative group work.

- Share positive personal anecdotes. Use humor.

- Reflect on your own feelings and allow AR students to do the same.

- Use art within assignments.

- Relate learning to film, television, and media. E.g., "Write ten new vocabulary words from your favorite tv show" or "Discuss how the title of a certain short story is like the title of a certain tv show."

- Offer optional techniques that use AR strengths: webbing, interviewing, working with a partner.

- Give your personal support to ARs as individuals. E.g., ask how a role in the school play is going.

- Ask personal questions, "What's the matter? You seem down today. Are you okay?" Take the initiative if communication seems poor.

- Let ARs know they pleased, not disappointed, you; don't assume they know.

Bridging to AR Learners in Concrete Random Activities

• Ask AR learners to compare a problem to a personal experience.

• Have students write their own word problems in math, and work with a partner to solve.

• Teach students to sketch word problems as a problem-solving strategy.

• Assign AR learners high-spirited characters in simulations.

• Include the way a problem might affect people.

• Give AR learners direct instructional support and time to work out problems.

• Don't allow the AR learner to get caught in the process of a CR activity without checking that he/she knows what to do.

• Provide extensive opportunities for AR students to sketch science experiments and demonstrations.

• Let AR learners know they were good team players.

Bridging to AR Learners in Abstract Sequential Activities

• Include a drawing or visual to show a concept.

• Use artwork to illustrate a point.

• Provide a cassette recorder for AR students who have great difficulty with standardized tests to use to supplement the test or explain their answers.

• Incorporate metaphors, similes, and stories into explanations of ideas and problems.

• Use interpretive ways to explain a concept: guided imagery, a cartoon, humor.

• Minimize lengthy readings.

• Use webbing as an outlining technique.

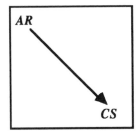

In the polar opposite style: Bridging to AR Learners in Concrete Sequential Activities

• Use a team approach to hands-on projects.

• Use visuals to support facts.

• Teach mnemonics as a technique for remembering specifics.

• Provide total and thorough directions that leave nothing to the imagination.

• Let AR learners know others depend on them to finish a task.

• Give a pre-deadline in which some aspect of their finished project is due. Give some flexibility to the final deadline.

• Help AR learners get started on a specific project by helping them to choose from among options.

• Have AR students keep journals in a sequential class as a means to pull information together. E.g., "In your mind, what were the most important points we discussed this week?" "What ideas seem most fuzzy to you still?"

• Use color coding to help them organize.

• Use boxes rather than file jackets to organize.

Bridges to
The Concrete Random Mind

BRIDGES TO THE CR MIND

- Use brainstorming approaches frequently.

- Seek alternatives, not just correct answers. E.g., "How else could we have solved this problem?" "What else could John have done?"

- Even when you provide a list of options, add a "write your own" or "see me for a special one."

- Pose questions such as,
  ~ What would happen if...?
  ~ How could we alter this to...?
  ~ How many different feelings...?
                          ideas...?
                          experiences...
                          ways could we...?

- Value CR students' divergent ideas, not just finished products.

- Allow revisions. Let CR students know it's okay to change their minds.

- Give CR students a sense of personal progress, not just product progress.

- Provide surprises (not surprise quizzes!).

- Work within guidelines, not restrictive rules, but stick to them.

- Call on CR students frequently to be productive problem solvers for you.

Bridging to CR Learners in Concrete Sequential Activities

• When definite rules are needed, ask the CR to tell you how he/she is working within the rules.

• Include "write your own question" on tests.

• Turn fact questions into problem questions that require facts to be used.

• Allow CR students to use their own approach to some CS material as long as they can be accountable for the information.

• Give a five-minute warning of closure of an activity.

• Give frequent reminders as deadlines approach.

• Ask CR students to tell you in their own words, or to show you, how they arrived at their answers.

• Ask CR students what guidelines or materials they need.

Bridging to CR Learners in Abstract Random Activities

• Encourage CR students to understanding feelings as a way to solve problems.

• Give CR students leadership or divergent-thinking roles in role-play assignments.

• Give CR students director roles in role-play assignments.

• Give CR learners license not to accept the activity. Ask them to redesign it to work better.

• Allow CR learners to opt out. E.g., "You don't have to do this. What do you need instead to learn about this?"

• Keep CR learners concretely busy. E.g., allow them to videotape the role play.

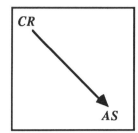

In the polar opposite style:
Bridging to the CR Learner in Abstract Sequential Activities

• Develop CR students' ability to web as a form of note-baking and as a writing pre-step.

• Use analogy as a means to explain an idea.

• Use analogy as a questioning technique.

• Use comparison and contrast statements to highlight differences.

• Minimize lengthy readings.

• Provide optional reading assignments.

• Give opportunity for hands-on projects after research has been completed.

• Recognize that CR learners like to consider possibilities but are bored with analytical arguments.

• Solicit many responses to a question.

Effective bridges build on learner strengths, and provide simple, basic accommodations to students' learning styles. Bridges can also help students to understand style demands. Let's take the example of brainstorming. Brainstorming requires basic concrete random thinking: divergency, open-endedness, connections, exploring. In most cases brainstorming uses knowledge-level thinking in the concrete random style. Most of us learn the techniques of brainstorming as a skill.

When we interviewed people with dominant styles, we found each style had definite perceptions about brainstorming. They also needed certain bridges in order to use brainstorming effectively. Without the bridges, other dominant styles simply endured the process or gave it lipservice.

The concrete sequential style thinkers said that brainstorming could be effective for them if participants followed brainstorming rules and someone kept a written record. They commented, "What's the job?" "Let's get it done." "Is it on the test?" Each liked to act as the recorder for the group. Participants in their group admired the fact that CS thinkers recorded their brainstorming list verbatim. The CSers, however, said that no matter how well they recorded, they still did not like to brainstorm. They suggested the following bridges:

- *"Give me written rules for the task."*

- *"Let me write or list my ideas."*

- *"Give me the option to 'pass' and just listen."*

- *"Make clear the relevancy of the assignment, 'Why are we doing this?'"*

Similarly, abstract sequential thinkers did not like the brainstorming process. They said that brainstorming could be effective for them, however, if they could do some private thinking or reading about the topic before brainstorming. In their minds, a worthwhile topic demanded time; otherwise on-the-spot brainstorming served as just an "entertaining or playtime" event. They offered the following bridging suggestions for meeting the AS mind:

- *"Allow me to think about the topic. Let me know that tomorrow we will spend ten minutes brainstorming about the topic."*

- *"Give me time to list my ideas independently before the group meets."*

- *"Understand me if I try to 'bring order' to the activity."*

- *"Let me choose my group. I will seek out some randoms because they help support the task beyond my comfort zone."*

- *"Tell me why the process of brainstorming is important to my understanding of the topic."*

Abstract random thinkers told us they enjoyed the group aspect of brainstorming, but they feared their own hurt feelings if others did not respond positively to their ideas. They needed the safety rule, that no one can judge others' ideas, guaranteed for them. ARs felt they needed to protect their own and others' feelings during the brainstorming process. They offered this bridging perspective:

- *"Help me to stay on task and to follow the rules of brainstorming."*

- *"Understand me when I want to explore ideas in greater detail and depth but should not elaborate. I will be frustrated."*

- *"Use large chart paper and colored markers. Let me make visual representations of our ideas, not just linear, written ones."*

- *"I need to feel an investment of 'self' in the process. Be sure to include all of us in discussing and piggybacking."*

Concrete random thinkers found brainstorming a process natural to them. They said they mentally brainstorm all the time as part of their natural thinking process. The key to maximizing their style, then, is freedom of thought. They want broad topics, not narrow ones. They wish to have their "zany" ideas accepted in the process by others. Just let their minds go!

Stretching Style

How might you help other styles understand the style demands of the brainstorming process? For sequential students, provide the rules of the brainstorming process and demonstrate those rules in action in a model brainstorming group. For random students, allow them to experience the brainstorming process (they can role model for the sequentials) with a simple question, such as "What mental abilities or qualities do inventors have?" After this experience, review the list of brainstorming rules.

Once you determine the definition and rules of brainstorming, discuss how different types of thinkers might react to the brainstorming process. You can suggest that some thinkers (concrete sequential learners) may feel foolish in listing impossible ideas, may be frustrated in trying to come up with more and more reactions after the obvious ones have been listed, or may not participate effectively because they cannot "see" any real value as yet. You might suggest that students who have these experiences remind themselves to remain open-minded, learn how to brainstorm by listening to others, be aware that their feelings are natural, and participate to the best of their ability even though they may be unsure.

You can explain that some thinkers (abstract random learners) may lose sight of the purpose of a group brainstorming activity and turn it into a social discussion. When they find this happening, these students need to bring themselves back to the task. You can also discuss the fact that some thinkers (abstract sequential learners) may not value brainstorming because answers do not have to be logical or verifiable. You can suggest that these students purposely try to forget logic temporarily in order to develop the ability to generate alternative ideas. They can logically apply them at a later phase of the process.

At this point ease students into brainstorming. Ask them to generate alternatives by using actual examples, such as "How many ways could I use this pencil in the classroom?" "How many reasons can you think of to explain why 'brainstorming' might be a useful technique?" You might also ask the students to illustrate how "right-answer" thinking may prevent brainstorming from taking place.

Finally, ask the class to identify the students who could do the brainstorming process most easily. Ask these students to lead individual brainstorming groups.

When students do brainstorm, bridge to other styles:

- *Ask students to keep a list of ideas.*

- *Keep the groups small and balanced for style.*

- *Make frequent personal checks.*

- *Give encouragement and approval of participation.*

- *Voice recognition of any frustrations with appropriate suggestions for relief.*

IN SUMMARY

Style bridging should serve to ease students through the process of understanding and working in mismatched styles at the rate of progress they are able to handle.

Like guides in a museum who point out significant features to first-time visitors, bridges guide students to work with nondominant styles. And, like guides who give return visitors a more thorough or advanced tour of the museum, the bridges aid students to advance their ability to work with mismatched style. Like visitors who join the museum as supporting members, students gradually taught to handle mismatch eventually help others to do the same.

Bridges help us to work slowly and steadily to understand how to work in another style, to gain insight into the demands of other styles, and to bring their own abilities into perspective to meet those demands.

The concept of bridging sounds easy in theory and seems obvious in practice. However, bridging to the learner in reality requires sensitive understanding of style and a willingness to meet the learner halfway, sometimes all the way. The missed connections to students because of style happen all too frequently, just as if teacher and learner arrived at the same junction at different times only to take different roads.

Can we give teachers all the bridging techniques they need? No. Teaching with style bridges is a personal, not a factual, process. The answer must lie in a teacher's own knowledge of style in self and others, and its translation to each classroom experience. Our suggestions provide guides to your thinking about bridging. Your questions and experience with style in the classroom must lead you to define and refine bridging techniques for yourself.

Are there techniques that I and others can share to expand your repertoire of bridging possibilities. Of course!

In this chapter we discussed basic ways to help a student meet a learning task by bridging to the learner's style. We suggested how to provide a simple, basic style accommodation to the learner so that the learner could rely on some aspect of his/her own style to complete a task, no matter what the style of the task. We suggested that a teacher's bridging attitudes and actions help all learners in any situation, but that bridging takes on special importance as a technique when the learner faces a mismatched situation. Teachers who bridge successfully understand style points of view and interact with learners from each learner's point of view.

A teacher's ability to bridge empowers him/her to reach learners through natural interaction, regardless of the mechanics of the situation. Teachers who

Learning and Teaching Style: In Theory and Practice

bridge successfully appear as natural counselors with children, able to understand perceptions and problems, and to act on them. Teachers who bridge effectively work from multiple points of view, even when all students work on the same assignment!

Bridging becomes more natural with experience in watching, listening to, and understanding different styles. You cannot learn bridging intellectually and apply it practically until you live it personally. The teacher must be able to step outside his/her own style and reenter from the learner's perspective. Bridging clearly requires the most psychological understanding of style. Not every teacher can or will bridge with equal effectiveness.

CHAPTER 10

STYLE DIFFERENTIATED INSTRUCTION: THE RELATION OF BLOOM'S TAXONOMY TO STYLE

It is high time we freed ourselves of attachments to old forms and eased the flight of the unfettered human mind.

—Marilyn Ferguson

We see that bridging integrates the personal teacher with the individual learner. Bridging techniques allow us to meet the day-to-day, lesson-to-lesson needs of learners, both psychological and instructional. But, the use of bridging represents only one important way to apply style in the classroom. When we bridge, we help learners work within one style. But, we can also plan for instruction in more specific, intentional, and direct ways that go beyond bridging if we understand how each style naturally thinks, performs, and processes information. To go beyond bridging, then, we must understand instructional preferences.

We can see that learning preferences and instructional activities within different styles range from simple to complex, from lower to higher levels. To provide for learning style preferences, then, we must understand not only the style preferences but also the levels of thinking within styles.

We found that Benjamin Bloom's taxonomy of education objectives (20) served as a helpful tool to clarify the level of thinking in each style. Although Bloom did not apply the taxonomy to style, we could see that the quality of a student's outcome depended as much on style as on the level of the activity. When we considered levels of thinking within styles, it shed light on the reasons that some able learners performed inconsistently at higher levels of thinking. They produced well within their own style, but performed poorly in mismatched situations.

In addition to findings among students, we saw that teachers could plan student options for different styles, but often did not offer options of equal value or at a similar level of thinking. Therefore, students chose activities not by style but by level of thinking—usually the lower level. It became clear that if teachers wanted to plan for higher-level thinking, they had to consider style. If they wanted to plan for style differences, they had to consider levels of thinking within style.

Bloom's Taxonomy identifies six levels. In the chart below, I have summarized the types of thinking expected at each level.

Bloom's Taxonomy: A Summary

- *Knowledge*

  Recognition or identification of simple knowledge, such as facts, definitions, theories, positions, and points of view, through such means as stating, listing, recalling.

- *Comprehension*

  An understanding or ability to show the elements that form knowledge, through such means as explanations, inferences, and use of examples.

- *Application*

  The ability to apply knowledge and comprehension to a specific situation, through such means as solving problems, demonstrating skill, or using knowledge and comprehension.

- *Analysis*

  The ability to break a whole into its constituent parts in order to understand the relationship of parts to the whole, through such means as descriptions and explanations for cause and effect, and the ability to show reasons among parts of the whole.

- *Synthesis*

  The ability to recombine constituent parts into new and significant relationships to create a new whole, through such means as design and creating new products.

- *Evaluation*

  The ability to assess the value of the new product by devising one's own evaluation system, or by using another's system.

**The Problem
Hierarchy**

Of equal significance, when we assessed the curriculum development process, we found that many teachers gave attention to Bloom's taxonomy but adopted a style hierarchy in the way they developed lessons or planned curriculum. Frequently, they began at the knowledge/comprehension level in one style (usually CS), then moved to higher levels in other styles, and, often ended with CR at the synthesis level. Such a hierarchy does not give students equal access to learning quality thinking in their own style, and often becomes the source of much frustration for students.

**STYLE AND
BLOOM'S TAXONOMY**

On the following pages you will find a summary of our observations and the results of interviews with teachers and students who showed a single dominant style as they operated along Bloom's taxonomy. Please keep in mind that the charts generalize the performance about styles of thinkers and their performance at Bloom's six levels.

You will have to translate the generalization to student behavior that also reflects a student's developmental stage. For example, Josh, a kindergarten boy, is in a concrete developmental stage in Piaget's terms but certainly could have an abstract sequential style. As a five-year-old, he will not produce research reports, but he may indeed love to find out how many books he and the librarian can turn up about the class science project.

" We gather factual information in hands-on ways, engage with structured learning experiences, and create our own real products."

Learning and Teaching Style: In Theory and Practice

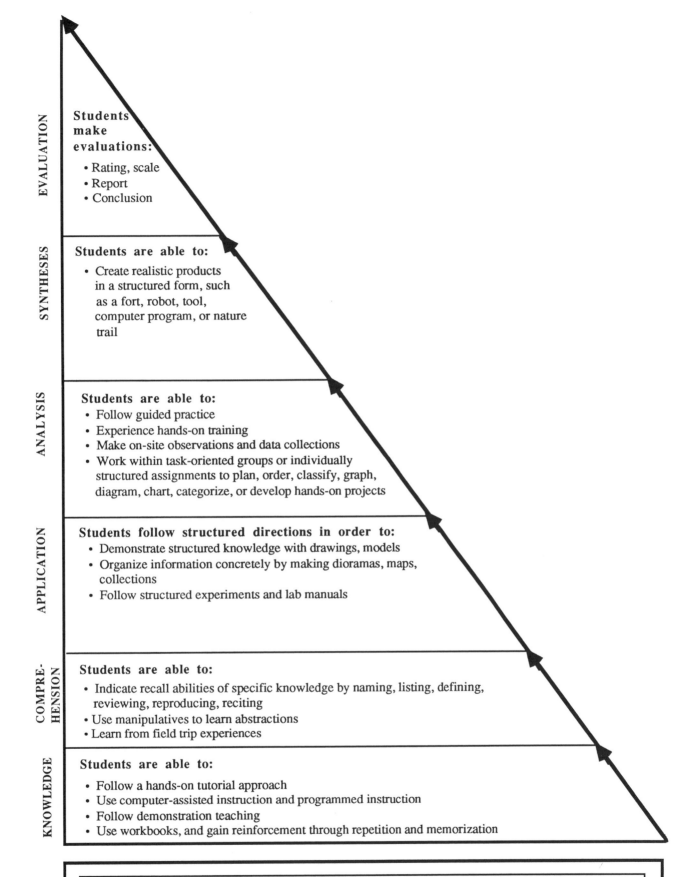

EVALUATION

Students make evaluations:

• Rating, scale
• Report
• Conclusion

SYNTHESES

Students are able to:

• Create realistic products in a structured form, such as a fort, robot, tool, computer program, or nature trail

ANALYSIS

Students are able to:

• Follow guided practice
• Experience hands-on training
• Make on-site observations and data collections
• Work within task-oriented groups or individually structured assignments to plan, order, classify, graph, diagram, chart, categorize, or develop hands-on projects

APPLICATION

Students follow structured directions in order to:

• Demonstrate structured knowledge with drawings, models
• Organize information concretely by making dioramas, maps, collections
• Follow structured experiments and lab manuals

COMPRE-HENSION

Students are able to:

• Indicate recall abilities of specific knowledge by naming, listing, defining, reviewing, reproducing, reciting
• Use manipulatives to learn abstractions
• Learn from field trip experiences

KNOWLEDGE

Students are able to:

• Follow a hands-on tutorial approach
• Use computer-assisted instruction and programmed instruction
• Follow demonstration teaching
• Use workbooks, and gain reinforcement through repetition and memorization

The Concrete Sequential Style: Levels of Student Performance

Chapter 10: The Relation of Bloom's Taxonomy to Style

" We gather information by reading and listening. We engage with learning by researching. Then, we create a product to instruct others or present a new idea."

Learning and Teaching Style: In Theory and Practice

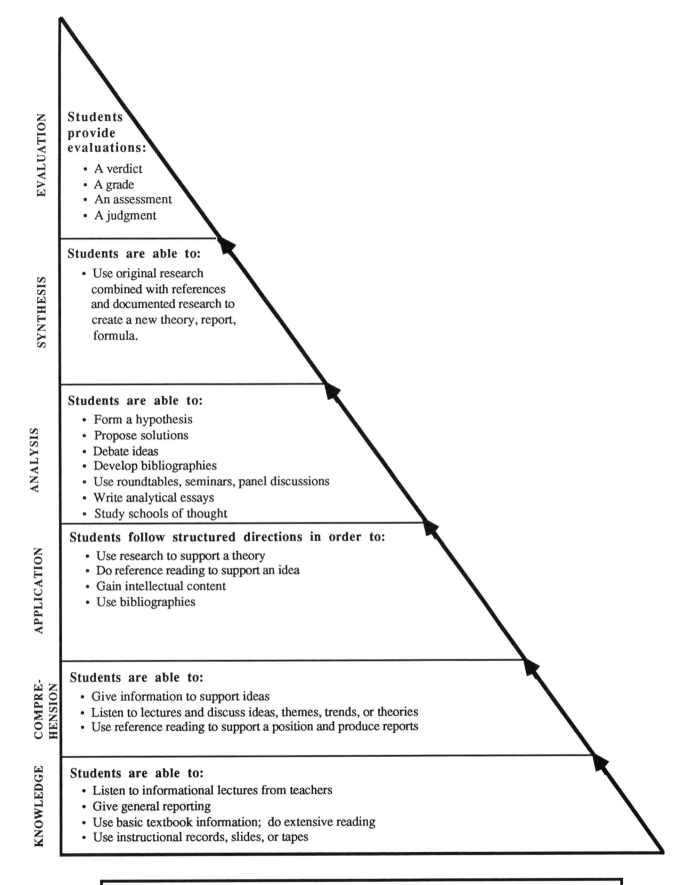

EVALUATION

Students provide evaluations:

- A verdict
- A grade
- An assessment
- A judgment

SYNTHESIS

Students are able to:

- Use original research combined with references and documented research to create a new theory, report, formula.

ANALYSIS

Students are able to:

- Form a hypothesis
- Propose solutions
- Debate ideas
- Develop bibliographies
- Use roundtables, seminars, panel discussions
- Write analytical essays
- Study schools of thought

APPLICATION

Students follow structured directions in order to:

- Use research to support a theory
- Do reference reading to support an idea
- Gain intellectual content
- Use bibliographies

COMPRE- HENSION

Students are able to:

- Give information to support ideas
- Listen to lectures and discuss ideas, themes, trends, or theories
- Use reference reading to support a position and produce reports

KNOWLEDGE

Students are able to:

- Listen to informational lectures from teachers
- Give general reporting
- Use basic textbook information; do extensive reading
- Use instructional records, slides, or tapes

The Abstract Sequential Style: Levels of Thinking

" We gather information by discussing plans and sharing ideas. We engage with learning by using our interpretive abilities to relate information. We create colorful and imaginary products."

Learning and Teaching Style: In Theory and Practice

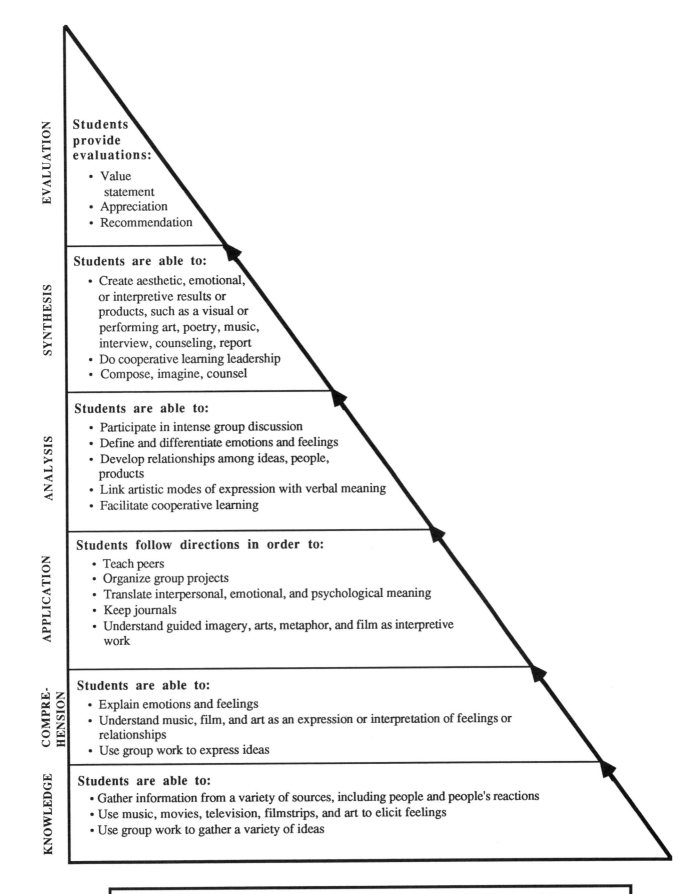

EVALUATION

Students provide evaluations:
- Value statement
- Appreciation
- Recommendation

SYNTHESIS

Students are able to:
- Create aesthetic, emotional, or interpretive results or products, such as a visual or performing art, poetry, music, interview, counseling, report
- Do cooperative learning leadership
- Compose, imagine, counsel

ANALYSIS

Students are able to:
- Participate in intense group discussion
- Define and differentiate emotions and feelings
- Develop relationships among ideas, people, products
- Link artistic modes of expression with verbal meaning
- Facilitate cooperative learning

APPLICATION

Students follow directions in order to:
- Teach peers
- Organize group projects
- Translate interpersonal, emotional, and psychological meaning
- Keep journals
- Understand guided imagery, arts, metaphor, and film as interpretive work

COMPRE-HENSION

Students are able to:
- Explain emotions and feelings
- Understand music, film, and art as an expression or interpretation of feelings or relationships
- Use group work to express ideas

KNOWLEDGE

Students are able to:
- Gather information from a variety of sources, including people and people's reactions
- Use music, movies, television, filmstrips, and art to elicit feelings
- Use group work to gather a variety of ideas

The Abstract Random Style: Levels of Thinking

" We gather information by exploring the facts. We engage with learning by investigating. We create our own new products and ideas."

Learning and Teaching Style: In Theory and Practice

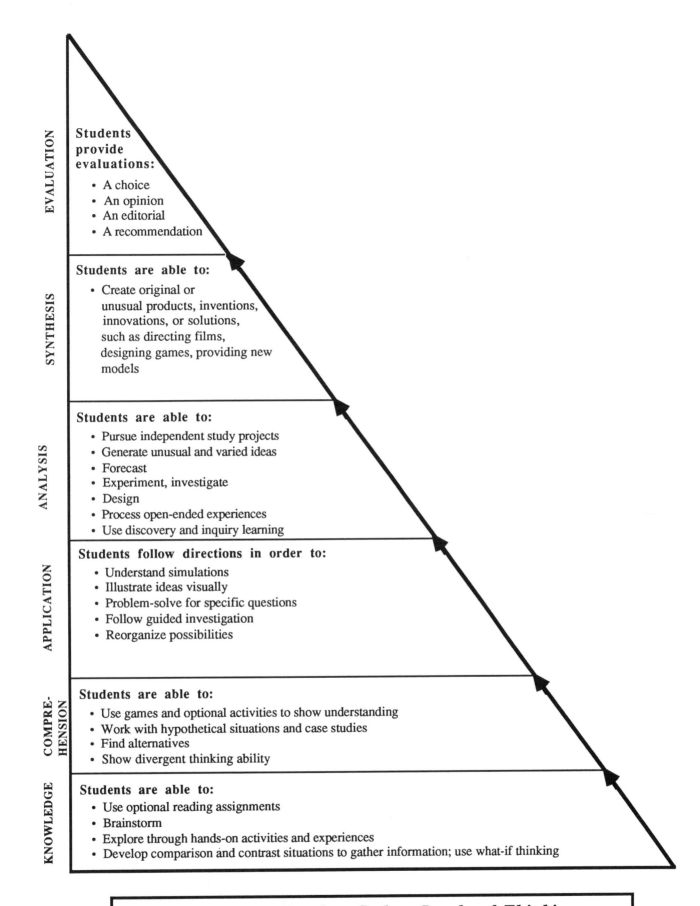

EVALUATION

Students provide evaluations:

- A choice
- An opinion
- An editorial
- A recommendation

SYNTHESIS

Students are able to:

- Create original or unusual products, inventions, innovations, or solutions, such as directing films, designing games, providing new models

ANALYSIS

Students are able to:

- Pursue independent study projects
- Generate unusual and varied ideas
- Forecast
- Experiment, investigate
- Design
- Process open-ended experiences
- Use discovery and inquiry learning

APPLICATION

Students follow directions in order to:

- Understand simulations
- Illustrate ideas visually
- Problem-solve for specific questions
- Follow guided investigation
- Reorganize possibilities

COMPRE-HENSION

Students are able to:

- Use games and optional activities to show understanding
- Work with hypothetical situations and case studies
- Find alternatives
- Show divergent thinking ability

KNOWLEDGE

Students are able to:

- Use optional reading assignments
- Brainstorm
- Explore through hands-on activities and experiences
- Develop comparison and contrast situations to gather information; use what-if thinking

The Concrete Random Style: Levels of Thinking

**Knowledge and
Comprehension
Level**

As a result of interviews with, observations of, and test results for students with dominant abilities in the four different styles, I have come to some interesting conclusions about style and levels of thinking.

At the Knowledge/Comprehension Level

Knowledge/comprehension level activities in any style do not require a significant amount of ability in that style for successful completion. Most students can operate at the knowledge/comprehension level in any style because most students can learn the coping skills for working in each style. In addition, most students can learn the thinking skills of each style at this level.

Success at the knowledge/comprehension level for most students depends on the teacher's using a variety of styles as a matter of daily teaching at this level of thinking. However, even at this basic level, we have sufficient reason to give attention to learning style. We have found that

- *Most students find considerable learning discomfort in their minor style and will not choose to use it even at this level.*

- *Students who can work in mismatch at this level, but who find it difficult or more time consuming than other students do, tend to develop self-esteem and self-concept problems.*

- *Disaffection with learning appears at this level when students have too few opportunities to use their own styles.*

- *A few students lose motivation when consistently matched to style at the knowledge/comprehension level. At this level they depend on mismatch for stimulation. Gifted students lose motivation or become bored at this level regardless of style.*

- *Underachievement at this level often results from mismatch of style.*

- *At-risk learners need a style match at the knowledge/comprehension level.*

- *At-risk learners can be misidentified as learning disabled if they do not have a match to style at this level.*

- *Some students appear to have a learning disability when they cannot work in a sequential style at this level.*

- *A teacher can create a learning disabled student at this level when he/she defines an "able" student as a sequential student.*

Application-level activities in any style require more style ability to do the task than at the knowledge/comprehension level. Students gain strong benefits from a match in style at the application level. If the student's style and the instructional style differ when the student works at the application level, then the student must *adapt* his/her style to meet the style demands of the activity. To adapt one's style means to control one's personal style in favor of the style of the activity. Coping strategies, effective for the knowledge/comprehension level, are no longer sufficient.

Most students work best at the application level in their strongest styles. Success at the application level in different styles for most students requires the teacher to vary the use of all four styles in the curriculum, to teach the thinking skill of the style as students work with it, and to use bridging techniques within each style as needed.

At application levels, we begin to see victims of style mismatch appear more frequently.

- *Students mismatched at this level have greater learning difficulties than when mismatched at lower levels.*

- *Students who cannot adapt to this level tend to lose motivation and self-esteem.*

- *At the application level, style mismatch affects most quickly the student whose style is the opposite of the activity: CS/AR; AS/CR.*

- *At-risk learners usually do not succeed when mismatched at this or higher levels.*

As an example of the student's need to adapt to the style demands of an activity, consider how students of different styles participate in a concrete sequential science lab. Whereas most students can adapt their styles to complete an application-level science lab, many style-dominant abstract random students (the opposite of concrete sequential) literally do not understand the lab, even when they have carefully completed it step by step. The material makes no connection to their thinking and no sense. In their minds, it becomes non-sense.

In this situation such abstract random learners require learning bridges that include their style: cooperative group process, a series of step-by-step visuals, a range of questions that use association; extra time to work; and a supportive attitude. For a few learners like this, only personal, interpretive work with a sensitive teacher will create authentic understanding.

At the Analysis Level

Analysis-level activities in any style require a significant amount of style flex-ability to meet the style demands of the activity. Students gain considerable benefit from a match in style at the analysis level, even more so than at the application level. Because analysis-level thinking often takes on a strong style point of view, students who cannot flex to meet the style demands of the activity rarely achieve analysis-level thinking in that style.

We find serious learning problems when students experience mismatch at this level.

- *A student mismatched to the style demands of the activity at this level must style flex into the style of the activity and use that style's point of view. Neither adaptation nor coping skills are sufficient to complete the task.*

- *Many students can style flex into a required style for short periods of time.*

- *Students who cannot style flex into a required style tend to lose confidence in their ability as learners.*

- *Bridging helps some students at this level, but not all.*

- *Success at analysis levels in different styles for most students requires the teacher to vary the use of all four styles in the curriculum, to use planned bridging techniques, and to give careful guidance.*

For example, when we ask students to analyze an issue, we demand analysis-level, abstract sequential thinking characterized by key ideas that are logically developed. Students who can flex into this way of thinking have no difficulty. Others often cannot. They required planned bridges from the teacher to help them meet the task.

At Synthesis and Evaluation Level

Synthesis and evaluation-level activities in any style require a natural style. Students should be matched in style at these levels. Given a choice at this level, learners choose higher-level activities within their natural styles rather than choose a nondominant style. We see the most important style issues for higher-level thinking at this level.

- *Interviews show that learners feel more fulfilled and satisfied by hard work at synthesis and evaluation levels in their own style.*

- *Learners' efforts to create usually result in a quality, authentic product when style is matched at this level.*

- *Learners' efforts to evaluate are superior when done from their own style viewpoints than when done from nondominant viewpoints.*

- *Students can technically create and evaluate out of their style. But, students and teachers alike report that the quality of their product and, often, the learner's degree of satisfaction do not approach those of the naturally matched style.*

- *Students may not show their true giftedness until they reach higher levels of thinking within their own style.*

- *Success at higher levels of thinking requires students to have a choice from among styles, to have support for skills needed, and to have the guidance of a mentor with a like style.*

At this level, we also see the most serious style issues for higher-level thinking.

- *When students are mismatched to a synthesis-level activity, bridging can help them complete the technical aspects of a synthesis-level activity, but bridging does not help much in generating a feeling of real creativity.*

- *For those who do not have the natural abilities required, hard work at these levels can be draining, difficult, and unrewarding, and may result in an inferior product.*

- *Continued expectations of students at higher levels of thinking in nondominant styles can cause poor performance, learning difficulties, and psychological problems.*

For example, think about Jessica, a strongly abstract sequential child required to make a diorama of a rain forest—a higher-level concrete sequential task. She not only has difficulty creating in the concrete but knows much more about the topic than she could possible portray in a shoebox. She feels the frustration of "having the answers, but no way to tell anyone."

In Jessica's situation, her teacher suggested an abstract sequential bridge, notecards attached to the back of the box that explained parts of the display. The bridge appeased Jessica's concerns and she finished the task. Jessica viewed her assignment as a job, which she completed. She certainly did not see it, or complete it, as a creative expression of her own mind.

Gifted individuals often becomes acutely aware of their natural mental powers at the analysis, synthesis, and evaluation levels. Many gifted students gather knowledge easily at lower levels in all styles, reaping "A" grades with ease. Educators usually define this group as the well-rounded learners. In fact, until these gifted children work through to the higher levels, we do not know whether their gifts shine through all channels or not.

Other gifted children excel at the lower levels in their dominant style but have greater difficulty in nondominant styles. We punish children in this situation with the "all-'A's" criterion for entrance into gifted programs. Often, we will not see the specialness of their abilities until they have opportunities to develop their gifts at high levels.

Furthermore, many "underachieving" gifted children "underachieve" because they are not allowed to learn and produce in their own style at higher levels. Instead, they find themselves required to work at low levels in mismatched styles, for which they seem to have few coping skills or tolerance.

Indeed, it does appear that many students can meet the style requirements of the material but may choose not to do so because the material provides no mental stimulation. In other cases, students can be given materials that match their learning style, but because the assignment requires low-level thinking, they have little motivation or willingness to do it.

All students, but especially gifted students, assume self-direction and self-organized learning within their own style more rapidly than they can in mismatch. We do well to provide them every opportunity to draw upon their own talents, even as they stretch to meet more difficult areas.

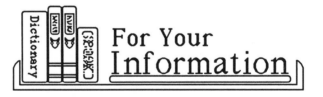

For Your
Information

**TO MATCH OR
NOT TO MATCH**

To match and mismatch requires an understanding of the student, a knowledge of style, and a recognition of levels of thinking. We see that matched learning experiences allow students to learn most efficiently, effectively, easily, and with greatest enjoyment. We see that guided mismatch through learning experiences helps students to gain and practice skills that they do not naturally use.

As we discussed earlier, at the knowledge/comprehension level, students gain from the experience of both matched and guided mismatched conditions. At the application and analysis levels, students need careful guidance and significant bridging. But at the synthesis and evaluation levels students need matched style conditions and opportunity to use their dominant, natural styles. Only under these conditions can students express their gifts and talents.

In working at the higher levels, students need to direct their own learning with guidance from teachers. At higher levels a student benefits most from a teacher who can match or flex into the student's style. At this level teachers and students with a style match think alike, share assumptions about the way they work, and have the best chance for creative success.

At the synthesis and evaluation level, a mismatch between student and teacher results, at best, in the student's pursuing independent projects without the benefit of guidance. If the teacher and student cannot identify with each other's thinking, the teacher may be tempted to let the student "do his/her own thing." For example, Anne liked to create her own experiments in science. Her teacher found theory more interesting than hands-on experiments. He encouraged Anne to try her experiments but could offer no guidance in helping her extend or refine her investigative thinking abilities. In fact, Anne surpassed her teacher's ability to design experiments because her teacher had minimal ability in this way. But with a natural problem-solving, experimental science teacher, Anne's fledgling talents could have been challenged rather than simply expressed. In this example, we see the results of a concrete random student mismatched in style at the mentoring level to an abstract sequential teacher.

At its worst, mismatch can result in students' inability to work in worthwhile ways with teachers. Several situations may arise from mismatch. For instance, a teacher may try to redefine a student's process or product as the teacher would like to see it. In this regard we might consider Dave, a divergent thinker and creative student. He wanted to write an original play. His teacher suggested that he research the style of playwrights instead. Again, the concrete random student feels the effects of mismatch at the synthesis level to an abstract sequential teacher.

In other situations students may become completely frustrated when they try to define or explain a process or product that does not reflect the teacher's vision. To illustrate: Joyce, a sensitive and interpretive student, wanted to start an interest group of students who write poetry as her project. However, Joyce's teacher could not understand that the process of intense group discussion stimulated imaginative thinking for students like Joyce and her teacher vetoed the project as not product-oriented. Here we see an abstract random creator mismatched to a concrete sequential creator.

Finally, students may even unknowingly accept a teacher's approach to a problem, abandoning their own. Peter planned to survey and graph a report on teenage accidents. His personalizing teacher reformulated it. She suggested he interview and write a news article about teenagers who had experienced an auto accident, an AR approach that Peter accepted even though he had no great interest in it. In this case, we see the concrete sequential creator mismatched to an abstract random creator.

Thus, at higher levels students achieve quality production when we match styles of teachers, students, and instruction. The match should not shape the student in the teacher's ways but allow like minds to open doors for each other.

Perhaps the poetic insight of Kahlil Gibran speaks most accurately to us about guiding others to the highest levels of human potential.

> Then said a teacher, Speak to us of
> Teaching.
> And he said:
> No man can reveal to you aught but that
> which already lies half asleep in the
> dawning of your knowledge.
> The teacher who walks in the shadow of
> the temple, among his followers, gives
> not of his wisdom but rather of his faith
> and his lovingness.
> If he is indeed wise he does not bid you
> enter the house of his wisdom, but rather
> leads you to the threshold of your own mind.
> The astronomer may speak to you of his
> understanding of space, but he cannot
> give you his understanding.
> The musician may sing to you of the
> rhythm which is in all space, but he
> cannot give you the ear which arrests
> the rhythm nor the voice that echoes it.
> And he who is versed in the science of
> numbers can tell of the regions of weight
> and measure, but he cannot conduct you thither.
> For the vision of one man lends not its
> wings to another man.
> And even as each one of you stands
> alone in God's knowledge, so must each
> one of you be alone in his knowledge of
> God and in his understanding of the
> earth. (21)

I believe that teachers must match a student's style to a significant degree to mentor and guide that learner. If we expect students to learn how to produce at higher levels, then schools must provide opportunities for teachers to develop their own natural style channels to the highest levels, and to become the mentors that students need at these levels.

Many educators criticize students' unwillingness to operate at higher levels of thinking. Perhaps they have not exposed their students to the higher levels, as Bloom suggested, or perhaps they have not opened the doors within the students' own styles. Possibly students cannot operate at, choose to ignore, see no significance in, or do not understand higher levels of operation in other than their own styles. Maybe teachers would see higher levels of operation and more quality from students if we challenged and developed students' natural abilities and capacities.

CHAPTER 11

STYLE DIFFERENTIATED INSTRUCTION: EXAMINING INSTRUCTIONAL OPTIONS WITHIN STYLES

...The forces of the Third Wave...fight for less standardization more individualization in the schools.

—Alvin Toffler

MEDIATION MESSAGES

In 1964 Marshall McLuhan's pronouncement "the medium is the message" caused many to consider the influence of technology on the development of the twentieth century. The electronic age, according to McLuhan, would shape our world just as the means by which people communicated throughout history determined the direction of thought, action, and life itself. McLuhan suggested that the media we choose to use are extensions of our minds. He said,

> *Every culture and every age has its favorite model of perception and knowledge that it is inclined to prescribe for everybody and everything. (22)*

What do McLuhan's comments have to do with style? Gregorc states, "'The medium is the message' and the massage." In effect the media we use—our instructional technologies—not only provide information to us in a certain way but also call upon us to use certain styles of thinking with them.

Each and every instructional tool or strategy that we use with our students can be analyzed for similar "messages" and "massages." Instructional technology biases the way we present information, and itdemands, to varying degrees, that we use certain styles of thinking. The learner, however, may or may not respond in the way the instructional material requires! The ultimate decision, as well as its consequences, rests with the individual.

In the previous chapter we discussed levels of thinking within styles and ways of learning from a style perspective. In this chapter we will finally move beyond research and theory to offer specific instructional guidelines. We will consider several aspects of style as it applies to instruction, including

> • *the style bias of the content*
>
> • *the style bias of the processes we use*
>
> • *the concern for levels of thinking*
>
> • *the style attraction of language*

THE STYLE BIAS OF CONTENT

Instructional content has style. Content such as colonial architecture lends itself to the concrete sequential style, but the lyrics of a social protest song attract the abstract random mind. The political history of an era naturally appeals in an abstract sequential way, yet a study of the future entices concrete random thinking. A rose may be a rose by any other name, but a history course, or any other course, clearly can take on a style by the style-focus of the content.

Do certain subjects have given styles? Yes and no. Remember, the mind of the teacher will impact the style of the content. Does math have a concrete sequential content? Often, yes. Will a random teacher work with this math content differently in tone, attitude, or technique than a concrete random teacher? Usually. Can students take the same course from two teachers, cover the same content, learn the same content, but have an altogether different experience? Witness style!

Think about the style focus of your content. A book about how trains work provides a different fourth grade reading experience than one called *Tales of a Fourth Grade Nothing*. Does the content style of a book attract children to read it or not? The answer is obvious.

THE STYLE BIAS OF PROCESS

Instructional processes—techniques, activities, and strategies—require us to process information in certain ways. For example, a classification chart and role play require very different types of thinking processes and different styles of thinking. If I ask students to complete a Venn diagram, I require their thinking to have a concrete sequential focus. If I ask students to do a research report, I require abstract sequential thinking. In effect, I can set expectations that require students to process their thinking in a certain style.

Style-Solid Activities

We call activities that demand one style of thinking, **style-solid.** The student must adapt to the style of the activity. For example, "Gather statistical data to produce a flowchart of information" requires concrete sequential thinking.

Style-Fluid Activities

We call activities that take on a style as a result of the student's style **style-fluid.** For example, the assignment "Write an essay about the Statue of Liberty" leaves room for the learner to use fact and detail, personalization, research, or divergent thinking—any style. The student's style will shape the results.

If your activities have style fluidity, you must recognize the different ways that each style can complete the assignment. But when you require students to complete a style-solid assignment, you will need to bridge to some learners whose difficulty in style mismatch precludes accomplishment.

LEVELS OF THINKING   Each of the styles clearly has instructional preferences, and as we saw in the previous chapter, each style shows lower levels of thinking to higher levels of thinking. For the sake of instructional planning, I have integrated learning style preferences with Bloom's Taxonomy and created three levels of thinking.

LEVEL I

- Emphasize knowledge and comprehension: the gathering and gaining of information.

- Use a variety of techniques from each style throughout teaching.

- Focus on students' ability to

  ~ process in their own styles;

  ~ respect the styles of others;

  ~ improve communication with other styles;

  ~ increase their ability to access content in a variety of ways.

LEVEL II

- Emphasize application and analysis: the engagement of the learner with the information.

- Use a variety of thinking processes from each style and carefully teach the thinking style process we require as well as the content.

- Focus on students' ability to

  ~ enhance critical thinking abilities in their own styles;

  ~ learn critical thinking skills in other styles;

  ~ appreciate the strengths of self and others in different ways.

LEVEL III

- Emphasize synthesis and evaluation: the dynamic thinking of the learner in his/her own way.

- Offer a choice of assignments from each style.

- Focus on students' ability to

  ~ create an authentic product reflecting quality and originality;

  ~ develop their own strengths to higher levels;

  ~ learn to respect others and their gifts.

When I devised levels of thinking, I did not intend to negate that application and analysis require two different processes. Rather, I suggest that both processes engage the learner actively with the content. I do not disregard that synthesis and evaluation are distinct. Rather, each requires an intrinsic response, an original interpretion.

When we teach critical thinking to students, we must distinguish among styles of thinking. Let us take care to develop many modes of thinking critically so that we include the natural bent of a learner's mind, not attempt to bend all minds to think in one style.

When we encourage creative and dynamic thinking, students should use the gifts of their own minds. We violate the very nature of creative and evaluative thinking when we require all students to "create" the same thing! It boggles my mind to hear a teacher tell all students to "create" an American Indian dwelling, explaining that they can create whatever they want—a teepee, a sugar-cube igloo, a hut!

When we mistake assignments like this for creative opportunities, we do not open the door to creativity but force conformity in style. When we add a style perspective to this assignment, we see the need for some children to have a hands-on, structured opportunity, like the dwelling. But we also realize that some children need to write stories and enact them, others need to do research and provide expertise on the subject, some need to investigate problems and offer new solutions. Creativity must be intrinsic. It flows only from an inner source, even when the request to create comes from without.

LINGUISTICS AND STYLE

We can address learners' styles by instructional content, the instructional process, and the level of thinking. We can also attract and repel learners by the choice of words we use to develop our activities. Our word choice should reflect an **intention** to ask students to process thinking in a style and level of thinking, or to engage with content in a certain style and level of thinking. For example, if I ask students "to *list* the *facts* about," I intend to encourage the process of CS thinking (list) with the content of CS thinking (facts) at Level I. If I ask students "to *forecast* the *many different* results," I intend to encourage a CR thinking process (forecast) and content (many different) at Level II.

> **Words attract us by their style.**
>
> **Which words appeal more to you?**
>
> **Categorize?   Forecast?**
>
> **Interpret?   Imagine?**

INSTRUCTIONAL PREFERENCES

Each style has preferred ways to learn. In Gregorc's original research he identified preferences for each style by screening 100 people with dominant scores in each style. He labeled learning style preferences for a style when 75 of 100 people chose an activity as a preference. (23) I have added to this list, and refined it, to show levels of thinking within preferences.

IN SUMMARY

In developing SDI, I looked for many ways in which style preferences impact on teachers, students, content, and activity. In the following section, you will assess each style as it relates to

- *The style's perspective*

- *The characteristics of content in that style*

- *The focus of objectives in that style*

- *The role of the teacher working from that style perspective*

- *Learning preferences from lower to higher levels of thinking for that style*

- *The linguistic implications for writing activities and questions with that style perspective*

- *Metacognitive notes for encouraging students to "think" within that style*

- *Evaluation preferences for students with that style*

- *Examples of activities that demand that style's thinking*

Instructional Applications:
The Concrete Sequential Style

THE CONCRETE SEQUENTIAL INSTRUCTIONAL PERSPECTIVE

FACTUAL   PRACTICAL

STRUCTURED   DETAILED

REALISTIC   HANDS-ON

THE CS FOCUS ON CONTENT

- A definite structure and pattern

- Details and facts

- Practical concerns

- Exact directions

- Realistic problems

THE CS FOCUS ON OBJECTIVES

The focus: skills, information, products

- To learn specific objectives

- To follow sequential directions

- To demonstrate specific skills

- To work with content in an organized way

- To create a practical, structured product

THE CONCRETE SEQUENTIAL ROLE OF THE TEACHER

When students work in a CS way, the teacher must

- organize the procedures

- present information

- establish clear directions

- give guided practice

- develop real and specific activities

- provide immediate feedback

CS INSTRUCTIONAL PREFERENCES

- Checklists
- Worksheets
- Outlines
- Charts
- Hands-on work
- Maps
- Computer programs
- Demonstrations
- Field trips
- Skills
- Memory games
- Information search
- Drill and practice

•• How-to projects
•• Practical problems
•• Learning packets
•• Directed activity
•• Diagramming
•• Flowcharting
•• Doing timelines
•• Hands-on activity
•• Venn diagrams
•• Attribute listing
•• Classification
•• Realistic writing

••• Making original, structured products
~ diorama
~ model
~ timeline
~ replica
~ demonstration
~ map
~ graph
~ diagram

CS LINGUISTIC PREFERENCES

- Describe
- Review
- Observe
- List
- Define
- Sort
- Group
- Name

•• Match
•• Collect
•• Measure
•• Organize
•• Plan
•• Graph
•• Classify
•• Diagram

••• Develop
••• Demonstrate
••• Prepare
••• Report
••• Devise
••• Construct
••• Build
••• Rate

CS METACOGNITIVE NOTES

When you assign tasks and activities that require CS thinking, prompt students' thinking to meet the style demands with suggestions that show them how to

- be specific and factual

- be organized and detailed

- use a task-oriented focus

- look to completion of a finished product

CS EVALUATION PREFERENCES

CS learners prefer to be evaluated in precise and efficient ways, such as with objective tests that have clear, correct answers.

They think in evaluative ways that are precise and structured, such as with rating scales.

The Concrete Sequential Mind

"I work best with clear time limits."

" I value order and structure in my work."

" I like to create real products in hands-on ways."

EXAMPLES OF CONCRETE SEQUENTIAL ACTIVITIES

The following activities demand concrete sequential thinking. They are ordered from lower to higher levels.

"Chart the effects of different insecticides on the life-cycle stages of the gypsy moth."

"Keep the class records for an experiment. Everyone will depend on the data in your records."

"Make and display a series of opinion polls illustrating student reaction to certain questions or topics."

"Build a step-by-step display showing the 'before,' 'now,' and 'after' of a solved problem."

"Visit a museum to find out what kind of information about gemstones can be learned there."

"Visit an ethnic restaurant. Take notes on the customs and culture represented there. Provide the class with a display that illustrates your conclusions."

"Trace the stages of a building project in your city."

"Work as an apprentice to a graphic designer. Use your knowledge to improve the school newspaper."

"Using colored transparencies, make a layered transparency to demonstrate the components of a volcano. Build the volcano according to your model."

"Survey your neighborhood to find out if...."

"Choose a political candidate. Compile a data book of statistics and information about the candidate."

"Select three jobs. Collect and organize facts about the qualifications necessary to hold each job."

"Make a diorama showing the meaning of the word billingsgate."

"Shadow a museum guide for a day. What did you learn?"

Instructional Applications:
The Abstract Sequential Style

THE ABSTRACT SEQUENTIAL INSTRUCTIONAL PERSPECTIVE

READING	REFERENCED
LOGICAL	ANALYZING
IDEA-ORIENTED	DEBATING

THE AS FOCUS ON CONTENT

- Structure
- Ideas and logic
- Intellectual approach
- Referenced
- Theory

THE AS FOCUS ON OBJECTIVES

The focus: in-depth content, information, and analysis of ideas

- to learn through lecture and reading
- to consider concepts and ideas
- to consider intellectual issues
- to research and create hypotheses

THE ABSTRACT SEQUENTIAL ROLE OF THE TEACHER

When students work in an abstract sequential way, the teacher must

- organize issues
- provide topical outlines
- present lectures
- develop analytical questions
- provide reading and research
- value theory

AS INSTRUCTIONAL PREFERENCES

- Lecture
- Text
- Notetaking
- Outlining
- Library work
- Documenting
- Lengthy reading
- Instructional media
- Audio tapes

- •• Writing reports
- •• Doing research and referencing
- •• Doing bibliographies
- •• Supplemental reading
- •• Individualized study
- •• Timeline essays
- •• Logic puzzles
- •• Term papers
- •• Content mastery

- ••• Conceptualizing and producing original ideas based on research
  - ~ Debate
  - ~ Theory
  - ~ Policy statement
  - ~ Formula
  - ~ Research paper
  - ~ Book
  - ~ Lecture
  - ~ Critique
  - ~ Argument

AS LINGUISTIC PREFERENCES

- Read
- Report
- Take notes
- Outline

- •• Explain
- •• Research
- •• Summarize
- •• Exemplify
- •• Infer
- •• Discriminate

- ••• Formulate
- ••• Speculate
- ••• Hypothesize
- ••• Debate
- ••• Verify
- ••• Critique
- ••• Argue
- ••• Judge

AS METACOGNITIVE NOTES

When you assign students tasks and activities that require abstract sequential thinking, prompt their thinking to meet the style demands with suggestions to

- check with expert sources

- organize researched information

- question ideas

- develop an understanding of issues

AS EVALUATION PREFERENCES

AS learners prefer to be evaluated as a result of writing analytical essays, doing take-home exams, and providing reports.

They themselves think in evaluative ways that offer critiques and judgments.

The Abstract Sequential Mind

"I like to gather much information."

"I value analysis in my work."

"I like to weigh and create new ideas."

EXAMPLES OF ABSTRACT SEQUENTIAL ACTIVITIES

The following activities demand abstract sequential thinking. They are ordered from lower to higher levels.

"Give an oral report on the use of robots in the auto industry."

"Write a report on the development of robotics."

"Attend the lecture 'Archeological Findings.'"

"Outline the main ideas in this chapter."

"Describe the history and growth of the country/western music industry."

"Identify the issues that led to the American Civil War."

"Research the background of Eleanor Roosevelt to explain her role in New Deal politics."

"Write a term paper on the economy of Japan."

"Debate the issue 'Computers are a more important invention than the car.'"

"Read four books by one author. Analyze the author's style."

"Discuss the following quotation, 'People learn differently.'"

"Explain the theory of limited nuclear war."

"Devise a theory to explain why people are nationalistic."

"Determine the criteria for judging the writing contest."

"Evaluate the usefulness of your criteria for judging the writing contest."

Instructional Applications:
The Abstract Random Style

THE ABSTRACT RANDOM INSTRUCTIONAL PERSPECTIVE

PERSONAL	RELATING
FLEXIBLE	FEELING
INTERPRETIVE	IMAGINATIVE

THE AR FOCUS ON CONTENT

• Personal understanding

• Interpretation

• Flexibility

• Appreciation for feelings

• Use of imagination

THE AR FOCUS ON OBJECTIVES

The focus: awareness, appreciation, and affective conclusions

• To use imagination, artistic sense, or emotions to gain data and interpret ideas

• To interpret in a personalized manner

• To work cooperatively with others

• To create an interpretive product

THE ABSTRACT RANDOM ROLE OF THE TEACHER

When students work in an abstract random way, the teacher

• shares personal experiences

• acts as a discussion facilitator

• provides a climate for personalized learning

• values individual interpretation

• maintains order within flexibility for groupwork and discussion

AR INSTRUCTIONAL PREFERENCES

- Mapping, clustering
- Groupwork
- Visual thinking
- Cartoons
- Mnemonics
- Music
- Poetry
- Humor
- Short reading or lecture with discussion
- Media
- Personalized examples

•• Group discussion and cooperative learning
•• Guided imagery
•• Role play, drama
•• Interviewing
•• Using metaphor
•• Relational thinking
•• Values clarification
•• Keeping journals
•• Interpretive writing or drawing

•••Composing original, interpretive products
~ Interview
~ Poetry
~ Visual arts
~ Performing arts
~ Creative writing
~ Songwriting
~ Peer counseling
~ Social leadership
~ Aesthetic products

AR LINGUISTIC PREFERENCES

- Remember
- Suppose
- Share
- Choose
- Tell
- Web

•• Relate
•• Express
•• Discuss
•• Imagine
•• Pretend
•• Suggest
•• Interpret

••• Illustrate
••• Compose
••• Perform
••• Translate
••• Perceive
••• Counsel
••• Write

AR METACOGNITIVE NOTES

When you assign students tasks and activities that require abstract random thinking, prompt their thinking to meet the style demands with suggestions to

- use group problem solving
- show personalized understanding
- value opinions and actions of others
- encourage communication
- consider values
- develop imagination

AR EVALUATION PREFERENCES

AR learners prefer to show their knowledge through short essay, interpretive writing, an interpretive product or oral explanation.

They themselves think in evaluative ways that show appreciation and concern for value.

The Abstract Random Mind

"I work best in shared learning times with others."

"Let me give you my interpretation."

"I create from my personal understandings."

EXAMPLES OF ABSTRACT RANDOM ACTIVITIES

The following activities demand abstract random thinking. They are ordered from lower to higher levels.

"Working in groups of four, discuss and answer the questions at the end of the chapter."

"After watching the film SAND PEBBLES, what was your reaction to the Chinese people?"

"Invite a scientist to class to discuss why he/she chose the field of science and how he/she feels about being a scientist."

"Copy the words to your favorite song. Find all adjectives. Replace each one with an adjective of similar meaning."

"In what ways does this poem illustrate the problem of communication between people?"

"Keep a daily class journal, recording your thoughts about...."

"Follow this guided imagery. Discuss your visualizations."

"Write a short story about your hike from the viewpoint of your hiking boots."

"Role play a discussion between parents and child about...."

"Illustrate one aspect of the presidential campaign, using an artistic form: editorial cartoon, poster, sketch...."

"Interpret the meaning of this poem, short story, photograph, painting...."

"Interview people from different generations to find out their feelings about computers."

"Rewrite this event story from the viewpoint of an eyewitness."

"Write an original song, poem, story, or speech to illustrate the main character's feelings in this movie."

"Evaluate the impact of your original composition on others."

Instructional Applications:
The Concrete Random Style

THE CONCRETE RANDOM INSTRUCTIONAL PERSPECTIVE

DIVERGENT   OPEN-ENDED

INVESTIGATIVE   PROBLEM-SOLVING

EXPERIENTIAL   INVENTIVE

THE CR FOCUS ON CONTENT

- Respect diversity

- Allow open-ended questions

- Encourage exploration and investigation

- Generate problems

THE CR FOCUS ON OBJECTIVES

The focus: divergent thinking, problem solving, considering ideas in new ways

- To use open-ended strategies for gathering information

- To use divergent thinking to analyze ideas

- To experiment with possibilities or options

- To create new and original products

THE CONCRETE RANDOM ROLE OF THE TEACHER

When students work in concrete random ways, the teacher must

- ask open-ended questions

- brainstorm

- withhold judgment

- encourage diversity

- provide opportunity for novel answers

CR INSTRUCTIONAL PREFERENCES

- Brainstorming
- Divergent thinking
- Gathering possibilities
- Hands-on experiences
- Open-ended activities
- Webbing, mapping
- Mini-lecture
- Optional reading

•• Simulation
•• Games
•• Experiments
•• Computer games
•• Forecasting
•• Finding alternatives
•• Problem-solving
•• Investigations
•• Divergent thinking
•• Case study
•• Independent study
•• Analogies

••• Creating original, unusual products as a result of experimentation and divergent thinking
  ~ Invention
  ~ Play
  ~ Video production
  ~ New solution
  ~ Innovation
  ~ Simulation
  ~ Game

CR LINGUISTIC PREFERENCES

- Brainstorm
- Web
- Explore
- What about

•• Reorganize
•• Forecast
•• Connect
•• Investigate
•• Illustrate
•• Solve
•• Find out

••• Design
••• Invent
••• Direct
••• Create
••• Editorialize
••• Recommend
••• Experiment

CR METACOGNITIVE NOTES

When you assign students tasks and activities that require concrete random thinking, prompt their thinking to meet the style demands with suggestions to

- look for many, varied, and unusual answers

- reorganize what is, in order to see what could be

- value trial and error

- investigate the unknown

CR EVALUATION PREFERENCES

CR learners prefer evaluation procedures that validate their knowledge through open-ended questions, writing assignments, problem solving, or producing a product.

They themselves think in evaluative ways by offering alternative recommendations and "editorial" positions.

The Concrete Random Mind

"I am interested in many possibilities."

"I like to investigate and discover."

"I create in the real world in my own way."

EXAMPLES OF CONCRETE RANDOM ACTIVITIES

The following activities demand concrete random thinking. They are ordered from lower to higher levels.

"Brainstorm all the ways you can think of to use music."

"Complete the following analogy: The blood stream is like a city because...."

"Play the economic game "Market to Market."

"Using the following case study, write a school policy for vandalism."

"Find as many alternative ways as possible to test for properties of flour and sugar."

"Choose from among the list of activities for homework."

"Run the simulation of leadership; conduct a feedback session on what you learned about leader behavior."

"Follow this guided investigation; record your findings; propose how to make the investigation better."

"If there were no fish remaining in a lake, what alternatives would you take to find the cause?"

"How many different ways can you design a city skyline?"

"What would happen if water and oil mixed?"

"Create a new way to arrange and design our classroom."

"Combine and recombine the attributes of a product to create a new product."

"Evaluate the need, feasibility, and use of your product."

"Take any of the above assignments and change them around to suit your way of doing things."

Research has shown that each learning style has specific learning preferences. That is, most people prefer to approach learning in the way their minds naturally function. This does not mean that individuals choose to learn only and always in one style. It means that most people learn with greatest ease, efficiency, effectiveness, and enjoyment in their preferred style with topics or problems that allow them to use their natural abilities.

There are some individuals who avoid, resist, or cannot function with any learning that is out of their style. Others are more amenable to developing a nondominant style channel or to using it to achieve a specific end. Still others have an easy time of using a nondominant channel, although it may not be a preferred channel.

For example, a naturally abstract random person faced with the task of wallpapering a room may avoid the job for months, argue with his/her spouse every time the project is mentioned, enlist a concrete sequential to help, or simply adopt concrete sequential behaviors to do the work.

Likewise, when abstract random students confront demands to produce a sequential science project, they may avoid it until the last minute; resist it by claiming, "I'm stupid in science"; put together a project, possibly with the help of others; or find out the requirements, directions, or procedures in order to complete the project as sequentially as possible. However, it does not take long for the AR student to "give up" sequential attempts if we always compare the random's work to the work of natural sequentials.

Style Demands

Every instructional strategy and activity has inherent style demands. When students encounter style demands outside their natural abilities, they could respond in one of several ways:

- *First, they could understand the demands of the activity and meet those demands.*

- *Second, they could use their own style, and inadvertently alter the demands of the activity.*

- *Third, they could miss or ignore the style demands of the lesson, use their own styles, work with the material incorrectly, and wonder why they failed.*

We have seen that all activities have a learning demand, but some activities are tighter in their demands than others. That is, some are style-solid, some style-fluid. Too often students do not learn because they do not understand how to meet the style requirements of the material, and do not realize that style mismatch is the problem. They may fault themselves, blame the teacher, develop a low self-concept, or become discipline problems in order to avoid the material and their own inability to handle it.

Instructional planning requires thoughtful and intentional planning. Using a perspective that includes style and level of thinking can only enhance the quality of our work and let us come closer to meeting the real needs of our learners.

MODALITY

Many people question the relationship of learning style to modality preferences. Learning style and modality are two different issues. Modality concerns one's preference for learning through visual, auditory, or kinesthetic means. Interviews with people who have a dominant learning style revealed that individuals in each style also have one or more modality preferences.

The interviews also revelealed that in regard to choice among learning activities, individuals would often reject a modality preference because it was strongly mismatched to their personal style. For example, a strong kinesthetic, abstract random learner preferred not to choose a concrete sequential project even though it met her modality preference. And, vice versa, some people said they might not choose a style preference because the modality was wrong for them. In one case, a strong concrete sequential teacher explained that she would not choose the concrete sequential activities developed by others because they were not kinesthetic, or hands-on. This teacher preferred to take his chances with another style in which he could use a kinesthetic approach.

On the following page, I have summarized the key findings that connect modality and learning style. As practitioners in the classroom, we must be aware and ready to adjust activities for modality when students need these changes. However, it is often quite simple to offer a choice of modality by allowing a choice of oral or written form, or a similar simple accommodation.

Check yourself after you have written your activities for style. Do they all require a one-modality preference? Or do you not address a certain modality at all? Could you make adjustments for modality without compromising the nature of the activity? If you require a strong modality preference for one style's activity, could you offer another choice in that style in addition?

If you find a student with a strong style who usually does not choose an activity in his/her style, check the modality requirements of the activity. And, as with style choices, talk with students about their modality preferences. Empower them to understand the nature of their own strengths and limitations.

Learning Style and Modality

	Visual *The visual learner needs to see, observe, record, and write.*	Auditory *The auditory learner needs to talk and to listen.*	Kinesthetic *The tactile-kinesthetic learner needs to do, touch, be physically involved.*
CS	See information • Diagram • Chart • List	Listen and respond to information	Needs structured, hands-on activity, such as building a replica of the Statue of Liberty, or using a salting process to feel the corrosion of metals.
AR	See meaning • Through imagined visualization • Interpretive illustration	Dialogue and discuss	Needs to be involved with "doing" activities, such as acting out an event in the dedication ceremony of the Statue of Liberty.
AS	See content • Reading • Through written description	Hear lecture and debate	Needs to touch what is being considered, such as holding and examining a model statue, visiting the Statue of Liberty, or analyzing and using the art of repousse.
CR	See possibilities • Through written brainstorming, such as webbing, mindmapping	Talk out ideas, interests, problems, possibilities	Needs to immerse in the trial and error of experimentation, such as building his/her own version of the Statue of Liberty.

CHAPTER 12

STYLE DIFFERENTIATED INSTRUCTION: PLANNING FOR LEVELS OF THINKING

Grow, move forward, with measured pace,
checking yourself all along the way. Observe
the situation closely and carefully, seeing all
facets, all possible sources of trouble.

—I Ching
The Book of Changes

When you plan a unit, a learning center, a test, or any series of activities for students, you begin with goals and objectives, and then develop teaching and learning activites for students. If you include style and levels of thinking in your planning, your unit will reflect diversity of thinking and a range of thinking levels. In this chapter, you will consider how to plan for style and levels of thinking in your instructional activities with students.

Remember the information on instructional preferences, levels of thinking, and linguistic implications developed in chapter 11? This information has been summarized in the ***SDI Strategy Chart for Levels of Thinking and Learning Styles***. The red ***SDI Strategy Chart*** can be found at the end of this book. The same information from the ***SDI Strategy Chart*** is shown in this chapter as I illustrate instructional examples.

AN ILLUSTRATION   Written by Ms. Bobby Prewitt, Hawley Elementary School, Newtown, CT

Unit: The Great Barrier Reef

This unit integrates science and social studies at the upper elementary level. The examples chosen represent only a few from the entire unit.

The key objectives of the Great Barrier Reef Unit: students will be able to
- demonstrate knowledge of the Great Barrier Reef's environment (CS)
- show appreciation for the aesthetic quality of the Great Barrier Reef (AR)
- have understanding of issues affecting the Great Barrier Reef (AS)
- explore the many and varied interests, and problems of the Great Barrier Reef (CR).

LEVEL I:
BASIC THINKING

When students work at Level I thinking, they learn basic processing skills and basic communication skills in each style. As students learn the basic skills of each style, they (1) learn how to gather information from many sources, (2) learn how to share information with thinkers whose styles are other than their own, and (3) have the opportunity to communicate their ideas in many ways.

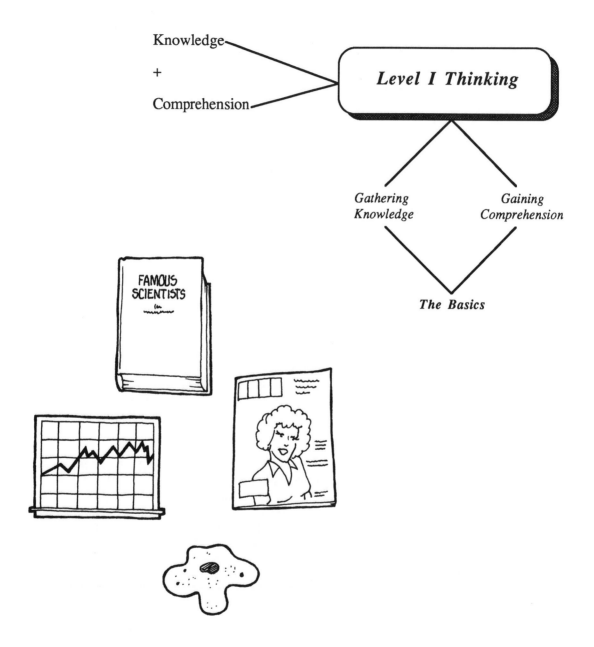

Knowledge

+

Comprehension

Level I Thinking

Gathering Knowledge

Gaining Comprehension

The Basics

Instructional activities that cause students to work at Level I are found in the *SDI Strategy Chart* and are summarized below with examples from a unit on the Great Barrier Reef.

Characteristics of Activities	Level I Basic Thinking	Examples from *The Great Barrier Reef Unit*
Concrete Sequential Factual Structured Realistic Practical Detailed Hands-on	**Describe Review Observe Restate** **Sort Group Name List** Checklists Summaries Patterns Worksheets Outlines Skills Charts Field trips Maps Computers SQ3R Examples Hands-on examples Demonstrations Using physical senses Practical reading	• *On a large chart, show the variety of marine life found in the Great Barrier Reef.*
Abstract Random Personal Relating Interpretive Flexible Feeling Imaginative	**Remember Suppose Tell** **Choose Share Web** Humor Poetry Webbing Music Groups Cartoons Feelings Flexible timelines Mnemonic devices Journal writing Visual thinking Short reading or lecture with discussion	• *Suppose you were a travel agent. Share highlights of the Great Barrier Reef in a collage with a brief taped or oral commentary.*
Abstract Sequential Reading Referencing Idea-oriented Logical Analyzing Debating	**Read Take notes Outline** **Report** Lectures Textbooks Instructional media Notetaking and outlining Library work Reading assignments	• *Write a two-page report on the ecosystem found in the Great Barrier Reef.*
Concrete Random Divergent Open-ended Investigative Problem-solving Experiential Inventive	**Brainstorm Web (Map, Cluster)** **Explore** Exploration Optional reading Options Mini-lectures Mapping Brainstorming Gathering possibilities Hands-on experiences Open-ended activities	• *Make a webbed map of the many, varied, and unusual characteristics used to describe the Great Barrier Reef.*

LEVEL II:
ENGAGED THINKING

When students work at Level II, they engage with their content. They apply information to a new context, or they analyze information to understand its components. But, they engage their minds with given content.

Most often, Level II thinking requires critical thinking. But Level II thinking advances critical thinking *abilities*—ways to engage for application and understanding. Learning to think critically from different style points of view provides students with a vast repertoire of options. But, remember, successful learning at Level II often requires that you bridge to students who are mismatched in style to the activity.

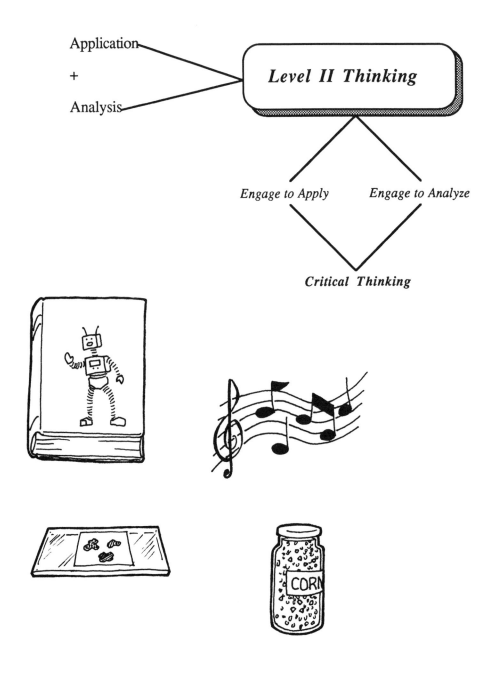

Application
+
Analysis

Level II Thinking

Engage to Apply   *Engage to Analyze*

Critical Thinking

Instructional activities that cause students to work at Level II are found in the *SDI Strategy Chart* and are summarized below with examples from a unit on the Great Barrier Reef.

Characteristics of Activities	Level II Engaged Thinking	*Examples from The Great Barrier Reef Unit*
Concrete Sequential Factual Structured Realistic Practical Detailed Hands-on	**Match Collect Measure Organize Plan** **Graph Classify Diagram Categorize** Labs with manuals How-to projects How-to discussions Diagramming Making models Doing timelines Direct learning Practical problem-solving Flowcharting Contract learning Doing computer applications	•• *Make a Venn diagram to show the overlapping and individual interests of six interest groups concerned with the Great Barrier Reef.*
Abstract Random Personal Relating Interpretive Flexible Feeling Imaginative	**Relate Express Wonder Discuss** **Imagine Pretend Suggest Interpret** Group discussion Cooperative learning Guided imagery Personalized examples Media Associative thinking Drama, role play Interviewing Cartooning Illustrating Using metaphor Value clarification Using imagination Doing interpretation	•• *Interpret the interests of the Great Barrier Reef though the eyes of a marine biologist, an artist, a skindiver, and a conchologist. Use oral or written form.*
Abstract Sequential Reading Referencing Idea-oriented Logical Analyzing Debating	**Explain Research Summarize** **Exemplify Discriminate Infer** General essay Report Summary Timeline essay Logic puzzle Referencing Term papers Idea sketches Reading Developing bibliographies Conceptual questioning Documenting	•• *Prepare and present a lecture entitled "Dangers of the Deep" for a skin-diving team undertaking a study of the Great Barrier Reef.*
Concrete Random Divergent Open-ended Investigative Problem-solving Experiential Inventive	**Illustrate Reorganize Generalize** **Forecast Connect Investigate** Simulations Experimentation Games Making analogies Computer games Forecasting Case studies Finding alternatives Independent study Problem-solving Investigations Divergent thinking	•• *Make a visual display illustrating what routes and means of transportation you would take to see significant parts of the Great Barrier Reef.*

Level III :
Dynamic Thinking

When students work at Level III, they create their own products in their own style and provide independent evaluation from their own style perspective. They think dynamically, which Webster's dictionary defines as energy or power in motion. Level III thinking promotes creativity or synthesis, and the highest level of critical thinking, evaluation.

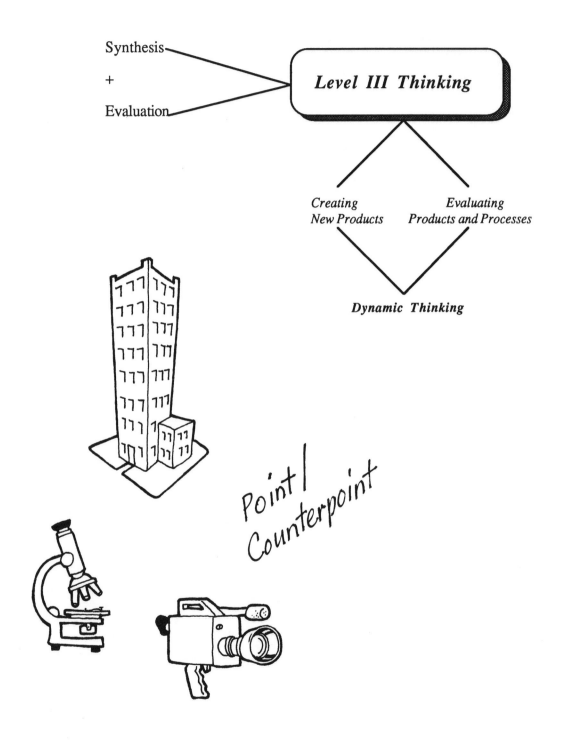

Synthesis

+

Evaluation

Level III Thinking

*Creating
New Products*

*Evaluating
Products and Processes*

Dynamic Thinking

Point / Counterpoint

Instructional activities that cause students to work at Level III are found in the *SDI Strategy Chart* and are summarized below with examples from a unit on the Great Barrier Reef.

	Characteristics of Activities	Level III — Dynamic Thinking	Examples from The Great Barrier Reef Unit
Concrete Sequential	Factual Structured Realistic Practical Detailed Hands-on	**Develop Demonstrate Prepare Report** **Devise Construct Build Rate** Original, structured or physical products Detailed, structured evaluations Action problems Work study Products such as diorama, flowchart, map, model, timeline, diagram, demonstration, graph, craft, tool, mobile, computer program, exhibit	••• *Study the species of shark in the GBR. Develop a questionnaire to determine people's perceptions of the shark. Compare your facts with perceptions. Report your findings in a brochure that corrects misperceptions. Evaluate your efforts.*
Abstract Random	Personal Relating Interpretive Flexible Feeling Imaginative	**Illustrate Compose Perceive Counsel** **Translate Perform Assess** Cooperative learning leadership Expressive or interpretive drawings Written expression Visual arts Performing arts Peer counseling Aesthetic products Emotional products Products such as art, writing, song, poem, journal, interview, essay, dramatic offering	••• *Imagine you are an old fisherman. You live near the waters of Australia. In presentation or written form, express your feelings about the Great Barrier Reef.*
Abstract Sequential	Reading Referencing Idea-oriented Logical Analyzing Debating	**Formulate Speculate Hypothesize** **Debate Critique Verify Judge** Original research Forming theories Conceptual problem solving Debating Conceptual analysis Policy line Products such as theory, report, formula, lecture, critique, thesis, persuasive argument	••• *Argue for or against the viewpoint that the Australian continental shelf should be used for oil exploration. Develop the campaign that your side would use to convince the Australian citizenry.*
Concrete Random	Divergent Open-ended Investigative Problem-solving Experiential Inventive	**Design Process Invent Direct** **Create Editorialize Recommend** Inventing Video productions Solutions Speech making Editorials Innovative products Products such as audio-visual products, simulations, games, inventions, editorials, directing, designing new methods	••• *Invent a board game in which three to five players search for buried treasure. During the game, the players are confronted or detained by the activities of the various interest groups concerned with the Great Barrier Reef.*

**THE SDI
STRATEGY CHART**

The **SDI Strategy Chart** provides an excellent resource for you to plan independent student activities. In the Appendix, you will find a working copy of the **SDI Strategy Chart**, called the **SDI Planning Chart**, for writing your own activities. In addition, you will see several examples of independent student activities written by classroom teachers. In addition to helping you plan independent student activities, the **SDI Planning Chart** also helps you as

* a planner to include critical thinking skills for all styles

* a planning approach for mini-units in which you require all students to participate in all styles at Levels I and II, but offer choices at Level III

* a planner for writing class discussion questions or homework questions

* a planner for developing learning centers

* a planning tool for special needs students so that student activities are matched to style

* an organizational chart for teacher-directed and student-directed activities

By using the **SDI Strategy Chart** and the **Planning Chart** you will be able to

* plan a variety of activities to ensure different levels of thinking

* plan activities within a given level of thinking to ensure equality of difficulty

* task analyze or to monitor the styles and levels used in a unit

APPLICATIONS

The **SDI Strategy Chart** does not intend for you to "teach to all twelve boxes!" In studying a novel, for example, you might concentrate on using Level II activities for style. In doing a science unit, you may find that you offer Level III activities in style for student projects and provide style-bridges rather than different styles in the rest of your unit. In doing an introductory French class, you may find that you concentrate on a style variety of Level I activities in the classroom and with homework assignments. During the course of a long assignment or an in-depth study of a topic, you may indeed wish to develop independent student activities for all levels and styles. In the next chapter, you will see how to work with one level of style thinking at a time.

INTENTIONS

A word about techniques...In the **SDI Strategy Chart** and the **Planning Chart,** I have abbreviated explanations of strategies into one-word summaries. When you consider the strategy, also consider how the student would use the strategy based on the level of thinking required. For example, at Level I in the CS style, students gather knowledge and gain information by *learning from* a classification chart. At Level II, in the CS style, students apply or analyze information so they *make* the classification chart. Likewise, at Level I in the AR style, students might learn information *from* a film, but at Level II they *produce* their own role play. Thus, keep the intention of the activity in mind as you plan.

CHAPTER 13

STYLE DIFFERENTIATED INSTRUCTION: TEACHING APPROACHES AND LESSON DESIGN

The natural tendency in problem-solving is to pick the first solution that comes to mind and run with it....A better strategy in solving problems is to select the most attractive path from many ideas, or concepts.

—James Adams

In the above quote from James Adams' book, *Conceptual Blockbusting*, we can hear him challenge our thinking about style. I hear him offer me the opportunity to solve the problem of meeting learning style needs in children from several possible approaches, rather than from one, good for all.

Style Differentiated Instruction attempts to avoid the one-right-way syndrome of organizing for style-based instruction in an attempt to provide many paths from which teachers may choose. The very notion of style difference defies one correct approach to teaching with style, and the actual reality of teaching prohibits one way for every one. We must consider that teachers with different styles need to choose from a variety of approaches that retain the integrity of their own teaching style yet help them expand their repertoire of teaching techniques with style. We realize that different content areas have style-biased objectives and performance demands that will not disappear even as we work for reform in these areas. We recognize that many concerns impact on a student's learning ability in addition to style. We acknowledge that change is a gradual process that layers itself invisibly toward a critical mass that eventually results in a real, not superficial, difference in instruction.

In the spirit of James Adams' words, SDI attempts to provide many ways to address style in the classroom. You need to select the "most attractive path" for your goals and objectives, teaching style, content, and students.

In this chapter, you will consider several ways to apply style practically in the classroom. First, we will look at three approaches that help you include style within your instruction: the Bridging Approach, the Choice Approach, and the Variation Approach. Each approach has its own function and results.

The Bridging Approach

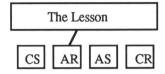

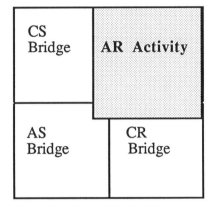

In this approach, all students do the activity together. The style demand is strongly in one style. The teacher offers bridging techniques to help students deal with the style and the content in a successful manner.

The Choice Approach

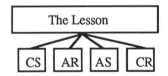

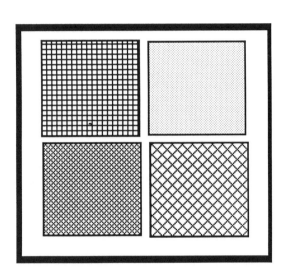

In the Choice Approach, the teacher offers a choice to students in each style. Students complete one activity.

The Variation Approach

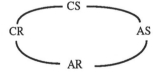

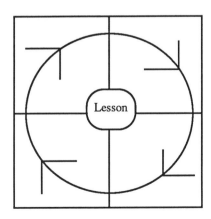

In the Variation Approach, the teacher rotates among the four styles. All students complete all the activities. There is no one correct style sequence.

THE BRIDGING APPROACH

In using the Bridging Approach, you will require all students to complete the same activity or develop the same knowledge, but you will provide assistance for the different styles of learners to achieve success with minimal frustration. In Part III: Student Styles, we explained bridging techniques for different learners, and in chapter 10, we explained informal and unplanned ways of bridging. Now you will take a closer look at these bridges in action—planned activity bridging. In order to bridge successfully, you will need to work from the viewpoint of each learning style.

The Bridging Approach

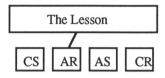

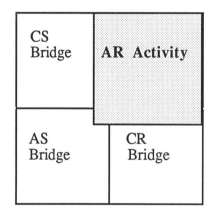

In this approach, all students do the activity together. The style demand is strongly in one style. The teacher offers bridging techniques to help students deal with the style and the content in a successful manner.

The Purpose

You will find frequent need for bridging to your students, especially when you need to teach a basic skill to all students (e.g., how to classify), when all students need to demonstrate their proficiency in a subject (e.g., on a spelling test), or to help students understand an activity that does not reach their style of thinking.

Procedure for Planning

When you plan an activity for students, decide how you will bridge.
- *Analyze the style of the activity.*
- *Consider which learners, if any, need a bridge.*
- *Think through the ways in which you will bridge to the whole class.*
- *Decide on the bridges you might need to use with some individuals.*
- *Form a clear way to explain the activity and the style demands of the activity to students.*

Procedure with Students

When you work with students, the following guidelines work well:
- *Introduce the topic and objective.*
- *Explain the stylistic expectations (e.g., this is an imaginative assignment).*
- *Show students how to work most efficiently with the assignment.*
- *Teach any skills needed to complete the work.*
- *Bridge to specific individuals as needed.*

Suppose I require all my sixth grade students to identify the parts and function of the parts of the microscope. A quick style-check tells me that the text's explanation about the parts and function of a microscope provide abstract sequential ways for students to learn the concrete sequential content. My class activities (a demonstration of the parts of a microscope and its use, and a worksheet assignment to label the parts of a microscope) provide concrete sequential ways for students to learn the concrete sequential content.

CS strategies in use: Demonstration Worksheet Hands-on use	How will I bridge to the AR? Visuals? Mnemonics? Groupwork? Writing? Personalization?
AS strategies in use: Text Lecture	How will I bridge to the CR? Open-ended activities? Divergent thinking? Computer game? Problem solving? Hands-on trials?

I decide to provide additional random processing techniques for all students by choosing intentionally to include visualization, personalization, and open-ended thinking. These techniques seem the most appropriate for my objectives, require no change of my objective, and do not penalize my students by deviating from the content.

I organize these activities on the following "bridging form" because it lends itself easily to the objective. In other circumstances, I would organize my activities differently. The activities used on this form were adapted from a science unit on the microscope written by teachers at the Westover School in Stamford, CT. (24)

Learning Bridges

Name_____

Date_____

Class_____

Key point or concept

To understand the parts and function of the microscope.

In your own words, write an explanation of how to use a microscope.

With a partner, sketch a microscope "person." Each part of the microscope should have a personal quality. For example, the eye equals the lens.

Label the parts of the microscope on the worksheet provided.

Identify the functions of each part on a separate sheet of paper and attach to this page with your worksheet.

Write creative synonyms for the parts of a microscope. E.g., the base equals a foundation.

Extra Credit   • Create a transformation of the microscope silhouette into another object.
Choose one   • Complete the word search for microscopical terms.
                 • Make a list of the many, varied, and unusual uses of a microscope.
                 • Write a paragraph in which you are the first microscope to witness the cure for cancer.
                   (You may create your own situation about the microscope to write about. See me.)

Procedure　　　　As you can see, all students faced the same objective task: to understand the parts and function of the microscope. In the bridging activities that I chose, I included paraphrasing so that I could be sure all students understood the text's meaning (AS). I included visualization, personalization, and work with a partner so that students could use and develop their imagination and learn by association (AR). I included the structured worksheet so that all students had exact information (CS). I included an open-ended activity so that all students could develop divergent thinking skills (CR). The last part of the bridging form, the extra credit, provides a choice of ways for students to continue interacting with the material. However, it is not necessary to use the extra credit portion when you bridge to an objective.

In working with bridging activities, check that you:

Explain the objectives of the assignment
- *To identify the parts of the microscope*
- *To determine the proper techniques for using it.*

Discuss the style demands of the objective and the need to bridge
- *Explain the concept of style: we learn in different ways; some ways are more comfortable and effective than others for different individuals; our topic has a style; we can use different methods to learn the topic.*

- *Ask students to describe the style of the topic. Expect to hear answers, such as "we must know facts and details about the microscope."*

- *Ask students to describe the ways we traditionally learn topics like this. They will probably reply: text, worksheets, quizzes, and tests.*

- *Note any bored, troubled, and confused looks in the class and suggest that we need to learn about the topic in many ways so that all students can understand, not just those who learn easily from texts and worksheets. Elicit suggestions with"How could we learn about the microscope?"*

Introduce and explain how we will bridge for this objective
- *Give students the bridging activities and explain how to complete them.*

Debrief through sharing groups
- *After students have completed their own sheets, ask them to review their work and assess their knowledge by comparing their forms with those of other in groups of three to five students. Establish the groups for a blend of styles. Avoid putting all sequential or all random children in the same group. Encourage students to add information to their own forms that they learn from others, but to do so in a different color pen from their own work.*

- *As a whole class, discuss the value of using many ways to learn, and the effectiveness of sharing work among students with different styles.*

Check students' achievement
- *Provide a variety of ways for students to show that they know the parts of the microscope and its use: quiz, taped explanation, demonstration.*

Help students think about their own thinking
- *Through class discussion, small groups, journal writing, or a letter to you, ask students to assess how they learned most effectively about the parts and use of the microscope, where they had difficulties, and how they might avoid those difficulties the next time they meet a similar situation.*

Advantages

There are several advantages in using the Bridging Approach:

- *You ensure that all students have a common skill or knowledge base.*

- *You can concentrate on one style of thinking.*

- *You help some students to stretch the style of thinking.*

- *You help some students to understand a nondominant style.*

Disadvantages

There are serious disadvantages to teaching without bridges:

- *Many students cannot learn well at Level I without bridges.*

- *Use of one style all the time, even if the students can perform in it, can lead to their frustration, stress, or boredom.*

- *Teachers who teach from one style do not develop other styles, and encourge one-dimensional thinking.*

OPPORTUNITIES

Opportunities to bridge occur all the time. You must use your teaching energies wisely, however, and bridge where it counts the most: in your interactions with students, and with the valuable learning activities that develop students' thinking. The example below illustrates effective use of activity bridging within a lesson—all students view a videotape but the key discussion questions address different styles.

Unit: "Non Verbal Language in Life and Literature," written by Patrick L. McKiernan, The Morgan School, Clinton, CT (25)

Lesson: 'Nonverbal Realms—Honeybees and Humans'

Objective: To compare the ways honeybees and human communciate

Approach: As part of a unit on nonverbal language, all students view a videotape about bees that the teacher created and produced himself. To draw in all the students to the video, he prepared this series of style differentiated questions for all students to answer.

- *List at least three ways honeybees communicate. (CS: factual)*

- *Explain the ways humans and honeybees communicate. (AS: logical)*

- *As a beekeeper, you developed a robot honeybee. How would you use it in the hive? Out in the fields where bees gather nectar and pollen? How would the robot bee communicate? (CR: divergent thinking)*

- *How do honeybees listen? Discuss how their "listening skills" help them to get along with one another. Consider the ways you use nonverbal behavior to improve your listening ability. (AR personalization)*

Bridging looks and sounds simple to do. It is not. Bridging requires your understanding of the viewpoint of each style and your willingness to invest time to develop or refine it. Rome was not built in a day, they say. Neither are bridges to students. Your caring time and persistence in learning how to plan bridges will, however, reap enormous rewards. Try style bridges, trust your intuition, check the authenticity of your bridges with individuals naturally dominant in a style, and give yourself time to grow in understanding.

When a teacher uses the Choice Approach, students choose the method, technique, activity, or assignment they prefer. Evaluation may differ for each activity. The Choice Approach can be used at Levels I, II, or III. If you can provide only a limited amount of choice for students, plan to use the Choice Approach at Level III. The Choice Approach is the easiest approach for most teachers because it requires the fewest changes in the teacher's operating style. The Choice Approach places the style issue in the hands of the learner.

The Choice Approach

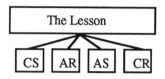

In the Choice Approach, the teacher offers a choice to students in each style. Students complete one activity.

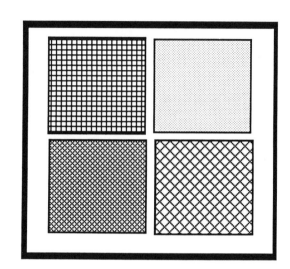

Purpose

The purpose of the Choice Approach is to provide teachers with a systematic way to offer students a choice of activities, usually in both content and process. Teachers find that the Choice Approach works naturally for independent assignments and homework assignments.

Procedure for Planning

When you plan activities for student choice, you will need to

• *Clarify your objectives*

• *Devise one or more activities for each style*

• *Give attention to*
  ~ *level of thinking and necessary bridges*
  ~ *time required*
  ~ *value*
  ~ *appropriateness to the objective*

Procedure with Students

When you work with students, the following guidelines work well:

- *Explain your objectives.*

- *Explain the objectives and activities in each style option if not evident.*

- *Explain the learning-style demands of the options, if not self-evident.*

- *Anticipate style problems and offer suggestions for solutions.*

- *Offer resource suggestions for different styles, if appropriate.*

- *Tell students your evaluation criteria for different styles of activities.*

- *Encourage students to use metacognition and to think stylistically about the task and their response to it, and why they chose it.*

- *Work with individuals as needed. Some may need coaching because they chose an option that stretches their style; others may need mentoring because they chose an assignment that deepens their style.*

An Example of the Choice Approach

The following examples illustrate the Choice Approach for style differentiated options for students. As you consider each selection, assess the reasons why such an activity might appeal to a certain style.

Unit	*Tokyo—Form and Spirit,* written by Bob Erickson, Global Studies Resource Center, St. Louis Park, MN (26)
Lesson	"Living—O-Hashi, The Use of Japanese Chopsticks"
Objectives	• To experience another culture's method of eating • To develop some dexterity with o-hashi
Approach	After students have experimented with using chopsticks and discussed the advantages and disadvantages of using them, students have a choice of the following activities.

Thinking Level I: Basic Thinking

Grade Level   6 - 10

Concrete Sequential Choice
• Find out which countries or cultures use chopsticks. Show the results on a world map. (Structured, information-oriented)

Abstract Random Choice
• Interview ten adults about their experiences using chopsticks. Share your findings in an article or tape. (Personal, relating)

Abstract Sequential Choice
• Write a short report on the history of chopsticks. Note cultural or religious implications as well as convenience and health considerations. (Research, reporting)

Concrete Random Choice
• Decorate or design a set of o-hashi. Use some aspect of Japanese tradition in your design. (Divergent, hands-on)

An Example of	**Unit**	Economics
the Choice Approach		

Lesson   "Consumer Spending"

Objective   To examine spending habits

Approach   As an introduction to a unit on consumer spending, students consider consumer spending habits.

Thinking Level II: Engaged Thinking

Grade Level 7 - 9

Concrete Sequential Choice

•• *You have $50.00 to spend on gifts for your family. Set up a budget for five people you must buy gifts for. Use catalogs to determine prices and good buys. Set up your work in chart or graph form.* (Factual, practical problem solving)

Abstract Random Choice

•• *Tape three different types of television commercials. Interpret how each attempts to appeal to the buyer through advertising techniques. In visual and/or written form, explain how advertisers attempt to appeal to emotions and why they are successful. You may make an appointment with the media center to use its videotape equipment.* (Interpretive, use of media)

Abstract Sequential Choice

•• *Credit Cards: Good News and Bad News*
Research the history of credit cards and summarize your findings in a short report. Wiith another student, present a "point/counterpoint" argument or write a pro/con one-page argument about credit cards. (Research, reporting)

Concrete Random Choice

•• *It is said that computers are changing the way people spend money. Interview a banker, a merchant, an adult who uses credit cards, and another person of your choice. In a colored mindmap show how each interviewee views how the computer changed his/her spending habits. From your information, write a one-page editorial.* (Investigative, open-ended)

*An Example of
the Choice Approach*

Unit Plants and Animals in Dependent Relationships, written by Bobby Prewitt, Hawley Elementary School, Newtown, CT

Lesson Final Project

Objectives
• To gain an understanding of the many dependent relationships between plants and animals
• To identify a desirable plant-animal relationship
• To predict what might happen if the plant or animal in the relationship became extinct
• To give one's opinion on whether or not the plant and/or animal should be saved if endangered.

Approach After the class study of plants and animals in dependent relationships, students chose a dependent relationship between a plant and animal on which to do research with specific guidelines from the teacher. Then, students addressed the above objectives in their criteria for a project chosen from the following selections.

Thinking Level III: Dynamic Thinking

Grade Level 3-4

Concrete Sequential Choices
••• Construct a diorama of the plant and animal showing them in their dependent relationship.
••• Make a mobile showing the plant and animal in their dependent relationship.

Abstract Random Choices
••• Compose a song or poem about the plant and animal showing them in their dependent relationship. Perform it for the class.
••• Pretend you are a reporter. Conduct an interview with your chosen plant and animal showing them in their dependent relationship.

Abstract Sequential Choices
••• Prepare a speech or article for the Ranger Rick Club in which you argue to preserve the environment for your plant and animal as you show the plant and animal in their dependent relationship.
••• With another student, debate the value of your plant-animal relationship as you show the plant and animal in their dependent relationship.

Concrete Random Choices
••• Design a puppet that could represent your plant and animal in their dependent relationship.   Present a puppet show to the class in which the plant and animal communicate with each other.
••• Create a cartoon strip in which your plant and animal are the main characters. Use at least four boxes in your cartoon and show your plant and animal in their dependent relationship.

**THE VARIATION
APPROACH**

In using the Variation Approach, teachers rotate among the four styles during the course of the lesson or unit, and all students take part in activities from each learning style area.

The Variation Approach

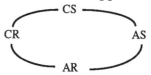

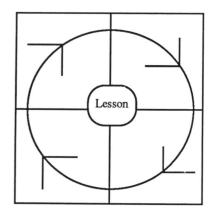

In the Variation Approach, the teacher rotates among the four styles. All students complete all the activities. There is no one correct style sequence.

Purpose

The purpose of the Variation Approach is to provide teachers with a systematic way to include all styles in lesson planning yet work with all students as a whole class. Use the Variation Approach, with bridges if needed, when you want students to work at Thinking Level I. Use the Variation Approach with bridges as a matter of course at Thinking Level II.

Procedure for Planning

When you plan a series of activities in different styles for all students to complete, you will need to

- *Clarify your objectives*

- *Plan the activities for each style in the desired sequence of styles*

- *Check to see that activities among the different styles are similar in*
  ~ *level of thinking (or provide appropriate bridges)*
  ~ *time required*
  ~ *value*
  ~ *appropriateness to the objective*

Procedure with Students

When you work with students, the following guidelines work well:

- *Clarify the goals of the topic and the objectives with all students.*

- *Explain the objectives and activities in each style option as you use them.*

- *Explain the learning-style demands of the options as you use them.*

- *Anticipate style problems and offer bridging suggestions for solutions when they occur, or plan bridging activities.*

- *Tell students your evaluation criteria for different styles of activities.*

- *Encourage students to use metacognition and to think stylistically about the task and their response to it.*

Often you will want students to build information from one style to another.

Unit   Inverse Operations, written by
Dan Zabriski, Haviland Junior High School, Hyde Park, NY

Lesson   An introduction to inverse operations

Objectives   • Students will learn how to solve inverse operation problems
• Students will understand the process of inverse operations

Approach   Students work in cooperative groups with a problem-solving focus to understand and apply the principle of inverse operations.

Grade Level 8

Abstract Random

In this example, the abstract random style is chosen first in order to provide students with a personal experience about the meaning of the concepts underlying inverse operations—opposite and backwards. Students complete the following task:

"Shannon leaves her room, walks down a corridor, turns left, walks up a flight of stairs, makes a right turn, takes the elevator down two floors to Renee's room, but forgets how to get back." Write a set of directions to help her back to her room.

Concrete Random

The concrete random style is chosen next in order to provide an opportunity for students to apply their new knowledge in an exploring and problem-solving way. In cooperative groups of three (cooperative grouping bridges to the abstract randoms), students complete the following tasks:

Discuss the two procedures Shannon used. Using these same procedures, solve this problem. "I start with the number N. I add 7, divide by 4, subtract 2, multiply by 9, and take half of what is left. I have 18. Find the value of N." Be ready to explain the steps of your procedure.

Concrete Sequential

Students tell the teacher the steps used to solve algebraic word problems like these:

The teacher facilitates and guides thinking as students explain the steps to solve these problems.

Abstract Sequential

Students work alone to solve algebraic word problems. They are given a series of problems like the one below to solve for a homework assignment.

"You are observing cells under a microscope. In one minute the cells split into two, so the number is doubled. Then you add 300 more. Now there are 1000 cells on the slide. Following the algebraic rules, find the number of cells you originally saw."

An Example of the Variation Approach

The following selections illustrate the Variation Approach to provide differentiated options for students as they read and analyze a novel:

Unit   *Johnny Tremain,* written by
Marcia O'Neil, Newburyport Public Schools, Newburyport, MA

Lesson   Chapters 4 - 6

Approach   As part of their study of *Johnny Tremain,* students answer questions about the content of the chapters. The selection below illustrates four styles of activities completed by all students.

Thinking Level II: Engaged Thinking for application or analysis

Grade Level 7-8

Concrete Sequential
•• *Use a line graph to identify and label the high and low points of Johnny's life to this point.*

Abstract Random
•• *Illustrate the scene that involved the butcher, the Webb twins and their cat Johnny, and Rab in cartoon form.*

Abstract Sequential
•• *Analyze the meaning of the British assumption that the colonists would "care more for their pocketbooks than their principles"?*

Concrete Random
•• *Predict another solution to the problem of freeing Cilla to testify, assuming Mrs. Lapham was literate.*

Advantages

We find several advantages to using the Variation Approach, especially for teacher-directed classroom instruction.

• *You can address each style of learning on a rotating basis.*

• *You can help students develop their strengths.*

• *You and students can develop abilities in each style.*

• *You have opportunity to discuss learning approaches with students, to validate different style points of view, and to value the strengths of your students in person.*

• *You can help students develop adapation skills but still encourage a positive self-concept.*

Disadvantages

We find, too, that the Variation Approach also has its disadvantages.

• *Some students will have considerable difficulty in any style but their own, even with bridging.*

• *Some students will complete the work but find little motivation except in their own style.*

• *Some students will recreate the activity in their own style because they have little ability to stretch their style.*

• Some students will complete activities in the different styles but with little quality.

• Teachers who do not understand a style of thinking will have difficulty planning a quality assignment in that style or teaching from that style.

**THE SDI
ACTION PLAN**

You have seen three ways to organize student activities: Bridging, Choice, and Variation. Each method brings its own outcome. Bridging helps students achieve an objective by providing a helping strategy. Bridging is most useful within a given activity that has a strong style demand. The Choice Approach allows students to choose their own way of processing information. The Choice Approach is most useful when the topic justifies many ways to consider a topic or concept. The Variation Approach allows students to develop a variety of ways of thinking about a topic or concept, and helps them systematically build information about a topic or concept.

Of the three, the Variation Approach requires more thoughtful planning for style because all students become involved with each activity and the content should not be repetitive from style to style. When teachers use the Variation Approach, it is important **not** to begin with the same style each time or that style will most likely be favored or penalized.

We have developed a convenient way for teachers to organize student activities using the ideas presented in this chapter, the **SDI Action Plan.** It pulls together the key ideas for providing for student learning styles that we have discussed. In the Appendix you will find additional examples of the Bridging, Choice, and Variation Approaches organized on the **SDI Action Plan** forms as well as an **SDI: Action Plan** chart that you may use for your own planning.

THE SDI APPROACH to LESSON DEVELOPMENT

In the next section of this chapter, you will find plans for creating lesson designs with style. Because some teachers work best when they have a structured lesson plan approach to follow, we have designed one that allows teachers to organize their own and the students' activities: the *SDI Lesson Developer*. The *SDI Lesson Developer* offers a structured lesson plan for the teacher's activities as well as for the students' activities. You will find the *SDI Lesson Developer* especially helpful when you need to develop a concept and then provide individual student choices to solidify the meaning of the concept. Within the *SDI Lesson Developer* you will use both the Variation and the Choice Approaches.

Some teachers prefer to design lessons using the Variation Approach in the classroom. The *SDI Lesson Developer Miniform* works very well for this purpose.

Both the *SDI Lesson Developer* and the *SDI Miniform* utilize a four phase process to organize instruction.

Phase I: Introduction

Phase II: Experience

Phase III: Meaning

Phase IV: Closure

In the next pages, I will explain these phases and provide a few examples of their application in both the *SDI Lesson Developer* and the *SDI Miniform*. I must stress that each method—Bridging, Choice, Variation, the Lesson Developer, or the Lesson Developer Miniform—have all brought fine results with students. The approach you choose to use depends on your style, your content, your students and their needs, your goals and objectives, and your desired outcomes. Each method has its own integrity. Give yourself time to try each one, then decide which ones best meet the students' needs and your own.

SDI: GUIDELINES for LESSON DEVELOPMENT

Whether you choose to use the **SDI Lesson Developer** or the **SDI Miniform,** certain guidelines help you develop a sound curricular plan to teach concepts and their relevant information. The SDI guidelines for lesson development incorporate the following key aspects:

- An effective teacher-directed SDI lesson is based on a concept and has clear objectives.

- An effective teacher-directed SDI lesson
  ~ gives students a motivational purpose for learning,
  ~ involves the learner in an active and problem-solving way,
  ~ aims for the learner to construct meaning, and
  ~ brings the lesson to closure.

- An effective teacher-directed SDI lesson attends to learning styles.

- An effective teacher-directed SDI lesson encourages higher-level thinking to occur.

- An SDI lesson defines its time-length by the amount of time needed to achieve the objective, not by the artificial time constraints of a school day's class period.

- In an SDI lesson, we discourage a standard sequence of learning styles and encourage your creativity to plan lessons in a variety of style sequences.

- We stress that the SDI Lesson-Developer Approach intends to develop students' understanding of concepts. If you do not intend to teach for concept attainment, then another, more simplified approach—Bridging, Variation, or Choice—may be more appropriate.

THE SDI LESSON: ORGANIZATION

The Content Example
As I explain the phases in the SDI Lesson Developer, I will illustrate them with examples from a social studies lesson.

Unit: "The Dust Bowl"
Developed by : Brian McIntyre, Haviland Junior High School, Hyde Park, NY

The key concepts:
~ the nature of political systems
~ the role of the environment in influencing the human condition
~ the meaning of empathy

The key objectives:
~ to identify the Dust Bowl phenomenon
~ to appreciate the effects of the Dust Bowl on human life
~ to assess governmental aid
~ to use group problem solving to find alternative solutions

Phase I:
INTRODUCTION
After you have determined the concepts and objectives of your lesson, you are ready to plan your teaching activities and the students' activities. In Phase I: Introduction, focus students' attention on the purpose of the lesson, use strategies to motivate student interest in the topic, and offer ways for students to explore the topic.

During Phase I, you usually emphasize information gathering as the basis for future applications and often work with Level I thinking activities. Use whole-class activities

~ to establish purpose,

~ to arouse interest and motivation,

~ to provide exploratory opportunity, and

~ to gather information.

The Dust Bowl Example: Phase I

Phase I: INTRODUCTION.   Purpose, motivation, exploration, gathering

---

Teacher uses a class whip to web key facts about the Dust Bowl with students. (CS facts, CR bridge)

Teacher shows a filmloop about the Dust Bowl. (AR: media; CS: factual and realistic)

Students answer key questions in their journals, then share their reactions to these questions:
• What grabbed my attention about the Dust Bowl in the filmloop?
• What did I think about as I watched?
• What problems do I foresee for the McCoys?
(AR: personalization)

Whole Class Activities: Level I

Phase II:
EXPERIENCE

In Phase II: Experience, you plan activities and experiences that actively involve students in the learning process and that encourage students to take a critical thinking role in their work. Students will have more opportunity to take an active part in their own learning when they apply and analyze (Level II thinking) in order to

~ raise concerns or interests,

~ consider issues or concepts,

~ develop questions or possibilities,

~ generate or solve problems, and

~ seek solutions

In the Experience Phase you will usually continue with whole-class activities that allow all students to gain a common body of knowedge, to have a common, baseline set of experiences, and to think in critical ways.

The Dust Bowl Example: Phase II

Phase II: EXPERIENCE.   Active involvement and personal relevance

Five students role play a prepared scene from the "The Okies."
(AR: role play, personalization)

Students complete response journals to the following questions, then discuss in cooperative groups:
• What are the options for the McCoys?
• In 1936, were there any New Deal programs to assist the McCoys?
• If you were a member of FDR's BrainTrust, what new programs would you suggest to help the Okies?
Be able to defend your reply.
(AS evaluative questions; AS text as source)

Teacher leads a whole-class discussion of responses.

Whole-Class Activities: Level II

In Phase III: Construction of Meaning, you give students the opportunity to construct their own meaning from gained knowledge and learning experiences. You encourage students' construction of personal meaning when you provide activities or options that ask for critical thinking through application and analysis (Level II), creative thinking (Level III), or evaluative thinking (Level III).

Phase III offers the ideal time to provide choices in style for students because they will construct meaning more efficiently, effectively, and with greater understanding from their own style point of view.

The Dust Bowl Example: Phase III

Phase III: CONSTRUCTION OF MEANING. Understanding	
Using the data sheet and a map, • *Trace the area affected by the Dust Bowl* • *Label the cities and states* • *List the causes of the Dust Bowl* • *List actions taken by the government to prevent another Dust Bowl* *Make a report to Congress with your findings* <div align="right">CS</div>	<div align="right">AR</div> *Write the last scene of the play "The Okies." Solve at least some of the problems in scene I. Include characters and an agricultural agent, and any other characters. Include ways in which feelings were affected and how they changed over time.*
<div align="right">AS</div>	CR
Argue for or against the hypothesis that "farming in Oklahoma is much different today than in the 1930s. No Dust Bowl or any other natural occurrence could threaten it now." Use two sources for your research.	*Take the role of the Grange president in Oklahoma. You have been invited to meet with Secretary of Agriculture Wallace in 1937. Make a list of six demands farm members want met; describe or draw three pictures you will bring with you to show Secretary Wallace.*
Individual choice: Level II or III	

Phase IV:
CLOSURE

In Phase IV: Closure, you check for students' accomplishment of the objectives and relate the objectives back to the concepts in the lesson. In order to gain closure, take one of three directions:

~ *Debrief*: guide students to analyze their learning and discuss their own thinking processes.

~ *Conclude*: facilitate students' sharing of Phase III products and results, draw conclusions about the concepts, or develop new problems from conclusions. Then, discuss students' own thinking processes.

~ *Culminate*: offer students the opportunity to elaborate upon their work by doing creative, independent activities that extend knowledge and practice into creative production.

Effective strategies for Phase IV include open discussion, small-group processing, personal conferencing, written tests, and student presentations.

The Dust Bowl Example: Phase IV

Phase IV: CLOSURE.   Debrief, conclude, culminate
Students share the results of homework assignment with the whole class.   *Teacher leads a discussion to draw conclusions about the concepts.*   *Students discuss their choice of homework assignments (reasons for) and consider thinking skills used (metacognition.)*

On the next pages, you will find three examples of the *SDI Lesson Developer* and two examples of the *SDI Miniform*.

SDI:™ Lesson Developer

Lesson by Nancy Boyles
North Haven School District
North Haven, CT
Grade 1

Student Objectives:

Children will understand "fair and unfair."

Children will understand "separate and unequal."

Key Concepts

Black people have experienced discrimination in many ways throughout history.

Phase I   INTRODUCTION: Purpose, motivation, exploration, gathering

Teacher shows a study print depicting an argument between two children over potentially unfair situations. (AR emotional connections)

Children hypothesize events that may have led to this confrontation as well as dialogue between the two children. (AS logic)

Children discuss the meaning of "fair and unfair." (AR discussion and AS analysis)

Whole Class Activities: Level I

Phase II   EXPERIENCE: Active involvement and personal relevance

Teacher conducts a large-group discussion in which children brainstorm situations in which they have been treated unfairly. (CR brainstorming; AR personalization)

Teacher lists data (concrete examples) on an experience chart.

Children explore feelings that evolve from unfair treatment.

Whole Class Activities: Level I

Phase III CONSTRUCTION OF MEANING: Understanding

Using your own words, turn the experience chart of unfair situations into a picture book to read to the kindergarten.	*Role play a situation in which several children want to help the teacher but the teacher always chooses the same helper.*
CS | AR	
AS | CR	
Go to the library. Find a couple of picture books with titles that are about "fair and unfair."	*Using the experience chart of unfair situations, think of different ways that each situation could have been solved.*

Choice Approach: Small group or individual   Levels II or III

Phase IV CLOSURE: Debrief, conclude, culminate

Teacher displays a poster, "Separate and Unequal," and indicates that each picture shows something that is unfair. (AS concept)

Children study poster at their leisure and hypothesize about what is unfair in each. (AS analysis)

During a large-group discussion, children share observations and hypotheses about pictures. (AS explanation)

Children make joint decisions concerning a good title for each picture. (AR shared learning)

Children show connections between their own activity (above) and the poster activity. (CS relate to their own work; CR divergent possibilities)

Whole Class Activities: Level II analysis and Level III evaluation

SDI:™ Lesson Developer

Student Objectives:

To read <u>The Bedspread</u> by Sylvia Fair.
To discuss the meaning of the book.
To complete an SDI activity related to the book.

Lesson by: Vicki Olsen and Kathy Herring, Independent School District 270 Hopkins, MN
Level: Intermediate Reading

Key Concepts

People have different viewpoints about the same event or situation.

We each have preferred ways of telling others about our experiences.

INTRODUCTION: Purpose, motivation, exploration, gathering

The teacher reads the story to the class and shares the pictures in the book. (AR storytelling; AS reading)

The teacher builds excitement about diversity by using voice inflection to point out differences. (AR emotion)

Whole-Class Activities: Level: I

EXPERIENCE: Active involvement and personal relevance

The teacher conducts a whole-group discussion of the book, including characteristics of the sisters and parts of the bedspread. (AR: viewpoints)

•Focus on the sisters—have students tell about the characteristics of Amelia and Maud. List these in two columns on a large sheet of paper. Students will need to use the pictures as well as the text to infer what the sisters were like. (AR: interpretation; CS: factual organization)

•Focus on the bedspread—ask students to recall some of the things the sisters sewed on the bedspread. Have them describe the differences in the ways the sisters remembered and created their home. List the items as students describe them. (AS: reference; CS: factual reference)

•Do a quick whip around the circle. Ask students to explain briefly which part of the bedspread they liked the best. Have them also tell which sister's version of the item they liked the best, i.e., Amelia's garden or Maud's door. Secretly record their choices. Report to them which sister was chosen most often as a group. Ask them to speculate on why so many of them chose work done by that sister. (AR: feelings)

Whole-Class Activities: Levels: I and II

Phase III CONSTRUCTION OF MEANING: Understanding

Write 5 - 7 questions that you will ask people. (E.g., what is your favorite ice cream flavor? If you could be an animal, what would it be?) *Answer the questions yourself.* *Find out who is most like you and unlike you.* *Make a chart that shows what you found out.* *How is you chart like the bedspread?* CS	*Think of a place that is special to you. Create a collage that shows this place and how it makes you feel. Use pictures from magazines, scraps of fabric and paper, markers and whatever else you wish in your collage.* AR
AS *Ask an adult you know to tell you about memories from his/her childhood. Work with him/her to draw the house, yard, garden, or whatever else he/she recalls.* *Write a short report with this information. In your report, describe the picture you drew. Tell what your person liked and didn't like. Tell your person's favorite story. Include your drawing at the end of your report.*	CR *Design and draw your own bedspread that shows important parts of your home. Remember that Amelia and Maud showed both the house and yard, and when they couldn't remember something exactly, they made things up a little.*

Choice Approach: individual   Levels II or III

Phase IV CLOSURE: Debrief, conclude, culminate

Provide sharing time for all projects.

Display the projects.

Discuss why children chose their option. (Metacognition)

Ask questions such as, What was appealing? Does a different option now seem more appealing? What things help you select the option for you?

SDI:™ Lesson Developer

Student Objectives:

Students will learn the meaning of point, line, plane.

Students will learn notation.

Students will see concrete examples from abstractions.

Students will learn about the relationship of intersections.

Students will begin to draw geometrically.

Lesson by: Nancy Duclos
Newburyport Public Schools
Newburyport, MA
Geometry

Key Concepts

Point, line, plane
Notation
Relationships

Phase I INTRODUCTION: Purpose, motivation, exploration, gathering

Teacher provides a clear explanation of expectations and outcomes.
Teacher asks a what-if question, "What if we had a system with nothing clearly defined?"

Students are asked to draw and define a point, line, and plane. The teacher expects the students to have difficulty expressing point, line, and plane in words. (CR exploration)

Students share their definitions and the class discusses the difficulty of working without clear definitions. This sets the stage for introducing the idea of notation and a universal understanding of notation. (AS concept and definition)

Whole-Class Activities: Level I

Phase II EXPERIENCE: Active involvement and personal relevance

Students walk around the room to find ten different items that can represent a line, point, and plane. (CS hands-on experience)

Students pair with another student to compare the items they found. They should be able to discover the answer to these questions:
 • Can or do two of your planes intersect?
 • Can or do two of your lines intersect?
 • Can or do a plane and a line of yours intersect? (CR investigation; AR shared processing)

Students transfer their findings in geometric terms and diagrams. The teacher reminds students to be very careful of notation, and reminds students to write an explanation if all attempts at drawing fail. (CS hands-on recording; AR pictorial visualization)

Teacher defines and draws diagrams of collinear points, coplanar points, noncollinear points, noncoplanar points, and space with colored chalk. (AS definitions) (Teacher suggests students use color pens, AR bridge)

Whole-Class Activities: Level: I

274   **Learning and Teaching Style: In Theory and Practice**

Phase III CONSTRUCTION OF MEANING: Understanding

Homework: Students choose one of the following activities

• *Write five statements that could be postulates for intersection of points, lines, and planes. Remember that these must be stated clearly and that a diagram should accompany each statement. (AS logic and theory)*

• *Create a three dimensional model that shows the intersection of relationships. You may use paper, boxes, straws, etc. (CS and CR, hands-on learning with opportunity for creativity.)*

• *Draw a picture that clearly shows all the intersection relationships. Write a story that accompanies this drawing. (AR visualization with opportunity for interpretation and personal expression.)*

Choice Approach: individual   Level II or III

Phase IV CLOSURE: Debrief, conclude, culminate

In small groups, students examine one another's homework assignments.

The teacher and students discuss problems and draw conclusions about the objectives.

SDI:™ Lesson Developer Miniform

This lesson is developed after students have read background
material about Freud. It illustrates a way in which whole-class
activities can move students to higher-level thinking.

Lesson by: Richard Gibbons
Amity Regional High School
Woodbridge, CT
Psychology

Major Concept

The Freudian concept of personality

Specific Objective

*Students will know the characteristics and
functions of id, ego, and superego*

---

1 ### Purpose, motivation, exploration, gathering

Introduction

(Students have read the text on Freud.)

*Ask students to diagram the id, ego, and superego on a
seesaw—how should it look? (CS specific fact)*

*From a Freudian perspective, students describe the
characteristics of persons who are dominated by the
id, ego, and superego. Students assess why each division of
the psyche is necessary. (AS: explanation of concept)*

Level I

---

2 ### Active involvement and personal relevance

Experience

*Students act out the role of the id, ego, and superego for each
of the following:*
  • *cheating on a test*
  • *breaking curfew (AR interpretation)*

*Students keep a journal of id/ego/superego conflicts of
which they become aware. (AR personal reflection)*

*Students bring in newspaper and magazine articles that
illustrate id, ego, superego control. Examples are
explained to the class. (CS specific examples)*

Levels I and II

---

3 ### Construction of meaning

Meaning

*Students respond individually to statements,
meet in small groups to compare ideas,
and then meet in a whole-class discussion
to analyze answers. (AS: applied logic)*

  • *From a Freudian perspective, explain why
  humans engage in warfare.*

  • *Explain whether violent sports perform
  a useful function in American society.*

Level II

---

4 ### Debrief, conclude or culminate

Closure

*Students form teams of three.
Using three characters from "M*A*S*H,"
students simulate the influence of the id, ego,
and superego in each character's personality.
(CR: simulation, divergent thinking, problem
solving)*

Level II

SDI: Lesson Developer Miniform

This lesson illustrates applications of styles and levels of thinking with the SDI Miniform. In this lesson students begin at Level I and progress to Level II. (28)

Lesson by: Patrick L. McKiernan
The Morgan School
Clinton, CT
English

Major Concept

Nonverbal cues occur in life and literature

Specific Objectives

• *to identify nonverbal behavior in visual presentations*
• *to recognize basic, emotional displays in facial expression*
• *to write simple dialogue to support verbal and nonverbal language*
• *to argue through supportive evidence*

1 Introduction — Purpose, motivation, exploration, gathering

Students observe enlarged photographs of facial expressions and label the emotional states. (CS: hands-on and specific)

Then they recall personal experiences with the same emotions and share their recollections with the class. (AR: personal experience)

Level I

2 Experience — Active involvement and personal relevance

Students complete a homework assignment that requires them to cut out and mount six facial expressions. On the reverse side of the display, they indicate what emotion each face reveals. (CS: hands-on, specific)

In class, students exchange homework and through group discussion agree or disagree about the labels chosen. (AR: interpretation, sharing viewpoints)

A class debate follows to determine, with teacher assistance, the six primary facial expressions of happiness, sadness, anger, fear, disgust, and surprise. (AS: analysis of correct answer in logical form)

The class receives a handout that contains illustrations of these basic displays. (CS: teacher verifies information)

Levels: I and II

3 Meaning — Construction of meaning

Independently, students collect three cartoon strips and "white out" the conversational balloons. In class students exchange cartoons and write dialogue to match and label the facial displays. The class discusses the results. (CR problem solving and divergent thinking)

Level: II

4 Closure — Debrief, conclude, or culminate

On a handout, students label the facial expressions of "affect blends": facial displays that represent multiple emotions simultaneously. (AR: interpretation of emotions)

Students discuss the possibilities for interpretations. (CR open-ended)

The teacher develops closure by summarizing and listing five statements about nonverbal language. (E.g., "the face elicits six primary emotional states.") (CS: verification)

Levels I and II

A COMPARISON CHART

	The SDI Lesson Developer	The SDI Lesson Developer Miniform
Phase I: Introduction	• Plan whole-class activities • Address one or more styles • Encourage Level I thinking	• Plan whole-class activities • Address at least one dominant style • Encourage Level I thinking unless building from a previous lesson
Phase II: Experience	• Plan whole-class activities • Address one or more styles • Attend to learning styles not addressed in Phase I • Include a choice approach if appropriate • Encourage Level II thinking	• Plan whole-class activities • Address a different or additional dominant style than in Phase I • Encourage Level II thinking
Phase III: Construction of Meaning	• Plan small-group or individual activities • Address all styles • Use a choice approach • Encourage Level II or Level III thinking	• Plan whole-class activities • Address a different dominant learning style than in Phases I and II • Encourage Level II or Level III thinking
Phase IV: Closure	• Plan whole-class, small-group, or individual activities • Encourage metacognition	• Plan whole-class activities • Address a different dominant learning style than in Phases I, II, III • Encourage metacognition

CHAPTER 14

SDI: FROM THEORY TO PRACTICE

...Growth takes place when the next step forward is subjectively more delightful, more joyous, more intrinsically satisfying than the previous gratification....

—Abraham Maslow

Philosophical Commitment

In order to implement STYLE DIFFERENTIATED INSTRUCTION within a school or system, the faculty must accept it as a worthy concept and agree that implementation of SDI is a worthy goal. If teachers and administrators do not value individual differences, then no amount of instructional training to accommodate differences will matter. Rather than work for implementation, teachers and administrators who have no commitment to style will invent every possilbe roadblock and excuse to avoid attention to differences in teaching.

In addition to a philosophical commitment, teachers and administrators must also share responsibility for development of SDI as an instructional process. Implementation of learning and teaching style concepts makes logical sense in theory, but poses considerable difficulty in practice because we simply cannot be all things to all people. Implementation of style cries out for cooperative teaching and peer coaching. Without individual commitment from teachers and administrators to work together in a cooperative learning fashion, at both a personal and professional level, implementation of SDI cannot reach full potential.

Personal Understanding

There are several key components to the process of adopting STYLE DIFFERENTIATED INSTRUCTION once a commitment to it has been made. First, teachers and administrators must understand style as a personal phenomenon and individual force. Unless educators understand the importance of their own style, they will not be able to understand others' styles. Unless they value and celebrate their own gifts and individuality, they will not do so for students.

Professional Reflection

Second, administrators and teachers must have the time to investigate without judgment how their own style works in the classroom. Only with this foundation can they begin to move outside their own minds to consider the impact of style for students, and ultimately for curriculum. Once teachers and administrators have developed a psychological understanding of their own style and have gained the knowledge base needed to work effectively with it, then they can look to application.

Knowledge of
Application Possibilities

Third, all interested teachers must have a general overview of style applications so that they can take charge of their own style problems in the classroom and enhance their own interests in the classroom. They need to have the tools to begin to address style differences at their own level of style ability and interest. This initial exposure to style applications provides the possibilities for exploring with style in the classroom without assessment from others. However, most will eventually need a significant amount of guidance and coaching in order to make style a working part of their classrooms.

Cadre
Leaders

Within this initial group, a number of teacher-leaders will emerge to form the style cadre in a school or district. They are driven by a commitment to style and its possibilities for students and for instruction. Within this group, each will work with style in a different way and become model examples of style variety in action. The teacher-leaders will become the true practitioners of style and, eventually, the peer coaches and trainers for other teachers if a caring facilitator invests time, energy, and support in them. The cadre will write and test SDI curriculum, and provide other teachers with realistic examples of effective lessons. In the cadre rests the future of districtwide style applications.

Administrators must be willing and able to provide political leadership and support for this group. They must have the personal ability to encourage the cooperative teamwork by teacher-leaders. They must help the cadre assume ownership of the style issue in a school or district.

Peer Coaching

The cadre of teachers provides a perfect role model for style differences when they bring a variety of personal styles to it. They will have more difficulty if the group lacks a variety of styles. Once the cadre members "know" style personally, professionally, and practically, they are ready to work with teachers if they can do so in a nothreatening manner. The cadre can encourage other teachers to develop the potential of their own natural styles, and to expand the breadth of their alternate styles to include more options and bridges for others. But, work with other teachers must be done within other teachers' styles and at the teachers' readiness levels.

Commitment

Without a doubt this approach demands commitment, sensitivity, knowledge, and the ability to examine the dynamics of teacher and student behavior and learning that result from a style differentiated approach to instruction.

Once teachers and administrators begin to address style, they extend their understanding of the many ways in which style impacts on a variety of issues: curriculum development, school leadership, school climate, teaching teams, guidance—in short, almost every aspect of school life. They will be ready to ask hard questions when they decide to pursue style beyond personal understanding and for implementation. For example, What style demands does our system place on educators and students as they pursue school goals? Do our teachers teach in the classroom with the same spirit of individual differences that we espouse in our curriculum guides? Do our administrators respect teachers' styles in the supervisory process? Do we treat our students as individuals with unique abilities or as children who must be shaped into the same mold?

Summary

In summary, the implementation of SDI involves several steps in staff development:

1. *Systemwide or schoolwide exposure to, and acceptance of, the concept of learning and teaching style; time for personalized meaning.*

2. *A broad-based overview of many style applications in the classroom and curriculum for teachers and administrators; time for professional reflection and training for selected style strategies.*

3. *Opportunity for a cadre of teacher-leaders who already have a natural ability in one or more styles, and who have the respect of other teachers, to receive further instruction and guided practice.*

4. *Coordination of the cadre group into a staff development team for the purposes of working with small groups and individual teachers in application strategies for the classroom.*

5. *Support for the cadre and new teachers to develop curriculum; time for resource development and networking.*

6. *Commitment to style as a high value by the system.*

7. *Evaluation of the effectiveness of Style Differentiated Instruction as it affects teachers' and students' well-being, teacher growth and effectivenss, and students' academic progress.*

8. *Personal support for student development as an ongoing feature of the students' involvement with style differentiated learning.*

The Teacher:
The Key

Why are individual teachers the key to the SDI approach? Teachers make critical decisions and evaluations about their use of style that ultimately affect the student—the teacher is the powerful force in the classroom. But we must remember that the ability to fulfill stylistic options ultimately comes from the learner's mind, not the teacher's activity. That is, it is the student's mind that actualizes SDI: that meets and matches stylistic demands of activities, that uses style flex-ability to accommodate the demands, that wills not to meet them, or that fails to understand and adjust appropriately to them. As Carl Rogers states:

> *There is the ridiculous question of*
> *coverage. What shall the course cover?*
> *This notion is based on the assumption*
> *that what is taught is learned, what is*
> *presented is assimilated. I know no*
> *assumption so obviously untrue. One does*
> *not need research to provide evidence*
> *that this is false. One needs only to talk*
> *to a few students.*

The idea that only the student can ultimately match style was illustrated clearly to me during a learning style course I was teaching to sixth-grade students. During the last class, I asked the students to choose an activity from a list of options. The activities were designed to match the four learning styles. Most of the children in the class chose the option that matched their style without any coaching from me. However, some did not. For example, Eric, a dominant concrete sequential, elected to make a poster that explained his style and illustrated how he interacted with others. In my mind, this activity was planned for AR learners. But by the end of the period, Eric had produced a perfectly divided poster using four magazine pictures captioned by neat, block lettering. In effect, he had translated his CS style into the activity.

On the other hand, Kim, a very bright girl with a strong CR style who was experiencing difficulty with her teachers, chose a variation of my CR activity. Kim is so independent that she created her own option rather than take one of mine. She presented a play in which she and a friend illustrated her perception of a random student's school experience. In the play, Kim took the dual role of a CS teacher as well as that of the random student's older sister. In the first scene, the girls showed the troubles of the random, which resulted in a referral to the principal's office. In the second scene, Kim confronted her "younger sister's" school problems with admonition, advice, and an extra dose of appreciation for her plight. It was as if Kim had stepped outside herself to view how others must see her. She understood the force of her CR nature and fully recognized what she labeled her "trouble spots."

FIVE STAGES

A teacher's ability to move from a simple bridging to student learning styles toward a sophisticated level of accommodation using SDI will parallel the teacher's personal growth and development within style. Several possible outcomes can occur when a teacher's knowledge, personal understanding, critical understanding, and experience with style unfold and evolve. The teacher can improve his/her ability to blend style-based theory and practice into the curriculum, understand the attitudes and forces behind different student styles, and help students achieve academic success, personal growth, and a working understanding of their stylistic differences—the goals of SDI.

The process of becoming a connoisseur of style parallels the psychological stages of comprehending personal learning style discussed in chapter 2.

Stage 1

At the first stage, teachers are introduced to the concept of style and are concerned with the question "What is style?" In effect, they enter a state of alertness—a feeling that something is in the wind. They ask, "What is my style?" They are interested in verifying the meaning of the Gregorc Style Delineator—an instrument designed to reveal an individual's personal style profile—for themselves. They enjoy applying their profile to life events and sharing their knowledge about style with significant others. At this stage, most teachers state that style "makes sense," has application to their own lives, and probably has more influence in their classrooms than they realized. Others find in style a new label for behaviors and forces they previously had recognized. Some choose to ignore the alert.

After gaining a little knowledge about style, most teachers reconsider some students' classroom behavior as characteristic of a learning style rather than as deviant behavior or as a learning difficulty. Interviews with teachers at the first level often brought out that they had gained a new tolerance for a learning style, but not necessarily that they understood, respected, appreciated, or cared to work with the style. Instead, the teachers said that they were pleased to identify a label for the students' behavior so that they could discover how "to help" the students. This usually meant bringing the students around to see learning in the teacher's way—the right way. For example, one science teacher felt fortunate in identifying an abstract random student's behavior so that he could more effectively help the student to "face the real sequential world of science."

At this level, teachers usually request a style "formula" to apply to their curriculum. Because their experience with the Gregorc model of style and with SDI is still limited, teachers assume that it will have the "kit for curriculum" so commonly and naively provided by some models designed to "save" education.

Although there is no "formula" for curriculum, guidelines help teachers to broaden the types of opportunities provided for students. These guidelines serve as a starting point and show teachers how to bridge to different learners. At this level, the teacher continues to use one style of teaching but provides style differentiated bridges to help all learners. This is the Bridging Approach discussed earlier.

Stage II

At the second stage individuals who have not paid attention to styles, other than their own, suspect that other styles may also be legitimate. Persons who have not respected their own style, or who have felt inferior about their style, infer that their own style may indeed be genuine. Teachers who realize that styles are valid express remorse over "all the children I haven't reached during the years." And, teachers who comprehend why they attempted to imitate another teacher, whose style differed from their own, free themselves to shed the mask of another style. As one teacher stated, "I worked myself into an ulcer trying to be the free-flowing, random teacher when all I should have done was be the best of sequential me."

Also at this stage of their development with style, teachers express a desire to meet styles more directly, but are concerned or fearful that they do not have the time, knowledge, or ability to address all four styles simultaneously. As teachers enter this phase, they are overwhelmed with insight into the implications of style. This is a normal reaction. Rather than worrying about making mistakes in their use of styles, teachers should continue to apply and progress. By their mistakes, they learn and grow. Given their concerns, teachers at this level are most comfortable with the Choice Approach to style.

Many teachers now ask for a questionnaire to identify the styles of their students. Their motives for this request vary. The majority of teachers who want an instrument for students are struck by the power of style identification for themselves. In their earnest desire to do well by their students, they assume that identification will be valid, accurate, free of bias, and a clear indicator of learning needs. They are impressed with the accuracy of their own profile within their own life experience. They assume they could interpret a student's profile with the same clarity. Without further training, however, this is not so.

Indeed, it is difficult to interpret the profile of styles other than one's dominant style. It is also inappropriate to make decisions for, or provide diagnoses of, mentally healthy others based on a profile, unless both parties can contribute a perspective.

Most educational systems provide little time for teachers to know their students in nonacademic ways. Teachers rarely have the opportunity to gain extensive background about their students or to develop an in-depth profile of learning abilities with the student. In the average junior or senior high school, it is likely that there would be little provision for teachers to discuss a profile with a student. Furthermore, in the specialty courses in which a teacher has a new group of students every nine weeks, most teachers would have the opportunity only to use raw style scores, with no personalization to the students, and of little use to the teacher.

Although many teachers have commendable intentions in seeking a style profile for students, others may be less ethical. Some teachers want profiles in order to label students, to define who matches their own style, or to avoid wasting time on styles they do not like. In the hands of such individuals, a style instrument for students is a lethal weapon.

At the present time, there are three alternatives to the problem of identifying student style. First, to provide student style instrumentation only to teachers who meet requirements in advanced training. Second, to provide an instructional arrangement—SDI—that allows teachers to address all styles of students by offering them qualitatively different learning options. Third, to teach students about style.

Stage III

Teachers who move into the third stage, an attitudinal one, begin a stage of introspection with the question "Why am I?" This stage is the most difficult, the one most strongly concerned with attitudes, and the one that lends itself to continuous reexamination as the individual grows throughout life.

This stage marks the point at which teachers begin to realize the potential of a psychological model of style. Their realization is apparent not by their knowledge about style but by the depth of their questions—about themselves in relation to style and mediation abilites, about their relationships with others, and about their awareness of the complexity of the human dimension.

At this stage, individuals examine their perceptions of self and others, and recognize their own worldviews in contrast to those of others. They talk to themselves in terms of style, and seem to "eat, breathe, and sleep the meaning of style." As individuals, they begin to listen carefully to the style signals of others, to seek verification of their views, and to begin a support network of people who share an interest is style.

In the classroom teachers continue to offer style bridges as an automatic part of their teaching, and increasingly use the Variation Approach in their daily instruction. They also offer qualitatively different stylistic options from which students may choose their preference.

Teachers, at this point, observe the effects of instructional options upon their students' behavior, achievement, and attitudes. And they actively seek student input and evaluation of the options' effectiveness.

As they probe the forces of style in their classroom, teachers at the attitudinal level show a psychological readiness to consider how to create personal and professional changes in their outlook and behavior toward other faculty and toward their students. Thus, during the attitudinal level, teachers experience the apparent paradox of searching inward for personal meaning at the same time that they begin to look outward at their relationships with others and to consider others' ways of thinking.

Stage IV

At the fourth stage, teachers begin to appreciate the styles of others, asking the question "Who are they?" More comfortable with their own sense of

Learning and Teaching Style: In Theory and Practice

self and continuing development, teachers begin to examine the styles of their students with the same care they gave to their own self-examination. At this stage, teachers automatically use the phenomenological process to understand their students, thereby trying to step into their students' shoes. The process usually results in the teachers' compassionate acceptance, appreciation, and adjustment to stylistic differences in their students.

Now teachers report a new interest in their students as people, a fascination with their interests and goals, and an enthusiastic willingness to help the students discover their own natural gifts. Consequently, teachers express a desire to explore the idea of style in depth with their students. Teachers are able to stress the concept of qualitative differences rather than the need to conform to the style of the environment, and to encourage their students to examine the importance of style.

At this stage, the teachers' motivation for sharing style with students is often based in their own need to be accepted as well as in their desire to show to students their acceptance of them. To some degree, teachers see their students through rose-colored glasses at this level. Teachers want to accept their students unconditionally as individuals, and they want to believe that all students would be highly motivated, high-achieving learners if they understood about the gifts of their own style and realized the necessity for learning style-flexing types of skills.

The assumptions about style that teachers bring to the classroom at this stage, however, transcend students' capacity for understanding about style. Because teachers usually have a renewed enthusiasm for teaching as a result of their own internal processing of style and wish all students to have the same experience with style, they forget the entry level of students' style knowledge. Thus, teachers are often disappointed when their students do not experience the same depth of realization about the powers of style or share the same revival of a love of learning.

Once they appreciate that style must be incorporated into the students' experience, teachers can help students see style as a component of all education and not merely a unit of study.

Stage V

At the fifth stage, teachers entertain the question "Who are we?" As individuals, they operate with ease and comfort from a highly developed, natural style base and serve as mentors to others of similar style. Because they have studied their own style as well as the styles of others and because they respect and appreciate other styles, their style-flex behavior is automatic and authentic. These teachers, then, provide truly qualitatively different options for students in their classrooms. They understand how different styles experience learning and instructional methods.

The teacher at this level accepts different readiness levels and learning motivations of students, does not need students to experience his/her level of style realization, and is able to organize content through many learning styles as a spontaneous process.

Teachers at this point are ready and able to help students experience the many facets of style without seeking the conversion of students to their own interests in style. They serve as effective guides and counselors for students in understanding the meaning of style channels and mental abilities. And teachers who operate at the activation level do not have a we-versus-them attitude toward different styles but know that others may indeed hold a we-versus-them attitude toward them. Finally, at the activation level, the individual teacher goes beyond the style understanding of others. The teacher does not attempt to convert others. Instead, he/she lives the life of one who knows that "all solutions must be sought, alone and together, in an unending universe of possibilities."

The Processing

As one might suspect, these five levels of SDI are not crisp, clean stages but guides to the types of thinking and behavior that occur as teachers change their scope of understanding about style. From simple solutions to complex realizations, the process of understanding a psychological model of style is personally absorbing and demands a considerable investment of personal energy.

STAGES OF UNDERSTANDING STYLE
FOR CLASSROOM APPLICATION

Stage	Development	Behavior and Need
I	Learn about style as a concept	*Ask for an instructional formula*
	Gain ability to solve basic style problems	*Need more knowledge*
		Ready to apply simple bridging
II	Investigate one's own style of learning and teaching	*Wish to identify student styles*
	Verify one's personal style	*Need basic applications*
	Curious about others' styles	*Ready to offer basic choices and to understand levels of thinking*
III	Consider effect of style on self and others	*Want to meet all needs*
	Recognize the strength of their own style viewpoint	*Want to bridge with sophistication*
	Assess teaching style with seriousness	*Need guided practice*
		Ready to use a variation approach
IV	Accept strengths and weaknesses of others and in self	*Have ability to apply style effectively in the class and to the curriculum in a variety of ways*
	Appreciate differences; seek them out	
	Create own adaptations for style	*Need support and networking*
V	Use style naturally in attitude and activity	*Provide real options for students and for adults with natural flex*
	Style flex with ease	*Ready to peer coach*
	Provide qualitatively different options	

Teaching by means of STYLE DIFFERENTIATED INSTRUCTION is a
complex process. SDI assumes that the teacher understands the philosophical
and theoretical approach to learning style as a theory and as a means to
understanding his/her personal mind qualities. It requires the teacher to have
assessed, evaluated, and internalized causes and effects of personal teaching
style. It demands that the teacher not only respect and appreciate individual
differences but value them too. It mandates that the teacher work with the
natural mind abilities of the student, yet help the student learn to work outside
natural style strengths as well.

          SDI does not ask, however, that the teacher be everything to everyone.
Rather, it maintains that each teacher has certain types of natural channels for
teaching and certain channels that need to be developed or uncovered. And it
maintains that a teacher cannot become another style. A teacher can
nonetheless learn how to recognize and work with other styles and to provide
freedom for other styles to learn and respond in qualitatively superior ways. SDI
also requires that the teacher find naturally matched materials, mentors, and
opportunities for others when the teacher can no longer meet the needs of
students of other styles.

MAJOR PRINCIPLES   Several key principles underlie the development of Style Differentiated
Instruction.

- STYLE DIFFERENTIATED INSTRUCTION has its philosophical and
  theoretical base in the Gregorc Energic Model of Style. Among SDI's
  assumptions derived from that model

    ~ People have natural mediation abilities, capacities, and
      potentialities. These are expressed through style channels labeled
      concrete sequential, abstract sequential, abstract random, and
      concrete random. The individual's way of showing a preferred
      channel is called his/her learning style.
    ~ The teacher needs to understand personal learning and teaching
      style.
    ~ Teaching style is the set of attitudes and activities that places
      mediation demands on the mind of the teacher and the learner.
    ~ The teacher's learning and teaching styles, together, create a
      psychological atmosphere for learning and determine instructional
      methods.
    ~ Every instructional method places demands on the mind of the
      learner.

- STYLE DIFFERENTIATED INSTRUCTION as an approach to group and
  individual instruction requires the use of diverse instructional methods
  among the four styles.

- STYLE DIFFERENTIATED INSTRUCTION as an approach to all
  individual instruction and most group instruction requires the use of
  distinguishable levels of instruction within each style.

- STYLE DIFFERENTIATED INSTRUCTION asserts the following:

    ~ Each learning style channel has definite preferences for
      instruction associated with it.
    ~ Each learning style channel has six qualitatively different levels of
      instruction and performance associated with it.

~ Each higher level of instruction within a style channel requires a higher degree of mediation ability in that style.

~ Basic skills for students are skills to operate at knowledge, comprehension, and application levels in each style channel.

~ Students learn basic skills when teacher, learner, and instructional styles are placed in matched as well as in guided mismatched experiences.

~ Minimum competencies for teachers are skills to operate at knowledge, comprehension, and application levels in each style channel.

~ Optimal performance by teachers and students occurs when they can tap natural mediation abilities.

~ Natural mediation abilities and channels must be used in order to create quality performances and products at the analysis, synthesis, and evaluation levels.

- STYLE DIFFERENTIATED INSTRUCTION maintains that

~ The teacher's understanding of style and its application to teaching and instruction increases gradually with study and application.

~ The teacher meets stylistic needs of groups of students best by guiding them in the use of qualitatively different learning options and opportunities, and by leading them to a working understanding of stylistic differences.

~ The teacher meets the stylistic needs of individual students best by observing, interviewing, and working directly one on one, and by helping them in the process of personal growth relative to style.

~ Learning styles of students and instruction are matched when students are able to use naturally dominant abilities and capacities to meet instructional demands.

You have begun the journey of style understanding. Your study is first a gift to your Self. When your Self is ready, it will then be your gift to others.

APPENDIX

Practice makes perfect.

—Teachers the whole world over

The SDI Planning Chart

The first section of the Appendix contains several examples of the *SDI Planning Chart* completed with teacher-developed activities for learning styles and levels of thinking within a unit. The following selections were chosen to illustrate different applications.

Heroes and Sheroes

The unit on "Heroes and Sheroes" by Stevie Cardamone illustrates independent student activities and enrichment activities for students as they read about famous men and women. Teachers in the Hopkins School District adapted this unit across many grade levels. With such activity options, the teacher might allow students to choose their own activities with a different point value at each level, or may, for example, require students to complete at least one activity of choice at different levels.

Learning about the Hospital

This unit gives an example of ways in which a teacher can preplan unit activities for style and level for use in the classroom, on a field trip, and for homework assignments. After doing such a plan, the teacher incorporates the variety into the lesson plans or transfers them into the *SDI Lesson Developer*.

Metric Measurement

Students often need additional practice with concepts and skills such as metrics. By providing style-based enrichment or extra-credit options like these, teachers give students the opportunity to practice skills on their own.

The Middle Ages and the Crusades

Teacher Peter Mongillo required students to complete basic activities in each style, then provided choices at higher levels. He found that students worked extremely well with this unit, gave him projects with more depth than before, extended themselves outside the classroom to enhance their projects (one group asked the music teacher to help them with music for a video interview), engaged with more content about the Middle Ages, and as a result, internalized an understanding of this time period in history.

Building and Marketing a Project

Some educators assume that learning style has a place in social studies or language arts, but are more skeptical of its applications elsewhere. This unit by an industrial arts teacher provides an illustration of the ways in which style and levels of thinking have value even in the industrial arts class.

The Impressionists

When students elect advanced, special classes such as art, they often want to dig deeply into the content. This unit on the Impressionists gives students an opportunity to develop an independent study project that provides both depth of content and different means to work with it.

The SDI Action Plan

The SDI Action Plan offers a way to plan for style in smaller sections of a lesson—the homework assignment, the test questions, the day's activities, the project assignments. The selections that use the **SDI Action Plan** illustrate a variety of ways that teachers incorporated style easily into their lessons.

Famous Women

In this third grade class, children were asked to read about a famous woman of their choosing. All children completed a small booklet of two questions from each style viewpoint; then, each child chose one method to report to the class about his/her famous woman. One shy child clearly revealed the benefits of this choice approach: she came to class wearing white makeup and confidently gave her presentation as the ghost of Mary, Queen of Scots.

Art with Style

The third grade students who worked with this lesson found many ways to learn about the ways body parts relate to each other. After a brief explanation of the concept (Lesson Developer—Phase I: Introduction) and a chance to experiment in a fail-safe way (Lesson Developer—Phase II: Experience), children chose one way to construct mearning for themselves (Lesson Developer—Phase III). With the levels of thinking in balance, the children's artwork clearly showed the differences in their styles.

Peace

The simplicity of this lesson shows one of the most practical aspects of planning with style. This lesson was one of several designed for a tabloid on global education. With limited space and time, students can experience many facets of the concept of peace in a real and practical way, on their own. What more important topic on which to use the Variation Approach—all children experiencing the meaning of peace from different style perspectives.

Measurement

This example could easily have been planned on the **SDI Planning Chart**. It provides for styles and levels of thinking. As an extension of the classroom work, such options cause students to continue their interaction with the content in a meaningful way.

RSL

An understanding of roots, stems, and leaves forms the purpose of these activities. All students complete the leaf-twig collection, then go about learning more with independent activities that supplement classroom work. If this teacher were to place these activities on the **SDI Lesson Developer**, they would fill Phase II: Experience and Phase III: Construction of Meaning.

Chaucer

We can also plan for style differences on our tests and quizzes. In this test, students worked from their own style perspective to show their understanding of Chaucer's *Canterbury Tales*.

SDI™ Planning Chart for Learning Styles and Levels of Thinking

Characteristics of Activities	Thinking Level I Knowledge/Comprehension			Thinking Level II Apply/Analyze				Thinking Level III Synthesize/Evaluate			
Concrete Sequential* Factual Structured / Realistic Practical / Detailed Hands-on	Describe Sort	Review Group	Observe Name	Restate List	Match Graph	Collect Classify	Measure Diagram	Organize Categorize	Plan	Develop Devise	Demonstrate Construct	Prepare Build	Report Rate
Abstract Random* Personal Relating / Interpretive Flexible / Feeling Imaginative	Remember Choose	Suppose Share	Tell Web		Relate Imagine	Express Pretend	Discuss Suggest	Interpret		Illustrate Translate	Compose Perform	Perceive Assess	Counsel
Abstract Sequential* Reading Referencing / Idea-oriented Logical / Analyzing Debating	Read Report	Take notes	Outline		Explain Exemplify	Research Discriminate	Summarize Infer			Formulate Debate	Speculate Critique	Hypothesize Verify	Judge
Concrete Random* Divergent Open-ended / Investigative Problem Solving / Experiential Inventive	Brainstorm Explore	Web (Map, Cluster)			Illustrate Forecast	Reorganize Connect	Generalize Investigate			Design Create	Process Editorialize	Invent Recommend	Direct

SDI Planning Chart

Characteristics of Activities	Thinking Level I — Knowledge/Comprehension	Thinking Level II — Apply/Analyze	Thinking Level III — Synthesize/Evaluate
Concrete Sequential* Factual Structured Realistic Hands-on Detailed Practical	List the biographies you have read. Describe the struggles your heroes and sheroes faced. Group these into either physical obstacles or political battles.	Organize your biographies into different historical periods of our country. Match the qualities your class admires most with the famous people in your biographies.	Develop a Hall of Fame for your school. Devise a nomination form for possible entrance into your Hall of Fame. Decide and report what kind of leaders we will need in the future. Develop a rating scale to rank these future leaders.
Abstract Random* Personal Interpretive Feeling Relating Imaginative Flexible	Write a letter to the family of your hero or shero discussing an event or accomplishment of the person. Suppose your hero or shero were alive today. What might that person be like? Draw a picture or make a collage of the things that person might be identified with.	Working in pairs, interview each other, and narrate a short biography. In a role play, to a partner, express your personality as a famous person.	Compose a limerick, song, ballad, or a poem about an event or accomplishment of one of your heroes or sheroes. Illustrate in an imaginative way, the significant people in your life who have helped you or taught you something important.
Abstract Sequential* Idea-oriented Logical Reading Referencing Debating Analyzing	Outline the struggles faced by the people in the biographies you have read. Prepare a short report for your class.	Research primary source materials about several heroes/sheroes. Explain how biographers use primary source information. Make a crossword puzzle using heroes and sheroes, and their contributions to society.	Debate with a classmate the differences or similarities between heroes/sheroes, and folk heroes/sheroes. Formulate a theory as to why terrorists villains, et al. are perceived by some groups as heroes.
Concrete Random* Divergent Open-ended Experiential Investigative Problem-solving Inventive	Brainstorm what biographies tell us about a particular period in history. Explore all the qualities your class admires most in heroes and sheroes. Map these.	Investigate ways in which each hero/shero is like the time and place in which he or she lived. Illustrate through visual display, how you reflect the time and place in which you live.	Predict where you see yourself in the 21st century. What struggles will you face that are like one of your heroes/sheroes? Design a new medium for presenting biographies of the future.

*Style terms used with permission of copyright owner, Anthony F. Gregorc, Ph.D.

Unit: "Heroes and Sheroes"
Written by Stevie Cardamone, Independent School District 270, Hopkins, MN
© Kathleen A. Butler, Ph.D.

SDI Planning Chart

Characteristics of Activities	Thinking Level I Knowledge/Comprehension	Thinking Level II Apply/Analyze	Thinking Level III Synthesize/Evaluate
Concrete Sequential* Factual/Structured, Realistic/Hands-on, Detailed/Practical	List types of workers in a hospital. Label pictures with different workers. See a demonstration of various instruments. Examine the floor plan of a hospital.	Take a field trip to a hospital. Look for items you have developed on a checklist. Record your observations and classify them into categories. Make your own "hospital chart" and keep a record of your daily temperature and pulse rate.	Develop a booklet about your field trip to a hospital. Make a model floor plan of the operating room. Find one problem concerning a hospital building itself and suggest how to solve it.
Abstract Random* Personal/Interpretive, Feeling/Relating, Imaginative/Flexible	Draw pictures of your feelings about hospitals. Read stories about being a patient. Watch the filmstrip about hospitals.	Role play a patient and doctor in a hospital. Convince the patient that doctor can help him/her. Interview a person who works in a hospital. Find out the most important part of his/her job.	Write a song or poem about your hospital field trip. Paint pictures for the children's wing of the hospital. Write a story for a child in the hospital.
Abstract Sequential* Idea-oriented/Logical, Reading/Referencing, Debating/Analyzing	Read about the various functions of a hospital. Find out about different types of hospitals. Find out about the books the school library has on medicine or famous doctors.	Write ten questions you could ask about an emergency room. Make an information booklet about your hospital.	Write your own story about the importance of a hospital to a community like yours. Make up a test about your field trip to see how how much we remember.
Concrete Random* Divergent/Open-ended, Experiential/Investigative, Problem-solving/Inventive	Develop a large web about the many, varied, and unusual happenings in a hospital. Brainstorm a list of problems a hospital might develop. Use medical instruments in the classroom.	Examine an X ray display. Figure out what is wrong from looking at the X ray. Make a web to show the many ways a hospital is a hospital like a shopping mall?	Design a bed/board game about hospitals. Create something new for the children's wing of the hospital: a toy, a sculpture, or something you would like to do.

Unit: "Learning about the Hospital"
Primary/Intermediate
© Kathleen A. Butler, Ph.D.

*Style terms used with permission of copyright owner, Anthony F. Gregorc, Ph.D.

SDI Planning Chart

Characteristics of Activities		Thinking Level I — Knowledge/Comprehension	Thinking Level II — Apply/Analyze	Thinking Level III — Synthesize/Evaluate
Concrete Sequential *	Factual / Structured	Estimate length and width of the room and your desk. Record estimates. Make actual measurements and record.	Measure the heights of students in the class and make a bar graph to show results.	Use measurements taken in the room and at home to make up five word problems.
	Realistic / Hands-on	Make an actual folding-size meter stick that shows dm, cm, mm.	Make a scale drawing of the classroom or a room at home.	Mark distance off on a cross country ski trail you make around the school yard. Figure the size of skis that would be needed by each member of your class.
	Detailed / Practical		Make a scale drawing of the lot your house or apartment is on. Give dimensions in metric.	
Abstract Random *	Personal / Interpretive	With a partner, estimate, then measure each other's hand, finger, foot, wrist, waist.	Interview a local business person. Find out how the metric system is used.	Plan an imaginary trip to several cities in the U.S. Make a map showing your travel, including distances and time it will take between destinations.
	Feeling / Relating	Secretly measure an object in the room. Give its measurements to a small group of students to guess the object.	Make a drawing or sketch or use pictures to illustrate three to five problems in the text. The illustrations should assist students in solving the problem.	Make a creative and colorful bulletin board that illustrates use of the metric system in the U.S. today.
	Imaginative / Flexible			
Abstract Sequential *	Idea-oriented / Logical	Make a chart that shows the relationship between metric units.	Make a chart that shows decimal and fractional relationships between metric units.	Hold a debate with a partner on the pro's and con's of the U.S. "going metric."
	Reading / Referencing	Make a set of vocabulary cards of new words that will be used in this unit. Include definitions.	Make a list of places that are approximately one km from the school.	Report to the class on the 10k runs held across the nation and what kind of training is needed for such events in relation to the distance.
	Debating / Analyzing	List metric abbreviations and their meanings.		
Concrete Random *	Divergent / Open-ended	Organize a collection of objects. Show their length in metric units.	Outline alternative routes of travel between Fairbanks and Seattle on a map. Show distance.	Choose an object for a measuring. Use this to devise your own measuring system.
	Experiential / Investigative	Make a concentration game that can be used for students to practice relationships between metric units.	Construct a dot-to-dot drawing on which another student can do the dot-to-dot and measure distances between each set of dots.	Organize a metric Olympics for the class.
	Problem-solving / Inventive			Make a map of the local community. Show distances between major centers.

Unit: "Metric Measurement"

Written by Tom Formella, Railbelt School District, Healy, AK

© Kathleen A. Butler, Ph.D.

SDI Planning Chart

Characteristics of Activities	Thinking Level I Knowledge/Comprehension	Thinking Level II Apply/Analyze	Thinking Level III Synthesize/Evaluate
Factual Structured **Realistic Hands-on** **Detailed Practical** Concrete Sequential*	* Show on a map of Europe and the Middle East the routes of the first three crusades and the years in which they began and ended. * Label the major towns, cities, and countries the crusaders passed through on the way to Jerusalem.	* On a chart or diagram show the different kinds of people within the ranks of the crusaders. * Measure the distance each crusade traveled on its way to the Middle East. Use your map.	• Construct a typical village in France A.D. 1350. Be sure to include some examples of food, shelter, clothing, and transportation. • Show illustrations of various kinds of knightly armor and weapons. Explain their value or use.
Personal Interpretive **Feeling Relating** **Imaginative Flexible** Abstract Random*	* Illustrate in cartoon form a typical "siege" of a Middle Eastern castle or city. Include participants, weapons, medical activity.	• Pretend you are in a castle or town that is under siege. Describe in diary form what takes place as the attack begins. Role play with two others a discussion of your fears during the siege. • Of the first three crusades you have studied, choose the one in which you would have liked to travel. Why? The crusades were made up of different kinds of people. Which would you have preferred to be with on this long journey? Why?	• Assume you are a reporter for the "Antioch Times." Interview a knight, a common soldier, and a townsperson. Report their feelings and views about the importance of the crusades.
Idea-oriented Logical **Reading Referencing** **Debating Analyzing** Abstract Sequential*	* Research the reasons for each of the three major crusades -- make an outline or web.	• Put your reasons for each of the three crusades in an essay form and indicate sources in your bibliography. • Present an oral report on the Children's Crusade. • Report on the geography of Europe and the Middle East. How might it have affected the Crusades?	• Analyze the results of the crusades. Might they have influenced the discovery of the New World? • Present a research paper summarizing the reasons for the failure of the crusades. Formulate a theory that suggests that the failure of the crusades would eventually benefit Western civilization.
Divergent Open-ended **Experiential Investigative** **Problem-solving Inventive** Concrete Random*	* Map a different route to the Middle East that would have made the journey less difficult for the crusaders. Work with a partner. Explain your reasons to a small group. Be prepared to debate or support your point of view.	* Illustrate on a map why the Middle East was called the "crossroads of the world." Include sea and land routes showing the transportation of silks, spices, gold, silver, jewels. Explain in a brief essay how these trade routes also encouraged the exchange of ideas and cultures.	• Devise a proclamation that would encourage various types of people to join a crusade. • Invent a strategy that might have eliminated the need for long sieges of castles and fortified towns.

Note: * Variation • Choice

Unit: "The Middle Ages and the Crusades"

Written by Peter Mongillo, North Haven School District, North Haven, CT

© Kathleen A. Butler, Ph.D.

SDI Planning Chart

Characteristics of Activities	Thinking Level I Knowledge/Comprehension	Thinking Level II Apply/Analyze	Thinking Level III Synthesize/Evaluate
Factual **Structured** **Realistic** **Hands-on** **Detailed** **Practical** *Concrete Sequential* *	~ Compile a list of woods that could be used for your project	• Collect samples of wood. Make a graph showing soft and hardwoods, and their uses. Construct a crossword puzzle for people to test their knowledge from your graph.	~ Build the project
Personal **Interpretive** **Feeling** **Relating** **Imaginative** **Flexible** *Abstract Random* *	~ Gather pictures and make a collage of functions of design.	• Interview a designer. Do a poster highlighting "Tips for Success," using the designer's work.	~ Illustrate the project at its location. Add a poem or essay from the viewpoint of the product, if you choose.
Idea-oriented **Logical** **Reading** **Referencing** **Debating** **Analyzing** *Abstract Sequential* *	~ Research and write a report on the processing of wood.	• Research and present a unit on methods of construction.	~ Establish criteria to judge the finished product.
Divergent **Open-ended** **Experiential** **Investigative** **Problem-solving** **Inventive** *Concrete Random* *	~ Experiment with the physical characteristics of wood. Develop a webbed map of wood by-products.	• Illustrate possible solutions to design problems identified in the resource book.	~ Develop a sales program for your project.

~ Variation Approach
• Choice Approach

Unit: "Building and Marketing a Project"
Written by Neil Richter, Bristol Public Schools, Bristol, CT
© Kathleen A. Butler, Ph.D.

SDI Planning Chart

Characteristics of Activities	Thinking Level I Knowledge/Comprehension	Thinking Level II Apply/Analyze	Thinking Level III Synthesize/Evaluate
Concrete Sequential * Factual / Structured Realistic / Hands-on Detailed / Practical	Sort and list the variety of sources one can use to gather information on Impressionism.	Collect sources of one Impressionist artist. Make a timeline of the artist's life and his/her art.	Develop a moveable bulletin board of teaching information on the artists' life and work. Include self-test quiz cards for the reader to take about the artist, a hands-on activity for the learner to use, and an evaluation form for the learner to rate the display.
Abstract Random * Personal / Interpretive Feeling / Relating Imaginative / Flexible	Choose one artist in the Impressionist period whose work you enjoy. Make a web of general information about him/her.	Choose one Impressionist artist. Relate the way his/her work reflected the social concern he/she felt.	Write a one-act play or interview showing how one Impressionist artist viewed his/her time or society. You may work with one or two people, perform the play, make a video, or tape the interview.
Abstract Sequential * Idea-oriented / Logical Reading / Referencing Debating / Analyzing	Read a variety of art history sources to define the term "Impressionism."	Research two varied sources on one Impressionist artist and explain how the time period in which he/she lived had a direct influence upon the art created.	Prepare a debate—orally with a partner or on paper with an invisible partner—arguing the artist's contribution as an Impressionist painter.
Concrete Random * Divergent / Open-ended Experiential / Investigative Problem-solving / Inventive	Observe several Impressionist paintings. How many and in what varied ways do they use color, theme, strokes? Explore your reactions in a web.	Investigate the background of one Impressionist artist, using at least one nonbook resource (video, artist, gallery). Develop a publicity campaign to bring the artist's work to the attention of an important gallery.	Choose two problems facing the world today. Create a painting, or write or present a statement, illustrating how one Impressionist artist would have reflected these problems in his/her work.

Unit: "The Impressionists"

Written by Dawn Chessman, Decatur Township Schools, Indianapolis, IN

© Kathleen A. Butler, Ph.D.

*Style terms used with permission of copyright owner, Anthony F. Gregorc, Ph.D.

SDI:™ Action Plan

Student Objectives:

   Process content in a factual, structured, realistic, or hands-on way.

   Process content in a personal, interpretive, feeling, or flexible way.

   Process content by reading, reporting, and researching in a structured way.

   Process content by using divergent thinking and exploring possibilities.

SDI™ Action Plan

Famous Women

Student Objectives: • To read for understanding about a woman's life
• To read for enjoyment

Children choose a book about a famous woman and complete a questionnaire about her. All students answer the questions listed below in italics in each style. Then, all students choose one project from among the choices listed below in plain type in each style.

Approach
__ Bridging
√ Choice   Variation Order:
√ Variation   1)____ 2)____
               3)____ 4)____

Activity
√ Homework __ Writing
__ In class   √ Independent

(Other)_____

Written by Beth Fox
Norfolk Public Schools
Norfolk, MA
Grade 3

   Process content in a factual, structured, realistic, or hands-on way.

Make a list of five things that you learned about this person.

Describe what this woman looked like.

•• Make a timeline of your woman's life. Remember to label important dates, such as birthdays, marriages, children's births, career dates, deaths. Then, draw a picture under each date or write one sentence under each date to describe it.

•• Find 10 objects around your house or even the school that remind you of your character. Place these small objects in a paperbag and bring them to school. Be prepared to describe the objects and how they remind you of your character.

   Process content in a personal, interpretive, feeling, or flexible way.

What did you like most about this person after reading about her? In what way was she most like you? In what way was she most unlike you?

•• Dress up like your character and make a speech in front of the class. Tell where you came from, why you are considered an important woman, and some events that happened in your life. If you choose this activity, see me to set up a date for you to give your speech. (Option: dress like the woman's husband. Adjust questions accordingly).

••• Pretend you and your characters are penpals. Write her a letter asking her questions. You may want to make some comments. Have her write back to you.

   Process content by reading, reporting, and researching in a structured way.

Why did you choose this woman to read about? What made her so interesting? What kind of person was she? What experiences do you think made her great?

•• Be a critic. Write a newspaper article about the book. Tell if you enjoyed reading it. Should someone else read it. If yes, why? If no, why not?

•• Make up a quiz about your character, such as a true/false fact sheet. List the answers separately so that we can take your quiz.

   Process content by using divergent thinking and exploring possibilities.

What would you have done differently if you were this woman? How might your different way have changed her life? Draw a picture of the woman you read about.

•• Make a large mural of your character's life. Draw pictures of the important things that happened to her. Make it colorful and completely colored in.

••• Add yourself into your character's life. Tell how you would effect or change her life. Write a short story about this change.

SDI:™ Action Plan

Art with Style

Student Objective:
To develop an awareness of body parts that move and their relation to one another

After an introduction to the concepts, use of demonstration and modeling, and analogy, students choose one of the following activities.

Written by M. Williamson
Barrington Public Schools
Barrington, RI
Art Department: elementary

Activity
__Homework   __Writing
√ In class   __Independent
(Other)_____

Approach
__Bridging   Variation Order:
√ Choice   1)____ 2)____
__Variation 3)____ 4)____

     Process content in a factual, structured, realistic, or hands-on way.

Create a realistic line drawing of your model to show details and textures of clothing with attention to proportion.

     Process content in a personal, interpretive, feeling, or flexible way.

Create a cartoon or comic strip that tells a story in three or four frames; keep the characters simple and easy to recognize.

     Process content by reading, reporting, and researching in a structured way.

Create a drawing from your model to show that parts of the body move, as in an action sport like baseball or basketball.

     Process content by using divergent thinking and exploring possibilities.

Create an imaginative drawing of yourself or of someone on a fantastic journey in a different environment or on a different planet, and the unusual human creatures found there.

SDI:™ Action Plan

Approach

__Bridging
__Choice
√ Variation

Variation Order:
1) CR   2) AR
3) CS   4) AS

Activity

__Homework   __Writing
√ In class   √ Independent

(Other)_____

Written by Robert Erickson
Global Studies Recource Center
St. Louis Park, MN

Global Education: Peace

Student Objectives:

As part of a unit on global education, students study the nature of peace in order
- *to understand that peace is a complex issue*
- *to understand that peace is a positive and active state*
- *to recognize that role models demonstrate peace*

   Process content in a factual, structured, realistic, or hands-on way.

   Process content in a personal, interpretive, feeling, or flexible way.

List all the Nobel Peace Prize recipients in the past 20 years. Read a biography about one of them and draw a timeline of significant events in his/her life.

Interview a peacemaker in your community. Find out how he/she creates an effort to promote peace.

   Process content by reading, reporting, and researching in a structured way.

   Process content by using divergent thinking and exploring possibilities.

Research how your political leaders stand on an issue important to you. Write them a letter expressing your opinion and soliciting their support.

Brainstorm in a group what peace means to you. Use a word cluster to record your ideas.

Voice your opinion on a global issue through active involvement with a local organization.

SDI:™ Action Plan

Approach

__ Bridging

√ Choice   Variation Order:

__ Variation   1)____ 2)____

    3)____ 4)____

Activity

__ Homework   __ Writing

__ In class   √ Independent

(Other)_____

Written by Michael Waters and
Michelle Warren, Seattle, WA

Measurement

Student Objectives:

• *To understand that mathematics has application to real-life problems*

• *To use measurement to solve real problems*

Students choose up to five activities for extra credit.

2 points for • activity   4 points for •• activity

6 points for ••• activity

   Process content in a factual, structured, realistic, or hands-on way.

• *Find odd measuring devices: pedometer, Geiger counter. Provide a demonstration to the class showing their use and importance.*

•• *Make a measurement of two variables in an everyday setting to determine the relationship between them.*

•• *Make representations of units of measure (such as a cubic foot) using cardboard models.*

•• *Demonstrate mastery of the relative sizes of all the units of measurement.*

••• *Devise electric quiz board for mastering the concept of measurement.*

••• *Write a computer program to solve a measurement problem.*

   Process content in a personal, interpretive, feeling, or flexible way.

• *Make a colorful poster showing samples of a variety of uncommon units of measure (furlong, Canadian gallon) .*

•• *View the movie on measurement with three other people. From the viewpoint of two types of measurement (square yard and cubic foot), explain your significance.*

•• *Show applications of measurement in advertising, the home, or art.*

•• *With a partner, make up your own measurement estimation test. Complete the test, score yourself, return to understand your mistakes, prove that you would not make the same mistake again.*

••• *Take slides of nature's applications of measurement. Write a script to teach others about the value of accurate measurement.*

••• *Redesign a room on paper, showing measurement applications.*

   Process content by reading, reporting, and researching in a structured way.

• *Choose an important measurement mathematician. Summarize the person's work and concepts.*

• *Define the difference between accuracy and precision. Apply these ideas to computations with measures.*

•• *Explain why progress in science in very dependent on precise measurement. Present in a written report with four resources.*

•• *Present a report on the approximate nature of measures and the necessary computational rules.*

••• *Research the use of congruence in indirect measurement in surveying. Report in depth.*

   Process content by using divergent thinking and exploring possibilities.

• *Practice your measurement skills with games.*

•• *Show the indirect measurement of an inaccessible distance with a hypsometer or with the use of similar triangle.*

•• *Measure an inaccessible height by measuring shadows and angles of elevation.*

•• *Show applications of measurement in highway construction, sports, architecture, carpentry, navigation, maps, or machinery.*

••• *Establish new, arbitrary units of measure. Use these units to make measurements and convert them from one unit to another.*

••• *Lay out a treasure hunt by establishing points, directions, and distances. Provide a unique treasure to discover.*

SDI:™ Action Plan

Approach
__Bridging   Variation Order:
√ Choice   1)_____ 2)_____
__Variation   3)_____ 4)_____

Activity
__Homework __Writing
__In class   √ Independent

(Other)_____

Written by Mark Anderson
Railbelt School District
Healy, Alaska
Science: secondary

RSL

Student Objectives:
- Students will further their understanding of the composition and function of roots, stems, and leaves.
- Students will make a leaf-twig collection of local trees and shrubs; for each plant, identify the kind of tree or shrub, the type of leaf (monocot or dicot; simple or compound) and the leaf arrangement (alternate, opposite, or whorled).

All students will complete one •• activity, and two ••• activities within the next fifteen class periods.

   Process content in a factual, structured, realistic, or hands-on way.

•• *Collect and diagram a twig. Include in the diagram all structures important to the twig and plant. Based on your diagram, predict what you think the purpose or function of each of the drawn structures may be. Compare your drawing with that in the text (p. 319). Label your diagram. How closely did your predicted functions match those listed in the book?*

•• *Make a chart of the various structures found in the cross-section of an herbacious and a wood stem. Label all parts and list their functions.*

••• *Prepare a clay model of the cross-sectional view of a leaf or stem. Label and describe in detail the function of each section or structure.*

   Process content in a personal, interpretive, feeling, or flexible way.

•• *Prepare a photographic display that compares and contrasts the root, leaf, and stem structure of "kitchen" and "lawn" monocots and dicots. Each picture should be titled and captioned. Add a creative one sentence description to help people remember facts.*

••• *Perform or write about the following: you operate an elevator in a large department store (really the side view of a leaf as magnified to show all the structures). Beginning on the ground floor (lower epidermis), take a group of people to the top floor (upper epidermis). Stop on each floor (layer) and tell passengers what it has to offer and its importance.*

••• *Pretend you are a tour guide and the rest of the class are molecules Tape or lead the class on a journey through the roots, stems, and leaves of a plant. Be informative and show the value of the parts.*

   Process content by reading, reporting, and researching in a structured way.

•• *Prepare a research report on the economic values of roots, stems, and leaves. Include their many uses in the world today. This report is not to include the uses of flowers, fruits, or seeds.*

•• *Do a three-page library research report on the various adaptations found in the roots, stems, and leaves of members of the flowering plants that allow survival in different environments (tundra, desert, tropical). Make copies to provide a reference for the class.*

••• *With three other students (two for monocots and two for dicots), debate for the class why your type of plant is vastly superior to the other type. (Why your arrangement of leaves, stems, and roots is the best). Each should prepare independently for the debate. (You may also assume the role of a biologist in support of one type if you wish).*

   Process content by using divergent thinking and exploring possibilities.

•• *Conduct a lab exercise to compare the fibrous and taproot root systems' holding ability in different types of soil. Prepare a lab write up for class discussion and pose one problem for the class to discuss.*

••• *Design a card game or a board game to test your classmates' knowledge of the root, stem, and leaf systems of plants.*

••• *Design an experiment to determine how much water is taken up in the roots of various plants and then released into the air. Write a procedure for the lab, conduct the experiment, and present your results to the class.*

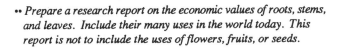

© Kathleen A. Butler, Ph.D.

SDI:™ Action Plan

Approach

__ Bridging
√ Choice
__ Variation

Variation Order:
1)_____ 2)_____
3)_____ 4)_____

Activity

__ Homework   __ Writing
__ In class   __ Independent
(Other) Exam _____

Written by Yvonne Klancko
Amity Regional High School
Woodbridge, CT
English: secondary

Chaucer

Student Objectives:
•*To show understanding of Chaucer's view of character.*
•*To analyze Medieval literature.*

Choose 4 questions
• *Write carefully planned essays to support your answers.*
• *Use an outline or web to organize your ideas.*
• *Choose according to your strengths.*
• *All questions are of equal weight.*

   Process content in a factual, structured, realistic, or hands-on way.

List four ways in which Chaucer reveals character. For each way, give an illustration, naming the pilgrim and also describing the way in which Chaucer presents the character.

Although Sir Gawain is a knight of great confidence and bravery, he is presented as someone with very human fears, failures, and misgivings. Write an essay in which you explain both the heroic and unheroic aspects of Gawain's behavior. Cite specific examples to support your position.

   Process content in a personal, interpretive, feeling, or flexible way.

Imagine that Chaucer has invited you as a guest pilgrim on the voyage to Canterbury. Your task is to judge who are the two most noble pilgrims. Name them, and compose a story that involves both. Be sure to reveal their personal characteristics.

You are one of the pilgrims. Recount a scene on the journey from the view of one of the pilgrims as he/she assesses the others.

   Process content by reading, reporting, and researching in a structured way.

It has been said that Chaucer "sees life in a true perspective." Do you agree? Write a carefully planned essay in which you support or reject this quotation on the basis of what you have read in the Prologue.

How does the literature of the medieval period reveal a change of attitudes and values? Give specific examples to support your analysis.

   Process content by using divergent thinking and exploring possibilities.

Explain the various leadership styles of Beowulf, Arthur, Leon, and Archie. Was each effective for his given circumstances? Would it have been just as successful if each tried to solve the challenges of one of the others' unique situations? In a well planned essay discuss the above questions.

Write your own significant question related to the Canterbury Tales and answer it.

SDI:™ Lesson Developer

Unit_____

Lesson_____

Student Objectives:

Teacher _____

Grade_____

Key Concepts

Phase I   INTRODUCTION: Purpose, motivation, exploration, gathering

Focus students' attention on the purpose of the lesson, motivate student interest, and offer exploration of the topic. Emphasize information gathering as a foundation for application.

Whole Class Activities: Level I   Choose one or more styles __CS   __AR   __AS   __CR

Phase II   EXPERIENCE: Active involvement and personal relevance

Actively involve students and encourage students to raise concerns, consider issues, develop questions, generate problems, or seek solutions using active participation and interactive processing.

Whole Class:
__Variation or __Choice   Choose styles not used in the Introduction __CS __AR __AS __CR Level: __II

Phase III CONSTRUCTION OF MEANING: Understanding

Give opportunity for students to construct meaning from knowledge and experience. Emphasize critical and creative thinking.	
Students construct meaning in a factual, structured, realistic, practical or hands-on way.	Students construct meaning in an interpretive, personal, feeling, or flexible way.
Students construct meaning in a conceptual, reporting, researching, or logical way.	Students construct meaning in a divergent, problem-oriented, investigative way.

___Small group (or) ___Individual choice   Level II or III

Phase IV CLOSURE: Debrief, conclude, culminate

Complete the objectives of the lesson and relate findings to concepts. Effective strategies include: open discussion, personal conferencing, small group processing, written comments, student presentations, Q/A discussion, "what-if" questions, or written evaluation.

Debrief	Conclude	Culminate
Guide students to analyze learning.	Facilitate students' sharing products and results, drawing conclusions about concepts, or developing new problems to study.	Offer students the opportunity to do creative, independent activities, extending knowledge and practice into creative production.

SDI™: Lesson Developer Miniform

Unit_____

Lesson_____

Grade_____

I Teach with Style

Major Concepts

Specific Objectives

1 Introduction

Purpose, motivation, exploration, gathering

This is a whole class introduction at Level I.
Styles addressed are:

2 Experience

Active involvement and personal relevance

This is a whole class activity at Level II.
Use styles not addressed in the Introduction.
(Option: provide choices)

3 Meaning

Construction of meaning

Level II___ or Level III___
Choices___ or Whole Group ___

4 Closure

Debrief, conclude or culminate

Whole class___ small group ___or individual___

NOTES

1. Carl Sagan, "Can we know the universe?" SATURDAY EVENING POST, July/August 1982, 46.

2. Anthony F. Gregorc, AN ADULT'S GUIDE TO STYLE. Maynard, MA: Gabriel Systems, Inc., 1982, v.

3. Ibid., 5.

4. Ibid.

5. Anthony F. Gregorc, INSIDE STYLE: QUESTIONS AND ANSWERS. Gregorc Associates, 15 Doubleday Road, Columbia, CT 06237 (original manuscript).

6. Anthony F. Gregorc, INSIDE STYLE: QUESTIONS AND ANSWERS. Maynard, MA: Gabriel Stytems, Inc., 1985, 7.

7. Gregorc, AN ADULT'S GUIDE TO STYLE. Maynard, MA: Gabriel Stytems, Inc., 1982, 5.

8. Ibid.

9. Ibid.

10. Ibid.

11. Ibid.

12. Don Idhe, LISTENING AND VOICE: A PHENOMENOLOGY OF SOUND. Athens: Ohio University Press, 1976, 17.

13. Arthur Combs, MYTHS IN EDUCATION. Boston: Allyn & Bacon, 1979, 134.

14. Ibid., 131.

15. Anthony F. Gregorc, GLOSSARY—THE ORGANON SYSTEM. Gregorc Associates, 15 Doubleday Rd., Columbia, CT 06237.

16. Ibid.

17. Frances Ilg and Louise Bates Ames, CHILD BEHAVIOR. New York: Harper & Row, 1955.

18. Butler, Kathleen, IT'S ALL IN YOUR MIND. Columbia, CT: The Learner's Dimension, 1987.

19. David Fontana, PSYCHOLOGY FOR TEACHERS. London: Macmillan Press, 1981, 2.

20. Benjamin Bloom et al., TAXONOMY OF EDUCATIONAL OBJECTIVES. HANDBOOK I: THE COGNITIVE DOMAIN. New York: David McKay, 1956.

21.   Kahlil Gibran, THE PROPHET. New York: Alfred A. Knopf, 1965.

22.   Marshall McLuhan, UNDERSTANDING MEDIA: THE EXTENSIONS OF MAN. New York: McGraw-Hill, 1964, 57-58.

23.   INSIDE STYLE: QUESTIONS AND ANSWERS (original manuscript).

24.   Westover Elementary School, Stillwater Avenue, Stamford, CT.

25.   Patrick L. McKiernan, LEARNING STYLES IN THE ENGLISH CLASSROOM: RIVALS OF THE WATCH. "Unit One—Nonverbal Language in Life and Literature," Curriculum Guide. Clinton, CT: The Morgan School, 1987.

26.   Robert Erickson, TOKYO: FORM AND SPIRIT, Walker Art Center, Minneapolis, MN, 1986, 9.

27.   McKiernan, "Unit One—Nonverbal Language in Life and Literature."

28.   Robert Erickson, GLOBAL EDUCATION, Minneapolis Star Tribune Tabloid, Minneapolis, MN, 1985, 20-21.

SELECTED READINGS

Adams, James. *Conceptual Blockbusting.* San Francisco: W.H. Freeman and Company, 1974.

Butler, Kathleen A. *It's All in Your Mind.* Columbia, CT: The Learner's Dimension. In press.

. "Learning Styles across Content Areas." In *Student Learning Styles and Brain Behavior.* Reston, VA: National Association of Secondary School Principals, 1982.

. "Learning and Teaching Styles Are Tools." *Marine Education* 3 (May 1983).

. "Learning Style, Competition, and Gifted Children." *Challenge* (Carthage, IL: Good Apple, Inc.), September 1983.

. "Learning Style: Let's Make a Match?" *Challenge* (Carthage, IL: Good Apple, Inc.), November 1983.

. "Stressing Style." *Challenge* (Carthage, IL: Good Apple, Inc.), March 1983.

. "Successful Learning Strategies for the Emerging Adolescent." *Oklahoma Middle Level Education Journal.* Oklahoma State Department, Oklahoma, City, OK. 1986.

. "Working Your Curriculum with Style," *Challenge* (Carthage, IL: Good Apple, Inc.), January 1984.

Cardamone, Stevie, and Butler, Kathleen. *The Constitution in Style.* Columbia, CT: The Learner's Dimension. 1987.

Chandler, Patricia. "A Staff Development Model for the Infusion of Style Differentiated Instruction into the Instructional Strategies of an Elementary School Staff (Grades K-6)". Seattle: Seattle University. Master's thesis. 1985.

Combs, Arthur. *Myths in Education.* Boston: Allyn & Bacon, 1979.

Cornett, Claudia. "What You Should Know about Teaching and Learning Styles." *Phi Delta Kappan Fastback 191* (1983).

Devine, Thomas. *Teaching Study Skills.* Boston: Allyn and Bacon, 1981.

Dewitt, Susan. *"The Effect of Style Differentiated Instruction on Content Mastery and Attitude."* St. Paul, MN: College of St. Thomas. Master's thesis. 1987.

Erikson, Erik H. *Identity: Youth and Crisis.* New York: Norton, 1968.

Erickson, Robert. *Developing the 21st Century Educator.* Available from St. Louis Park Staff Development Program, 6425 West 33rd St., St. Louis Park, MN. 55426.

Fontana, David. *Psychology for Teachers.* London: Macmillan Press, Ltd., 1981.

Frankl, Victor. *The Unheard Cry for Meaning.* New York: Simon & Schuster, 1978.

Ferguson, Marilyn. *The Aquarian Conspiracy.* Los Angeles: J.P. Tarcher,Inc., 1980.

Gardner, Howard. *Frames of Mind: The Theory of Multiple Intelligences.* New York: Basic Books, 1983.

Ginnot, Haim. *Teacher and Child.* New York: Macmillan, 1972.

Gregorc, Anthony, and Butler, Kathleen. "Learning/Teaching Style: A Status Report," *NASSP CURRICULUM REPORT.* Reston, VA: National Association of Secondary School Principals, Volume 12, No. 4, June 1983.

Gregorc, Anthony, and Ward, Helen. "A New Definition for Individual: Implications for Learning and Teaching." *NASSP Bulletin,* February 1977.

Gregorc, Anthony. "Learning/Teaching Styles: Potent Forces behind Them" (editorial statement). *Educational Leadership,* January 1979.

. "Learning Styles: Differences Which the Profession Must Address." In *Reading Through Content,* ed. R. Vacca and J. Meagher. Storrs: University of Connecticut, 1979.

. "Learning/Teaching Styles: Their Nature and Effects." In *Student Learning Style: Diagnosing and Prescribing Programs.* NASSP Monograph, October/November 1979.

. "Learning Style/Brain Research: Harbinger of an Emerging Psychology." In *Student Learning Styles and Brain Behavior.* Reston, VA: National Association of Secondary School Principals,1982.

. "An Open Letter to an Educator, Parts I - VI." *Challenge* (Carthage, IL: Good Apple, Inc.), 1981-82.

. *An Adult's Guide to Style.* Maynard, MA: Gabriel Systems, Inc., 1982.

. *Inside Style: Questions and Answers.* Gregorc Associates,15 Doubleday Road, Columbia, CT. 06237, original manuscript.

. *Inside Style: Questions and Answers.* Maynard, MA: Gabriel Systems, Inc., 1985.

Guild, Pat, and Garger, Stephen. *Marching to Different Drummers.* Alexandria, VA: Association for Supervision and Curriculum Development, 1985.

Hampden-Turner, Charles. *Maps of the Mind.* New York: Collier Books, 1981.

Hays, Edward. *Twelve and One-Half Keys.* Easton, KS: Forest of Books, 1981.

Hord, Shirley, et al. *Taking Charge of Change.* Alexandria, VA: Association for Supervision and Curriculum Development, 1987.

Ilg, Frances, and Ames, Louise. *Child Behavior.* New York: Harper & Row, 1955.

Jersild, Arthur. *In Search of Self.* New York: Teachers College, Columbia University, 1952.

Johnson, David, and Johnson, Roger. *Learning Together and Alone.* Englewood Cliffs, NJ: Prentice-Hall, 1975.

Kagan, Jerome, and Coles, Robert. *12 to 16: Early Adolescence.* New York: Norton, 1972.

Leonard, Joan; Fallon, John; and von Arx, Harold. *General Methods of Effective Teaching: A Practical Approach.* New York: Thomas Y. Crowell, 1972.

Link, Frances, ed. *Essays on the Intellect.* Alexandria, VA: Association for Supervision and Curriculum Development, 1985.

Litts, Cynthia, and Novosel, James. *SDI-CT: A Peer Coaching and Implementation Model.* Project Reports available from Ms. Litts, Decatur Township Staff Development Program, 5108 High School Road, Indianapolis, IN 46241.

Maslow, Abraham. *Toward a Psychology of Being.* New York: Van Nostrand, Reinhold, 1968.

McLuhan, Marshall. *Understanding Media.* New York: McGraw-Hill, 1964.

Pearce, Joseph Chilton. *The Crack in the Cosmic Egg.* New York: Pocket Books, 1973.

Rawitch, Don. "The Effect of Computer Use and Student Work Style on Database Analysis Activities in the Social Studies." Minneapolis: University of Minnesota. Doctoral dissertation, 1987.

Siegler, Robert. *Children's Thinking.* Englewood Cliffs, NJ: Prentice-Hall, 1986.

Sperry, Len. *Learning Performance and Individual Differences.* Glenview, IL: Scott, Foresman and Company, 1972.

Stewart, John. *Bridges, Not Walls.* Reading, MA: Addison-Wesley Publishing Co., 1977.

Student Learning Styles and Brain Behavior. Reston, VA: National Association of Secondary School Principals, 1982.

Toffler Alvin. *The Third Wave.* New York: William Morrow and Company,1980.

The Author

Kathleen A. Butler, Ph.D. is the founder and director of The Learner's Dimension, a firm specializing in professional development for educators. She is an internationally recognized researcher and writer on learning and teaching styles and developer of the Style Differentiated Model for application of style in the classroom. She has provided programs across the United States and Canada for education and business.

Dr. Butler received her degree from The University of Connecticut in 1981 where she studied under the direction of Dr. Anthony F. Gregorc, a pioneer in styles research. She is a former university instructor, high school social studies teacher, teacher of the gifted, adult education instructor and staff development coordinator. She serves on the editorial advisory board for The Clearinghouse Bulletin and the steering committee of the ASCD Learning Style Network. Her newest work is entitled It's All in Your Mind: A Student's Guide to Style.